GERALD DURRELL

Birds, Beasts and Relatives

HOUSE OF
STRATUS

B DUR
150497

This edition published in 2003 by House of Stratus, an imprint of House of Stratus Ltd, Thirsk Industrial Park, York Road, Thirsk, North Yorkshire, YO7 3BX, UK.

www.houseofstratus.com

Typeset by House of Stratus, printed and bound by Short Run Press Limited.

A catalogue record for this book is available from the British Library and the Library of Congress.

ISBN 0-7551-1181-8

To Theodore Stephanides,
in gratitude for laughter
and for learning

CONTENTS

FOREWORD

by Desmond Morris

There are a few people who can light up a room simply by walking through the door. Gerry Durrell was one of them. Even before he opened his mouth to speak, the warmth of his personality was evident, and once he started speaking, the room was instantly filled with good humour. In his later years, he looked remarkably like every child's idea of Santa Claus, and the presents he brought us were his hilarious anecdotes and his delightful books. He never took himself seriously, for although animals were a serious subject to him, he himself was not.

During the forty years that we knew one another, I don't ever recall a solemn encounter. Sarah Kennedy once said, 'Gerry is only rude to people he is very fond of', in which case he must certainly have been very fond of me because he was always blasting away at me, given half the chance! After our very last meal together, not long before he died, he wrote to me in typical vein saying, 'So appalled was I by your alcoholic intake and general bad behaviour that I completely forgot to give you the enclosed book. I know, since recently you learned to read, that you may possibly already have a copy of this from the public library – thus not increasing my income at all – but nevertheless, I felt you might like a copy signed by the author.'

Inside the book was a characteristic drawing by Gerry of a large, heavy-set rodent carrying a butterfly net with a butterfly sitting on the animal's Panama hat. Even though he was terribly ill, with both hips replaced and his liver collapsing, he was incapable of writing a boring sentence. What he had forgotten was that he had already sent me a copy of the book in question with another drawing in it, this time of two mongoosey creatures, one holding a dagger and the other offering it a flower, with the caption, 'The sex life of the lesser red-rumped tootle-whistle is filled with doubt.' Needless to say, I have kept both copies.

I have a whole shelf devoted to Gerry's books and I challenge anyone to take one down, open it and not become immediately absorbed in his skilfully woven accounts of his encounters with animals of all kinds. He was a born storyteller and it is great news that House of Stratus is republishing his works. Like all his friends, I only wish he was here to enjoy the occasion.

CONVERSATION

It had been a hard winter, and even when spring was supposed to have taken over, the crocuses – which seemed to have a touching and unshaken faith in the seasons – were having to push their way grimly through a thin crust of snow. The sky was low and grey, liable to discharge another fall of snow at any minute, and a biting wind howled round the house. Taken altogether, weather conditions were not ideal for a family reunion, particularly when it was my family.

It was a pity, I felt, that when they had all forgathered in England for the first time since World War II, they should be treated to something approaching a blizzard. It did not bring out the best in them; it made them more touchy than usual, quicker to take offence, and less likely to lend a sympathetic ear to anyone's point of view but their own.

They were grouped, like a pride of moody lions, round a fire so large and flamboyant that there was immediate danger of its setting fire to the chimney. My sister Margo had just added to it by the simple method of dragging in the carcass of a small tree from the garden and pushing one end into the fireplace, while the remainder of the trunk lay across the hearth-rug. My mother was knitting, but you could tell by the slightly vacant look on her face and the way her lips moved occasionally, as if she were in silent prayer, that she was really occupied with the menu for tomorrow's lunch. My brother Leslie was buried behind a large manual on ballistics, while my elder brother Lawrence, clad in a roll-top pullover of the type usually worn by fishermen (several sizes too large for him), was standing by the window sneezing wetly and regularly into a large scarlet handkerchief.

"Really, this is a *frightful* country," he said, turning on us belligerently, as though we were all directly responsible for the climatic conditions prevailing. "You set foot on shore at Dover and you're met by a positive barrage of cold germs... D'you realize that this is the first cold I've had in twelve years? Simply because I had the sense to keep away from Pudding Island. Everyone I've met so far has a cold. The entire population of the British Isles seems to do absolutely nothing from one year's end to another except shuffle round in small circles sneezing voluptuously into each other's faces...a sort of merry-go-round of re-infection. What chance of survival has one got?"

"Just because *you've* got a cold you carry on as though the world was coming to an end," said Margo. "I can't understand why men always make such a fuss."

Larry gave her a withering look from watering eyes. "The trouble with you all is that you like being martyrs. No one free from masochistic tendencies would stay in this – this virus' paradise. You've all stagnated; you *like* wallowing here in a sea of infection. One excuses people who have never known anything else, but you all had a taste of the sun in Greece; you should know better."

"Yes, dear," said Mother soothingly, "but you've just come at a bad time. It can be very nice, you know. In the spring, for example."

Larry glared at her. "I hate to jolt you out of your Rip Van Winkle-like trance," he said, "but this is supposed to be the spring…and look at it! You need a team of huskies to go down to post a letter."

"Half an inch of snow," snorted Margo. "You do exaggerate."

"I agree with Larry," Leslie said, appearing from behind his book suddenly. "It's bloody cold out. Makes you feel you don't want to do anything. You can't even get any decent shooting."

"Exactly," said Larry triumphantly, "while in a sensible country like Greece one would be having breakfast outside and then going down to the sea for a morning bathe. Here my teeth chatter so much it's only with difficulty that I can eat any breakfast."

"I do wish you'd stop harping on Greece," said Leslie. "It reminds me of that bloody book of Gerry's. It took me ages to live that down."

"Took *you* ages?" said Larry caustically. "What about me? You've no idea what damage that Dickens-like caricature did to my literary image."

"But the way he wrote about me, you would think I never thought about anything but guns and boats," said Leslie.

"Well, you never do think about anything but guns and boats."

"I was the one that suffered most," said Margo. "He did nothing but talk about my acne."

"I thought it was quite an accurate picture of you all," said Mother, "but he made me out to be a *positive imbecile.*"

"I wouldn't mind being lampooned in decent prose," Larry pointed out, blowing his nose vigorously, "but to be lampooned in bad English is unbearable."

"The title alone is insulting," said Margo. "*My Family and Other Animals!* I get sick of people saying, 'And which other animal are you?' "

"I thought the title was rather funny, dear," said Mother. "The only thing I thought was that he hadn't used all the best stories."

"Yes, I agree," said Leslie.

"What best stories?" Larry demanded suspiciously.

"Well, what about the time you sailed Max's yacht round the island? That was damned funny."

"If that story had appeared in print I would have sued him."

"I don't see why, it was very funny," said Margo.

"And what about the time you took up spiritualism – supposing he'd written about that? I suppose you'd enjoy *that?*" inquired Larry caustically.

"No, I would not – he couldn't write that," said Margo in horror.

"Well, there you are," said Larry in triumph. "And what about Leslie's court case?"

"I don't see why you have to bring me into it," said Leslie.

"You were the one who was going on about him not using the best incidents," Larry pointed out.

"Yes, I'd forgotten about those stories," said Mother, chuckling. "I think they were funnier than the ones you used, Gerry."

"I'm glad you think that," I said thoughtfully.

"Why?" asked Larry, glaring at me.

"Because I've decided to write another book on Corfu and use all those stories," I explained innocently.

The uproar was immediate.

"I forbid it," roared Larry, sneezing violently. "I absolutely forbid it."

"You're not to write about my spiritualism," Margo cried out. "Mother, tell him he's not to write about that."

"Nor my court case," snarled Leslie. "I won't have it."

"And if you so much as mention yachts…" Larry began.

"Larry dear, do keep your voice down," said Mother.

"Well, forbid him to write a sequel then," shouted Larry.

"Don't be silly, dear, I can't stop him," said Mother.

"Do you want it all to happen again?" demanded Larry hoarsely. "The bank writing to ask if you will kindly remove your overdraft, the tradesmen looking at you askance, anonymous parcels full of strait-jackets being left on the doorstep, being cut dead by all the relatives. You are supposed to be head of the family – stop him writing it."

"You do exaggerate, Larry dear," said Mother. "Anyway, I can't stop him if he wants to write it. I don't think it will do any harm and those stories are the best ones, I think. I don't see why he shouldn't write a sequel."

The family rose in a body and told her loudly and vociferously why I should not write a sequel. I waited for the noise to die down.

"And apart from those stories, there are quite a number of others," I said.

"Which ones, dear?" inquired Mother.

The family, red-faced, bristling, glowered at me in an expectant silence.

"Well," I said thoughtfully, "I want to give a description of your love affair with Captain Creech, Mother."

"What?" squeaked Mother. "You'll do no such thing…love affair with that disgusting old creature, indeed. I won't have you writing about *that*."

"Well, I think that's the best story of the lot," said Larry unctuously, "the vibrant passion of the romance, the sweet, archaic charm of the leading man…the way you led the poor old chap on…"

"Oh, do be quiet, Larry," said Mother crossly. "You do make me angry when you talk like that. I don't think it's a good idea for you to write this book, Gerry."

"I second that," said Larry. "If you publish we'll sue you in a body."

Faced with such a firm and united family, bristling in their resolve to prevent me at all costs, there was only one thing I could do. I sat down and wrote this book.

Writing something of this sort presents many pitfalls for the author. His new readers do not want to be constantly irritated by references to a previous book that they have not read, and the ones who have read the previous book do not want to be irritated by constant repetition of events with which they are familiar. I hope that I have managed to steer a fairly steady course between the two.

PART ONE

Perama

Here great trees cool-shaded grow, pear, pomegranate, rich apple, honey-sweet fig and blossoming olive, forever bearing fruit, winter and summer never stripped, but everblowing the western wind brings fruit to birth and ripens others. Pear follows pear, apple after apple grows, fig after fig, and grape yields grape again.

— HOMER

1

THE CHRISTENING

The island lies off the Albanian and Greek coast-lines like a long, rust-eroded scimitar. The hilt of the scimitar is the mountain region of the island, for the most part barren and stony, with towering rock cliffs haunted by blue rock-thrushes and peregrine falcons. In the valleys in this mountain region, however, where water gushes plentifully from the red-and-gold rocks, you get forests of almond and walnut trees, casting shade as cool as a well, thick battalions of spear-like cypress and silver-trunked fig trees with leaves as large as a salver. The blade of the scimitar is made up of rolling greeny-silver eiderdowns of giant olive trees, some reputedly over five hundred years old and each one unique in its hunched, arthritic shape, its trunk pitted with a hundred holes like pumice-stone. Towards the tip of the blade you have Lefkimi, with its twinkling, eye-aching sand dunes and great salt marshes, decorated with acres of bamboos that creak and rustle and whisper to each other surreptitiously. The island is called Corfu.

That August, when we arrived, the island lay breathless and sun-drugged in a smouldering, peacock-blue sea under a sky that had been faded to a pale powder-blue by the fierce rays of the sun. Our reasons for packing up and leaving the gloomy shores of England were somewhat nebulous, but based loosely on the fact that we were tired of the drab suburbanness of life in England and its accompanying bleak and unpleasant climate. So we had fled to Corfu, hoping that the sunshine of Greece would cure us of the mental and physical inertia which so long a sojourn in England had brought about. Very soon after we had landed, we had acquired our first villa and our first friend on the island.

The friend was Spiro, a waddling, barrel-shaped man with huge powerful hands and a brown, leathery, scowling face. He had perfected an odd but adequate command over English and he possessed an ancient Dodge which he used as a taxi. We soon found that Spiro, like most of the Corfu characters, was unique. There seemed to be no one that he did not know and nothing that he could not obtain or get done for you. Even the most bizarre requests from the family would be met by him with the remark, "Don'ts yous worrys about thats. I'll fixes thats." And fix it he would. His first major piece of fixing was the acquisition of our villa, for Mother had been insistent that we must have a bathroom, and this very necessary adjunct of wholesome living was in short supply in Corfu. But, needless to say, Spiro knew of a villa with a bath, and very soon, after much shouting and roaring, gesticulation, sweating, and waddling to and fro carrying armfuls of our goods and chattels, Spiro had us safely installed. From that moment he ceased to be merely a taxi-driver that we hired and became our guide, philosopher, and friend.

The villa that Spiro had found was shaped not unlike a brick and was a bright crushed-strawberry pink with green shutters. It crouched in a cathedral-like grove of olives that sloped down the hillside to the sea, and it was surrounded by a pocket-handkerchief-size garden, the flower-beds laid out with a geometrical accuracy so dear to the Victorians, and the whole thing guarded by a tall, thick hedge of fuchsias that rustled mysteriously with birds. Coming, as we had done, from a number of years' torture in the cold grey of England, the sunshine and the brilliant colours and scents it evoked acted on us all like a heady draft of wine.

It affected each member of the family in a different way. Larry wandered about in a sort of daze, periodically quoting long stanzas of poetry to Mother, who either did not listen or else said, "Very nice, dear," absently. She, entranced by the variety of fruit and vegetables available, spent most of her time closeted in the kitchen preparing complicated and delicious menus for every meal. Margo, convinced that the sunshine would do for her acne what all the pills and potions of the medical profession had so far failed to do, sunbathed with strenuous earnestness in the olive groves and in consequence got herself badly burnt. Leslie discovered, to his delight, that one could purchase lethal weapons without a permit in Greece and so he kept disappearing into town and reappearing carrying a variety of fowling pieces ranging from ancient Turkish muzzle-loaders to revolvers and shotguns. As he insisted on practising with each new acquisition, our nerves became somewhat frayed, and as Larry remarked somewhat bitterly, it was rather like living in a villa surrounded by revolutionary forces.

The garden, for long untended, was an overgrown riot of uninhibited flowers and weeds in which whirled, squeaked, rustled, and jumped a multi-coloured merry-go-round of insect life, and so it was the garden that held my immediate attention.

However luxurious our various gardens had been in England, they had never provided me with such an assortment of living creatures. I found myself prey to the most curious sensation of unreality. It was rather like being born for the first time. In that brilliant, brittle light I could appreciate the true huntsman's-red of a ladybird's wing case, the magnificent chocolate and amber of an earwig, and the deep shining agate of the ants. Then I could feast my eyes on a bewildering number of creatures unfamiliar to me: the great, furry carpenter bees, which prowled like electric-blue teddy bears, humming to themselves, from flower to flower; the sulphur-yellow, black-striped swallow-tailed butterflies, with their elegant cut-away coats, that pirouetted up and down the fuchsia hedge doing complicated minuets with each other; and the hummingbird hawkmoths that hung, stationary, suspended by a blur of wings, in front of the flowers, while they probed each bloom with their long, delicate proboscises.

I was exceedingly ignorant as to even the simplest facts about these creatures and I had no books to guide me. All I could do was to watch them as they went about their business in the garden or capture them so that I could study them more carefully at first hand. Very soon my bedroom was filled with a battalion of jam-jars and biscuit tins containing the prizes that

I had found in our tiny garden. These had to be smuggled surreptitiously into the house, for the family, with the possible exception of Mother, viewed the introduction of this fauna into the villa with considerable alarm.

Each brilliant day brought some new puzzles of behaviour to underline my ignorance. One of the creatures that intrigued and irritated me most was the dung-beetle. I would lie on my stomach with Roger, my dog, squatting like a mountain of black curls, panting, by my side, watching two shiny black dung-beetles, each with a delicately curved rhino horn on its head, rolling between them (with immense dedication) a beautifully shaped ball of cow dung. To begin with I wanted to know how they managed to make the ball so completely and beautifully round. I knew from my own experiments with clay and plasticine that it was extremely difficult to get a completely round ball, however hard you rubbed and manipulated the material, yet the dung-beetles, with only their spiky legs as instruments, devoid of calipers or any other aid, managed to produce these lovely balls of dung, as round as the moon. Then there was the second problem. Why had they made it and where were they taking it?

I solved this problem, or part of it, by devoting one entire morning to a pair of dung-beetles, refusing to be deviated from my task by the other insects in the garden or by the faint moans and yawns of boredom that came from Roger. Slowly, on all fours, I followed them foot by laborious foot across the garden, which was so small to me and yet such a vast world to the beetles. Eventually they came to a small hummock of soft earth under the fuchsia hedge. Rolling the ball of dung uphill was a mammoth task, and several times the beetle's footwork was at fault and the ball would break away and roll back to the bottom of the little incline, the beetles hurrying after it and, I liked to imagine, shouting abuse at each other. Eventually, however, they got it to the top of the rise and started down the opposite slope. At the bottom of the slope, I noticed for the first time, was a round hole like a well, which had been sunk into the earth, and it was for this that the beetles were heading. When they were within a couple of inches of the hole, one of the beetles hurried ahead and backed into the hole where he sat, gesticulating wildly with his front legs, while the other beetle, with a considerable effort (I could almost convince myself that I heard him panting), rolled the ball of dung up to the mouth of the burrow. After a considerable length of time spent in pushing and pulling, the ball slowly disappeared into the depths of the earth and the beetles with it. This annoyed me. After all, they were obviously going to do something with the ball of dung, but if they did it underground, how could I be expected to see what they did? Hoping for some enlightenment on this problem, I put it to the family at lunch-time. What, I inquired, did dung-beetles do with dung? There was a moment's startled silence.

"Well, I expect they find it useful, dear," said Mother vaguely.

"I trust you're not hoping to smuggle some into the house?" Larry inquired. "I refuse to live in a villa whose decor consists of balls of dung all over the floor."

"No, no, dear, I'm sure he won't," said Mother peaceably and untruthfully.

"Well, I'm just warning you, that's all," said Larry. "As it is, he appears to have all the more dangerous insects out of the garden closeted in his bedroom."

"They probably want it for warmth," said Leslie, who had been giving the matter of dung-beetles some thought. "Very warm stuff, dung. Ferments."

"Should we, at any time, require central heating," said Larry, "I'll bear that in mind."

"They probably eat it," said Margo.

"Margo, dear," said Mother. "Not while we're having lunch."

As usual, my family's lack of biological knowledge had let me down.

"What you want to read," said Larry, absentmindedly helping himself to another plateful of stew, which he had just described to Mother as being lacking in flavour, "what you want to read is some Fabre."

I inquired what or who Fabre was, more out of politeness than anything else, because, as the suggestion had come from Larry, I was convinced that Fabre would turn out to be some obscure medieval poet.

"Naturalist," said Larry, his mouth full, waving his fork at me. "Wrote about insects and things. I'll try and get you a copy."

Overwhelmed with such unlooked-for magnanimity on the part of my elder brother, I made a point of being very careful within the next two or three days not to do anything to incur his wrath; but the days passed and no book appeared and eventually I forgot about it and devoted my time to the other insects in the garden.

But the word "why" pursued and frustrated me on every hand. Why did the carpenter-bees cut out little circular pieces from the rose leaves and fly away with them? Why did the ants conduct what appeared to be passionate love affairs with the massed battalions of greenfly that infested many of the plants in the garden? What were the strange, amber, transparent insect corpses or shells that I found sticking to grass stalks and to olive trees? They were the empty skins, as fragile as ash, of some creature with a bulbous body, bulbous eyes, and a pair of thick, well-barbed forelegs. Why did each of these shells have a split down its back? Had they been attacked and had all their life juices sucked out of them? If so, what had attacked them and what were they? I was a bubbling cauldron of questions which the family were unable to answer.

I was in the kitchen when Spiro arrived one morning some days later, as I was showing Mother my latest acquisition, a long, thin, caramel-coloured centipede which I was insisting, in spite of her disbelief, glowed with a white light at night. Spiro waddled into the kitchen, sweating profusely, looking, as he always did, truculent and worried.

"I've broughts yours mails, Mrs Durrells," he said to Mother, and then, glancing at me, "Mornings, Masters Gerrys."

Thinking, in my innocence, that Spiro would share my enthusiasm for my latest pet, I pushed the jam-jar under his nose and urged him to feast his eyes upon it. He took one swift look at the centipede, now going round and round in the bottom of the jar like a clockwork train, dropped the mail on the floor, and retreated hurriedly behind the kitchen table.

"Gollys, Masters Gerrys," he said, "what's you doing with *thats?*"

I explained it was only a centipede, puzzled at his reaction.

"Thems bastards are poisonous, Mrs Durrells," said Spiro earnestly, to Mother. "Honest to Gods Masters Gerrys shouldn't *have* things like thats."

"Well, perhaps not," said Mother vaguely. "But he's so interested in all these things. Take it outside, dear, where Spiro can't see it."

"Makes me scarce," I heard Spiro say as I left the kitchen with my precious jar. "Honest to Gods, Mrs Durrells, makes me scarce what that boy *finds.*"

I managed to get the centipede into my bedroom without meeting any other members of the family and I bedded him down in a small dish, tastefully decorated with moss and bits of bark. I was determined that the family should appreciate the fact that I had found a centipede that glowed in the dark. I had planned that night to put on a special pyrotechnic display after dinner. However, all thoughts of the centipede and his phosphorescence were completely driven from my mind, for in with the mail was a fat, brown parcel which Larry, having glanced at, tossed across to me while we were eating lunch.

"Fabre," he said succinctly.

Forgetting my food, I tore the parcel open, and there inside was a squat, green book entitled *The Sacred Beetle and Others* by Jean Henri Fabre. Opening it, I was transported by delight, for the frontispiece was a picture of two dung-beetles, and they looked so familiar they might well have been close cousins of my own dung-beetles. They were rolling a beautiful ball of

17

dung between them. Enraptured, savouring every moment, I turned the pages slowly. The text was charming. No erudite or confusing tome, this. It was written in such a simple and straightforward way that even I could understand it.

"Leave the book till later, dear. Eat your lunch before it gets cold," said Mother.

Reluctantly I put the book on my lap and then attacked my food with such speed and ferocity that I had acute indigestion for the rest of the afternoon. This in no way detracted from the charm of delving into Fabre for the first time. While the family siestaed, I lay in the garden in the shade of the tangerine trees and devoured the book, page by page, until by teatime – to my disappointment – I had reached the end. But nothing could describe my elation. I was now armed with knowledge. I knew, I felt, everything there was to know about dung-beetles. Now they were not merely mysterious insects crawling ponderously throughout the olive groves – they were my intimate friends.

About this time another thing that extended and encouraged my interest in natural history – though I cannot say that I appreciated it at the time – was the acquisition of my first tutor, George. George was a friend of Larry's, tall, lanky, brown-bearded and bespectacled, possessed of a quiet and sardonic sense of humour. It is probable that no tutor has ever had to battle with such a reluctant pupil. I could see absolutely no reason for having to learn anything that was not connected with natural history, and so our early lessons were fraught with difficulty. Then George discovered that, by correlating such subjects as history, geography, and mathematics with zoology, he could get some results, and so we made fair progress. However, the best thing as far as I was concerned was that one morning a week was devoted exclusively to natural history, when George and I would peer earnestly at my newly acquired specimens and endeavour to identify them and work out their life histories. A meticulous diary was kept which contained a large number of flamboyant and somewhat shaky pictures, purporting to be of the specimens in question, done by me in a variety of coloured inks and watercolours.

Looking back, I have a sneaking feeling that George enjoyed the mornings devoted to natural history as much as I did. It was, for example, the only morning during the week that I would go to meet him. I would amble through the olive groves halfway to the tiny villa that he occupied, and then Roger and I would conceal ourselves in a clump of myrtle and await his approach. Presently he would appear, clad in nothing but a pair of sandals, faded shorts, and a gigantic, tattered straw hat, carrying under one arm a pile of books and swinging a long, slender walking-stick in the other hand. The reason for going to meet George, I regret to say, was of an entirely mercenary nature. Roger and I would squat in the sweet-scented myrtles and lay bets with each other as to whether or not, on this particular morning, George was going to fight an olive tree.

George was an expert fencer and had a quantity of cups and medals to prove it, so the desire to fight something frequently overcame him. He would be striding along the path, his spectacles glittering, swinging his walking-stick, when suddenly one olive tree would become an evil and malignant thing that had to be taught a lesson. Dropping his books and hat by the side of the path, he would advance cautiously towards the tree in question, his walking-stick, now transformed into a sword, held in his right hand at the ready, his left arm held out elegantly behind him. Slowly, stiff-legged, like a terrier approaching a bull mastiff, he would circle the tree, watching with narrowed eyes for its first unfriendly move. Suddenly he would lunge forward and the point of his stick would disappear in one of the holes in the olive tree's trunk and he would utter a pleased "Ha," and immediately dodge back out of range, before the tree could retaliate. I noticed that if he succeeded in driving his sword into one of the smaller of the olive tree's holes, this did not constitute a death wound, merely a slight scratch which apparently had the effect of rousing his antagonist to a fury, for in a second he would be fighting grimly for his life, dancing nimble-footed round the olive tree, lunging and parrying, leaping away with a downward slash of his sword, turning aside the vicious lunge that the olive tree had aimed at him, but so rapidly that I had missed the move. Some olive trees he would finish off quickly with a deadly thrust through one of the larger holes, into which his sword disappeared almost up to the hilt, but on several occasions he met with an olive tree that was almost more than a match for him, and for perhaps a quarter of an hour or so, it would be a fight to the death, with George, grim-faced, using every cunning trick he knew to break through the defences of the giant tree and kill it. Once he had successfully killed his antagonist, George would wipe the blood off his sword fastidiously, put on his hat, pick up his books, and continue, humming to himself, down the path. I always let him get a considerable distance away before joining him, for fear he should realize I had watched his imaginary battle and become embarrassed by it.

It was about this time that George introduced me to someone who was going to become immediately the most important person in my life, Dr Theodore Stephanides. To me, Theodore was one of the most remarkable people I had ever met (and thirty-three years later I am still of the same opinion). With his ash-blond hair and beard and his handsome aquiline features, Theodore looked like a Greek god, and certainly he seemed as omniscient as one. Apart from being medically qualified, he was also a biologist (his particular study being freshwater biology), poet, author, translator, astronomer, and historian, and he found time between these multifarious activities to help run an X-ray laboratory, the only one of its kind, in the town of Corfu. I had first met him over a little problem of trapdoor spiders, a creature that I had only recently discovered, and he had imparted to me such fascinating information about them, so diffidently and shyly, that I was captivated, not only by the information, but by Theodore himself, for he treated me exactly as though I were an adult.

After our first meeting, I was convinced that I should probably never see him again, as anyone as omniscient and famous as he was could not possibly have the time to spare for a ten-year-old. But the following day I received a present of a small pocket microscope from him and a note asking me to go to tea with him in his flat in town. Here I plied him with eager questions and breathlessly ran riot through the enormous library in his study and peered for hours through the gleaming barrels of microscopes at the strange and beautiful forms of pond life that Theodore, like a magician, seemed able to conjure out of any drab, dirty stretch of water. After my first visit to Theodore, I asked Mother tentatively whether I might ask him to come to tea with us.

"I suppose so, dear," said Mother. "I hope he speaks English, though."

Mother's battle with the Greek language was a losing one. Only the day previously she had spent an exhausting morning preparing a particularly delicious soup for lunch, and having concluded this to her satisfaction, she put it into a soup tureen and handed it to the maid. The maid looked at her inquiringly, whereupon Mother used one of the few Greek words that she had managed to commit to memory. "*Exo*," she had said firmly, waving her arms. "*Exo*." She then went on with her cooking and turned round just in time to see the maid pouring the last of the soup down the sink. This had, not unnaturally, given her a phobia about her linguistic abilities.

I said indignantly that Theodore could speak excellent English – in fact, if anything, better English than we could. Soothed by this, Mother suggested that I write Theodore a note and invite him out for the following Thursday. I spent an agonizing two hours hanging about in the garden waiting for him to arrive, peering every few minutes through the fuchsia hedge, a prey to the most terrible emotions. Perhaps the note had never reached him. Or perhaps he had put it in his pocket and forgotten about it and was, at this moment, gallivanting eruditely at the southernmost tip of the island. Or perhaps he had heard about the family and just didn't want to come. If that was the case, I vowed, I would not lightly forgive them. But presently I saw him, neatly tweed-suited, his Homburg squarely on his head, striding up through the olive trees, swinging his stick and humming to himself. Hung over his shoulder was his collecting bag, which was as much a part of him as his arms and legs, for he was rarely seen anywhere without it.

To my delight, Theodore was an immediate, uproarious success with the family. He could, with a shy urbanity, discuss mythology, Greek poetry, and Venetian history with Larry, ballistics and the best hunting areas on the island with Leslie, good slimming diets and acne cures with Margaret, and peasant recipes and detective stories with Mother. The family behaved much in the same way that I had behaved when I went to tea with him. He seemed such an endless mine of information that they bombarded him ceaselessly with questions, and Theodore, as effortlessly as a walking encyclopaedia, answered them all, adding for good measure a sprinkling of incredibly bad puns and hilarious anecdotes about the island and the islanders.

At one point, to my indignation, Larry said that Theodore ought to desist from encouraging me in my interest in natural history, for, as he pointed out, the villa was a small one and already stuffed to capacity with practically every revolting bug and beetle that I could lay my hands on.

"It isn't that," said Mother, "that worries me. It's the mess that he gets himself into. Really, Theodore, after he's been out for a walk with Roger he has to change into completely clean clothes. I don't know what he does with them."

Theodore gave a tiny grunt of amusement.

"I remember once," he said, popping a piece of cake into his mouth and chewing it methodically, his beard bristling and his eyes kindling happily, "I was coming to tea with some…um…you know, *friends* of mine here in Perama. At that time I was in the army and I was rather proud of the fact that I had just been made a captain. So…er…you know…er…to show off I wore my uniform, which included beautifully polished boots and spurs. I was rowed across by the ferry to Perama, and as I was walking through the little marshy bit I saw a plant that was new to me. So I stepped over to collect it. Treading on what…you know…seemed to be firm ground, I suddenly found that I had sunk up to my armpits in very foul smelling mud. Fortunately there was a small tree nearby and I… er…managed to grab hold of it and pull myself *out*. But now I was covered from the waist downwards with stinking black mud. The sea was…er, you know…quite close, so I…er… thought it would be better to be wet with clean seawater than covered with mud, so I waded out into it and walked up and down. Just at that moment, a bus happened to pass on the road above and as soon as they saw me with my cap on and my uniform coat, walking about in the sea, the bus driver immediately stopped so that all his passengers could…er…get a better view of the spectacle. They all seemed considerably puzzled, but they were even more astonished when I walked out of the sea and they saw that I was wearing boots and spurs as well."

Solemnly, Theodore waited for the laughter to subside.

"I think, you know," he said meditatively and quite seriously, "that I definitely undermined their faith in the sanity of the army."

24

Theodore was a huge success with the family and ever after that he came out to spend at least one day a week with us, preferably more if we could inveigle him away from his numerous activities.

By this time we had made innumerable friends among the peasant families that lived around us, and so vociferously hospitable were they that even the shortest walk was almost indefinitely prolonged, for at every little house we came to we would have to sit down and drink a glass of wine or eat some fruit with its owners and pass the time of day. Indirectly, this was very good for us, for each of these meetings strengthened our rather shaky command over the Greek language, so that soon we found that we were fairly proficient in conducting quite complicated conversations with our peasant friends.

Then came the accolade, the gesture that proved to us we had been accepted by the community in general. We were asked to a wedding. It was the wedding of Katerina, the sister of our maid, Maria. Katerina was a voluptuous girl, with a wide, glittering smile and brown eyes as large and as soft as pansies. Gay, provocative, and as melodious as a nightingale, she had been breaking hearts in the district for most of her twenty years. Now she had settled on Stephanos, a sturdy, handsome boy whom the mere sight of Katerina rendered tongue-tied, inarticulate, and blushing with love.

When you were invited to a wedding, we soon discovered, the thing was not done in half-measures. The first festivity was the engagement party, when you all went to the bride's house carrying your presents and she thanked you prettily for them and plied you with wine. Having suitably mellowed the guests, the future bride and groom would start walking to what was to be their future home, preceded by the village band (two violins, a flute, and a guitar) playing sprightly airs, and followed by the guests, all carrying their presents. Katerina's presents were a fairly mixed bag. The most important was a gigantic double brass bed and this led the procession, carried by four of Stephanos' friends. Thereafter followed a string of guests carrying sheets, pillowcases, cushions, a wooden chair, frying pans, large bottles of oil, and similar gifts. Having installed the presents in the new cottage, we then drank to the health of the couple and thus warmed their future home for them. We then all retired to our homes, slightly light-headedly, and waited for the next act in the drama, which was the wedding itself.

We had asked, somewhat diffidently, if Theodore might attend the wedding with us and the bride and her parents were enchanted with the idea, since, as they explained with becoming ingenuousness, very few weddings in the district could boast of having a whole English family *and* a genuine doctor as guests.

The great day came, and donning our best clothes and collecting Theodore from town, we made our way down to Katerina's parents' house, which stood among olive trees overlooking the sparkling sea. This was where the ceremony was to take place. When we got there we found it a hive of activity. Relatives had come on their donkeys from villages as far as ten miles away. All round the house, groups of ancient men and decrepit old women sat engulfing wine in vast quantities, gossiping as ceaselessly and as animatedly as magpies. For them this was a great day, not only because of the wedding, but because, living as much as ten miles distant, they were probably having their first opportunity in twenty years to exchange news and scandal. The village band was in full spate – the violins whining, the guitar rumbling, and the flute making periodic squeaks like a neglected puppy – and to this all the younger guests were dancing under the trees, while nearby the carcasses of four lambs were sizzling and bubbling on spits over a great chrysanthemum blaze of charcoal.

"Aha!" said Theodore, his eyes alight with interest. "Now that dance they are doing is the Corfu dance. It and the...er...tune *originated* here in Corfu. There are some authorities, of course, who believe that the dance...that is to say, the *steps*...originated in Crete, but for myself, I believe it is...um...an entirely Corfu product."

The girls in their goldfinch-bright costumes revolved prettily in a half-moon while ahead of them pranced a swarthy young male with a crimson handkerchief, bucking, leaping, twisting, and bowing like an exuberant cockerel to his admiring entourage of hens. Katerina and her family came forward to greet us and ushered us to the place of honour, a rickety wooden table that had been spread with a white cloth and at which was already sitting a magnificent old priest who was going to perform the ceremony. He had a girth like that of a whale, snow-white eyebrows, and moustache and beard so thick and luxuriant that almost all that could be seen of his face were two twinkling, olive-black eyes and a great, jutting, wine-red nose. On hearing that Theodore was a doctor, the priest, out of the kindness of his heart, described in graphic detail the innumerable symptoms of his several diseases (which God had seen fit to inflict him with) and at the end of the recital laughed uproariously at Theodore's childish diagnosis that a little less wine and a little more exercise might alleviate his ailments.

Larry eyed Katerina, who, clad in her white bridal gown, had joined the circle of the dancers. In her tight, white satin, Katerina's stomach was more prominent and noticeable than it would have been otherwise.

"This wedding," said Larry, "is taking place not a moment too soon."

"Do be quiet, dear," whispered Mother. "Some of them might speak English."

"It's a curious fact," said Theodore, oblivious to Mother's stricture, "that at a lot of the weddings you will find the bride in…er…um…a *similar* condition. The peasants here are very Victorian in their outlook. If a young man is…er…seriously *courting* a girl, neither family dreams for a moment that he will not marry her. In fact, if he did try to…um…you know…run off, both his family and the bride's family would be after him. This leads to a situation where, when the young man is courting, he is…er…chaffed, that is to say, has his *leg* pulled by all the young men of the district, who say that they doubt his… um…prowess as a…um…you know…potential father. They get the poor fellow into such a state that he is almost forced to…er …you know…um…*prove* himself."

"Very unwise, I would have thought," said Mother.

"No, no," said Theodore, endeavouring to correct Mother's unscientific approach to the problem. "In fact, it is considered quite a *good* thing for the bride to be pregnant. It proves her…um…fecundity."

Presently the priest heaved his vast bulk onto his gouty feet and made his way into the main room of the house, which had been prepared for the ceremony. When he was ready, Stephanos, perspiring profusely, his suit half a size too small for him and looking slightly dazed at his good fortune, was propelled towards the house by a laughing, joking band of young men, while a group of shrilly chattering young women fulfilled the same function for Katerina.

The main room of the house was extremely tiny, so that by the time the bulk of the well-larded priest had been inserted into it, plus all the accoutrements of his trade, there was only just about enough room for the happy couple to stand in front of him. The rest of us had to be content with peering through the door or through the windows. The service was incredibly long and, to us, incomprehensible, though I could hear Theodore translating bits of it to Larry. It seemed to me to involve quite an unnecessary amount of intoning, accompanied by innumerable signs of the cross and the splashing of tidal waves of holy water. Then two little garlands of flowers like twin haloes were held over the heads of Katerina and Stephanos, and while the priest droned on, these were exchanged at intervals. As it had been some considerable time since the people who held these garlands had been to a wedding, they occasionally misinterpreted the priest's instructions and there was, so to speak, a clash of garlands over the heads of the bridal pair; but at long last rings were exchanged and placed upon the brown, work-calloused fingers, and Katerina and Stephanos were truly and, we hoped, irretrievably wed.

The silence during the ceremony had been almost complete, broken only by the odd, drowsy chuckle of a hen or the shrill, and instantly repressed, squall of a baby; but now the stern part of the ceremony was over and the party blossomed once again. The band dug down into its repertoire and produced gayer and more sprightly tunes. Laughter and raucous badinage arose on every side. The wine flowed guggling from the bottles and the guests danced round and round and round, flushed and happy, as inexorably as the hands on a clock-face.

The party did not end till well after twelve. All the older guests had already made their way homewards on drooping donkeys. The great fires, with the remains of the sheep carcasses over them, had died in a shroud of grey ash with only a sprinkling of garnet embers winking in it. We took a last glass of wine with Katerina and Stephanos and then made our way sleepily through the olive groves, silvered by a moon as large and as white as a magnolia blossom. The scops owls chimed mournfully to each other, and the odd firefly winked emerald-green as we passed. The warm air smelled of the day's sunshine, of dew, and of a hundred aromatic leaf scents. Mellow and drugged with wine, walking between the great hunched olives, their trunks striped with cool moonlight, I think we all felt we had arrived, that we had been accepted by the island. We were now, under the quiet, bland eye of the moon, christened Corfiotes. The night was beautiful, and tomorrow, we knew, another tiger-golden day lay ahead of us. It was as though England had never really existed.

2

THE BAY OF OLIVES

As you left the villa and walked down through the olive groves, you eventually reached the road with its thick coating of white dust, as soft as silk. If you walked along this for half a mile or so, you came to a goat track which led down a steep slope through the olives and then you reached a small half-moon bay, rimmed with white sands and great piles of dried ribbon-weed that had been thrown up by the winter storms and lay along the beach like large, badly made birds' nests. The two arms of the bay were composed of small cliffs, at the base of which were innumerable rock pools, filled with the glint and glitter of sea life.

As soon as George realized that to incarcerate me every morning of the week in the villa impaired my concentration, he instituted the novel educational gambit of "outdoor lessons". The sandy beach and the shaggy piles of weed soon became scorching deserts or impenetrable jungles, and with the aid of a reluctant crab or sand-hopper to play the part of Cortez or Marco Polo, we would explore them diligently. Geography lessons done under these circumstances I found had immense charm. We once decided, with the aid of rocks, to do a map of the world along the edge of the sea, so that we had real sea. It was an immensely absorbing task, for, to begin with, it was not all that easy to find rocks shaped like Africa or India or South America, and sometimes two or three rocks had to be joined together to give the required shape to the continent. Then, of course, when you were obtaining a rock, you turned it over very carefully and found a host of sea life underneath it which would keep us both happily absorbed for a quarter of an hour or so, till George realized with a start that this was not getting on with our map of the world.

This little bay became one of my favourite haunts, and nearly every afternoon while the family were having their siesta, Roger and I would make our way down through the breathless olive groves, vibrating with the cries of the cicadas, and pad our way along the dusty road, Roger sneezing voluptuously as his great paws stirred up the dust, which went up his nose like snuff. Once we reached the bay, whose waters in the afternoon sun were so still and transparent they did not seem to be there at all, we would swim for a while in the shallows and then each of us would go about his own particular hobbies.

For Roger, this consisted of desperate and unsuccessful attempts to catch some of the small fish that flicked and trembled in the shallow water. He would stalk along slowly, muttering to himself, his ears cocked, gazing down into the water. Then, suddenly, he would plunge his head beneath the surface, and you heard his jaws clop together and he would pull his head out, sneeze violently, and shake the water off his fur, while the goby or blenny that he had attempted to catch would flip a couple of yards farther on and squat on a rock pouting at him and trembling its tail seductively.

For me the tiny bay was so full of life that I scarcely knew where to begin my collecting. Under and on top of the rocks were the chalky white tunnels of the tube-worms, like some swirling and complicated pattern of icing on a cake, and in the slightly deeper water there were stuck in the sand what appeared to be lengths of miniature hose-pipe. If you stood and watched carefully, a delicate, feathery, flowerlike cluster of tentacles would appear at the ends of the hose-pipes – tentacles of iridescent blue and red and brown that would revolve slowly round and round. These were the bristle-worms; a rather ugly name, I felt, for such a beautiful creature. Sometimes there would be little clusters of them and they looked like a flower-bed whose flowers could move. You had to approach them with infinite caution, for should you move your feet too rapidly through the water you would set up currents that telegraphed your approach and the tentacles would bunch together and dive with incredible speed back into the tube.

Here and there on the sandy floor of the bay were half-moons of black, shiny ribbon-weed, looking like dark feather boas, anchored to the sand, and in these you would find pipefish, whose heads looked extraordinarily like elongated sea horses, perched on the end of a long, slender body. The pipe-fishes would float upright among the ribbon-weeds, which they resembled so closely it required a lot of concentrated searching to find them.

Along the shore, under the rocks, you could find tiny crabs or beadlet anemones like little scarlet-and-blue jewelled pincushions, or the snakelocks anemones, their slender, coffee-coloured stalks and long, writhing tentacles giving them a hair-style that Medusa might well have envied. Every rock was encrusted with pink or white or green coral, fine forests of minute seaweeds, including a delicate growth of *acetabularia mediterranea* with slender threadlike stalks, and perched on the top of each stalk something that looked like a small green parasol turned inside out by some submarine wind. Occasionally a rock would be encrusted with a great black lump of sponge covered with gaping, protuberant mouths like miniature volcanoes. You could pull these sponges off the rocks and split them open with a razor blade, for sometimes, inside, you would find curious forms of life; but the sponge, in retaliation, would coat your hands with a mucus that smelt horribly of stale garlic and took hours to wear off.

Scattered along the shore and in the rock pools, I would find new shells to add to my collection; half the delight of collecting these was not only the beautiful shapes of the shells themselves, but the extraordinary evocative names that had been given to them. A pointed shell like a large winkle, the lip of whose mouth had been elongated into a series of semi-webbed fingers, was, I discovered to my delight, called the pelican's foot. An almost circular, white, conical, limpet-like shell went under the name of Chinaman's hat. Then there were the ark-shells, and the two sides of these strange, boxlike shells, when separated, did look (if one used a modicum of imagination) like the hulks of two little arks. Then there were the tower-shells, twisted and pointed as a narwhal's horn, and the top-shells, gaily striped with a zigzag pattern of scarlet, black, or blue. Under some of the bigger rocks, you would find keyhole limpets, each one of which had, as the name implied, a strange keyhole-like aperture in the top of the shell, through which the creature breathed. And then, best of all, if you were lucky, you would find the flattened ormers, scaly grey with a row of holes along one side; but if you turned it over and extracted its rightful occupant, you would find the whole interior of the shell glowing in opalescent, sunset colours, magical in their beauty. I had at that time no aquariums, so I was forced to construct for myself, in one corner of the bay, a rock pool some eight feet long by four feet wide. Into this I would put my various captures so that I could be almost certain of knowing where they were on the following day.

It was in this bay that I caught my first spider crab, and I would have walked right past him, thinking him to be a weed-covered rock, if he had not made an incautious movement. His body was about the size and shape of a small flattened pear, and at the pointed end it was decorated with a series of spikes, ending in two hornlike protuberances over his eyes. His legs and his pincers were long, slender, and spindly. But the thing that intrigued me most about him was the fact that he was wearing, on his back and on his legs, a complete suit of tiny seaweeds, which appeared to be growing out of his shell. Enchanted by this weird creature, I carried him triumphantly along the beach to my rock pool and placed him in it. The firm grip with which I had had to hold him (for once having discovered that he was recognized as a crab, he made desperate efforts to escape) had rubbed off quite a lot of his seaweed suit by the time I got him to the pool. I placed him in the shallow, clear water, and lying on my stomach, watched him to see what he would do. Standing high on his toes, like a spider in a hurry, he scuttled a foot or so away from where I had put him and then froze. He sat like this for a long time, so long in fact that I was just deciding that he was going to remain immobile for the rest of the morning, recovering from the shock of capture, when he suddenly extended a long, delicate claw and very daintily, almost shyly, proceeded to pluck a tiny piece of seaweed that was growing on a nearby rock. He put the seaweed to his mouth and I could see him mumbling at it. At first I thought he was eating it, but I soon realized I was mistaken, for, with an angular grace, he placed his claw over his back, felt around in a rather fumbling sort of way, and then proceeded to plant the tiny piece of weed on his carapace. I presumed that he had been making the base of the weed sticky with saliva or some similar substance to make it adhere to his back. As I watched him, he trundled slowly round the pool, collecting a variety of seaweed with the assiduous dedication of a professional botanist in a hitherto unexplored jungle. Within an hour or so his back was covered with such a thick layer of growth that, if he sat still and I took my eyes off him for a moment, I had difficulty in knowing exactly where he was.

Being intrigued by this cunning form of camouflage, I searched the bay carefully until I found another spider crab. For him I built a special small pool with a sandy floor, completely devoid of weed. I put him in and he settled down quite happily. The following day I returned, carrying with me a nail-brush (which subsequently, rather unfortunately, turned out to be Larry's) and taking up the unfortunate spider crab, I scrubbed him vigorously until not an atom of weed remained upon his back or legs. Then I dropped into his pool a variety of things: a number of tiny top-shells and some broken fragments of coral, some small sea anemones and some minute bits of bottle-glass that had been sandpapered by the sea so that they looked like misty jewels. Then I sat down to watch.

The crab, when returned to his pool, sat quite still for several minutes, obviously recovering from the indignity of the scrubbing I had given him. Then, as if he could not quite believe the terrible fate that had overtaken him, he put his two pincers over his head and proceeded to feel his back with the utmost delicacy, presumably hoping against hope that at least one frond of seaweed remained. But I had done my task well and his back was shining and bare. He walked a few paces tentatively and then squatted down and sulked for half an hour. Then he roused himself out of his gloom and walked over to the edge of the pond, where he endeavoured to wedge himself under a dark ridge of rock. There he sat brooding miserably over his lack of camouflage until it was time for me to go home.

I returned very early the following morning, and to my delight, I saw that the crab had been busy while I had been away. Making the best of a bad job, he had decorated the top of his shell with a number of the ingredients that I had left for him. He looked extremely gaudy and had an air of carnival about him. Striped top-shells had been pasted on, interspersed with bits of coral, and up near his head he was wearing two beadlet anemones, like an extremely saucy bonnet with ribbons. I thought, as I watched him crawling about the sand, that he looked exceedingly conspicuous, but, curiously enough, when he went over and squatted by his favourite overhang of rock, he turned into what appeared to be a little pile of shell and coral debris, with a couple of anemones perched on top of it.

To the left of the little bay, a quarter of a mile or so from the shore, lay an island called Pondikonissi, or Mouse Island. It was shaped not unlike an isosceles triangle and was thick with elderly cypress trees and oleander bushes, which guarded a small snow-white church and tiny living quarters adjoining it. This island was inhabited by an elderly and extremely verminous monk, with long black robes and a stove-pipe hat, whose major function in life appeared to be ringing the bell in the match-box-size church at intervals and rowing slowly over to a neighbouring headland in the evening, where there was a small nunnery, inhabited by three ancient nuns. Here he would partake of ouzo and a cup of coffee and discuss, presumably, the state of sin in the world today, and then, as the sun set and turned the calm waters round his island to a multi-coloured sheet of shot-silk, he would row back again, like a hunched black crow, in his creaking, leaking boat.

Margo, having discovered that constant sunbathing, if anything, inflamed her acne, now decided on another of Mother Nature's cures – sea-bathing. Every morning she would get up at about half past five, rout me out of bed, and together we would make our way down to the shore and plunge into the clear water, still chilly from the moon's gaze, and then swim slowly and languidly across to Pondikonissi. Here Margo would drape herself on a rock and I would potter happily in the rock pools on the shore. Unfortunately, our visitations to the island seemed to have a detrimental effect upon the monk, for no sooner had Margo landed and arranged herself attractively on a rock than he would come stamping down the long flight of stone steps that led up to the church, shaking his fist at her, and mouthing incomprehensible Greek from the depths of his long, unkempt beard. Margo would always greet him with a bright smile and a cheerful wave of her hand, and this generally made him almost apoplectic with rage. He would stamp to and fro, his black robes swishing, pointing one dirty and trembling finger at the heavens above and another at Margo. After this had happened on numerous occasions, I managed to commit to memory several of the monk's favourite phrases, for his vocabulary was not an extensive one. I then asked my friend Philemon what they meant. Philemon was convulsed with laughter. He laughed so much that he was almost incapable of explaining to me, but I at length understood that the monk had several derogatory terms that he used for Margo, the mildest of these being "white witch".

When I related this to Mother, she was, to my astonishment, considerably shocked.

"Really," she said, "we ought to report him to somebody. They'd never be able to carry on like that in the Church of England."

Eventually, however, the whole thing became a sort of game. When Margo and I swam across, we would take some cigarettes over for the monk and he would come flying down the stone steps, shaking his fist and threatening us with the wrath of God, and then, having done his duty, as it were, he would hitch up his robes, squat on the wall, and with great good humour smoke the cigarettes we had brought him. Occasionally he would even trot back to the church to bring us a handful of figs from his tree or a few almonds, milky and fresh, which we would crack between the smooth stones on the beach.

Between Pondikonissi and my favourite bay there stretched a whole string of reefs. Most of these were flat-topped, some of them only the size of a table and others the size of a small garden. The majority of them lay perhaps two inches below the surface of the water, so that if you hauled yourself out and stood on them, from a distance it looked exactly as though you were walking on the surface of the sea. I had long wanted to investigate these reefs, for they contained a lot of sea life that you did not find in the shallow waters of the bay. But this presented insurmountable difficulties, for I could not get my equipment out there. I had tried to swim out to one reef with two large jam-jars slung round my neck on a string and carrying my net in one hand, but halfway there the jam-jars suddenly and maliciously filled with water, and their combined weight dragged me under. It was a few seconds before I managed to disentangle myself from them and rise gasping and spluttering to the surface, by which time my jars were lying glinting and rolling in a fathom of water, as irretrievable as though they had been on the moon.

Then, one hot afternoon, I was down in the bay turning over rocks in an effort to find some of the long, multi-coloured ribbon-worms that inhabited that sort of terrain. So absorbed was I in my task that the prow of a rowing-boat had scrunched and whispered its way into the sandy shore beside me before I was aware of it. Standing in the stern, leaning on his single oar – which he used, as did all the fishermen, twisting it in the water like a fish's tail – was a young man, burnt almost black by the sun. He had a mop of dark, curly hair, eyes as bright and as black as mulberries, and his teeth gleamed astonishingly white in his brown face.

"*Yasu*," he said. "Your health."

I returned his greeting and watched him as he jumped nimbly out of the boat, carrying a small rusty anchor which he wedged firmly behind a great double bed of drying seaweed on the beach. He was wearing nothing but a very tattered singlet and a pair of trousers that had once been blue, but were now bleached almost white by the sun. He came over and squatted companionably beside me and produced from his pocket a tin containing tobacco and cigarette papers.

"It is hot today," he said, making a grimace, while his blunt, calloused fingers rolled a cigarette with extraordinary deftness. He stuck it in his mouth and lit it with the aid of a large, tin lighter, inhaled deeply, and then sighed. He cocked an eyebrow at me, his eyes as bright as a robin's.

"You're one of the strangers that live up on the hill?" he inquired.

By this time my Greek had become reasonably fluent, so I admitted that, yes, I was one of the strangers.

"And the others?" he asked. "The others in the villa, who are they?"

I had quickly learned that every Corfiote, particularly the peasants, loved to know all about you and would, in return for this information, vouchsafe to you the most intimate details of their private lives. I explained that the others at the villa were my mother, my two brothers, and my sister. He nodded gravely, as though this information were of the utmost importance.

"And your father?" he continued. "Where is your father?"

I explained that my father was dead.

"Poor thing," he said, quickly commiserating. "And your poor mother with four children to bring up."

He sighed lugubriously at this terrible thought and then brightened.

"Still," he said philosophically, "thus is life. What are you looking for here under these stones?"

I explained as best I could, though I always found it difficult to get the peasants to understand why I was so interested in such a variety of creatures that were either obnoxious or not worth worrying about and all of which were inedible.

"What's your name?" he asked.

I said that it was Gerasimos, which was the closest approach to Gerald that one could come to in Greek. But, I explained, my friends called me Gerry.

"I'm Taki," he said. "Taki Thanatos. I live at Benitses."

I asked him what he was doing up here so comparatively far from his village. He shrugged.

"I have come from Benitses," he said, "and I fish on the way. Then I eat and I sleep and when it's night I light my lights and go back to Benitses, fishing again."

This news excited me, for not long before, we had been returning late from town, and standing on the road by the little path that led up to the villa, we had seen a boat passing below us, being rowed very slowly, with a large carbon lamp fixed to the bows. As the fisherman manoeuvred the boat slowly

THE BAY OF OLIVES

through the dark, shallow waters, the pool of light cast by his lamp had illuminated great patches of seabed with the utmost vividness, reefs smouldering citron green, pink, yellow, and brown as the boat moved slowly along. I had thought at the time that this must be a fascinating occupation, but I had known no fishermen. Now I began to view Taki with some enthusiasm.

I asked him eagerly what time he intended to start his fishing and whether he meant to go round the reefs that lay scattered between the bay and Pondikonissi.

"I start about ten," he said. "I work round the island, then I head towards Benitses."

I asked him whether it would be possible for me to join him, because, as I explained, there were lots of strange creatures living on the reef which I could not obtain without the aid of a boat.

"Why not?" he said. "I shall be down below Menelaos'. You come at ten. I'll take you round the reefs and then drop you back at Menelaos' before I go to Benitses."

I assured him fervently that I would be there at ten o'clock. Then, gathering up my net and bottles and whistling for Roger, I beat a hasty retreat before Taki could change his mind. Once I was safely out of earshot, I slowed down and gave a considerable amount of thought to how I was going to persuade the family in general, and Mother in particular, to let me go out to sea at ten o'clock at night.

Mother, I knew, had always been worried about my refusal to have a siesta during the heat of the day. I had explained to her that this was generally the best time for insects and things like that, but she was not convinced that this was a valid argument. However, the result was that at night, just when something interesting was happening (such as Larry locked in a verbal battle with Leslie), Mother would say, "It's time you went to bed, dear. After all, remember, you don't have a siesta."

This I felt might be the answer to the night fishing. It was scarcely three o'clock and I knew that the family would be lying supine behind closed shutters, only to awake and start to buzz at each other, drowsily, like sun-drugged flies, at about half past five.

I made my way back to the villa with the utmost speed. When I was a hundred yards away, I took off my shirt and wrapped it carefully round my jam-jars full of specimens so that not a chink or a rattle would betray my presence; then, cautioning Roger upon pain of death not to utter a sound, we made our way cautiously into the villa and slipped like shadows into my bedroom. Roger squatted panting in the middle of the floor and viewed me with considerable surprise as I took off all my clothes and climbed into bed. He was not at all sure that he approved of this untoward behaviour. As far as he was concerned, the whole afternoon stretched ahead of us, littered with exciting adventures, and here was I preparing to go to sleep. He whined experimentally and I shushed him with such fierceness that his ears drooped, and putting his stumpy tail between his legs, he crept under the bed and curled up with a rueful sigh. I took a book and tried to concentrate on it. The half-closed shutters made the room look like a cool, green aquarium, but in fact the air was still and hot and the sweat rolled in rivulets down my ribs. What on earth, I thought, shifting uncomfortably on the already sodden sheet, could the family possibly see in a siesta? What good did it do them? In fact, how they managed to sleep at all was a mystery to me. At this moment I sank swiftly into oblivion.

I woke at half past five and staggered out, half-asleep, to the veranda, where the family were having tea.

"Good heavens," said Mother. "Have you been sleeping?" I said, as casually as I could, that I thought a siesta a good thing that afternoon.

"Are you feeling well, dear?" she asked anxiously.

I said, yes, I felt fine. I had decided to have a siesta in order to prepare myself for that evening.

"Why, what's happening, dear?" asked Mother.

I said, with all the nonchalance I could muster, that I was going out at ten o'clock with a fisherman who was going to take me night-fishing, for, as I explained, there were certain creatures that came out only at night and this was the best method of obtaining them.

"I hope this does not mean," said Larry ominously, "that we're going to have octopus and conger eels flopping around the floor. Better stop him, Mother. Before you know where you are the whole villa will look and smell like Grimsby."

I replied, somewhat heatedly, that I did not intend to bring the specimens back to the villa, but to put them straight into my special rock pool.

"Ten o'clock's rather late, dear," said Mother. "What time will you be back?"

Lying valiantly, I said I thought I would be back at about eleven.

"Well, mind you wrap up warmly," said Mother, who was always convinced that, in spite of the nights being warm and balmy, I would inevitably end up with double pneumonia if I did not wear a jersey. Promising faithfully to wrap up warmly, I finished my tea and then spent an exciting and satisfying hour or so in marshalling my collecting gear. There was my long-handled net, a long bamboo with three wire hooks on the end for pulling interesting clumps of seaweed nearer to one, eight wide-mouthed jam-jars, and several tins and boxes for putting such things as crabs or shells in. Making sure that Mother was not around, I put on my bathing trunks under my shorts and hid a towel in the bottom of my collecting bag, for I felt sure that I might have to dive for some of the specimens. I knew that Mother's fears of double pneumonia would increase a hundredfold if she thought I was going to do this.

Then at a quarter to ten I slung my bag on my back and, taking a torch, made my way down through the olive groves. The moon was a pale, smudged sickle in a star-lit sky, shedding only the feeblest light. In the black recesses among the olive roots, glow-worms gleamed like emeralds, and I could hear the scops owls calling "toink, toink" to each other from the shadows.

When I reached the beach I found Taki squatting in his boat, smoking. He had already lighted the carbon lamp and it hissed angrily to itself and smelt strongly of garlic as it cast a brilliant circle of white light into the shallow water by the bows. Already I could see that a host of life had been attracted to it. Gobies and blennies had come out of their holes and were sitting on the seaweed-covered rocks, pouting and gulping expectantly like an audience in the theatre waiting for the curtain to go up. Shore crabs scuttled to and fro, pausing now and then to pluck some seaweed delicately and stuff it carefully into their mouths; and everywhere there trundled top-shells, dragged by small, choleric-looking hermit crabs, who now occupied the shells in place of their rightful owners.

I arranged my collecting gear in the bottom of the boat and sat down with a contented sigh. Taki pushed off and then, using the oar, punted us along through the shallow water and the beds of ribbon-weed that rustled and whispered along the side of the boat. As soon as we were in deeper water, he fixed both his oars and then rowed standing up. We progressed very slowly, Taki keeping a careful eye on the nimbus of light that illuminated the sea bottom for some twelve feet in every direction. The oars squeaked musically and Taki hummed to himself. Along one side of the boat lay an eight-foot pole ending in a five-pronged, savagely barbed trident. In the bow I could see the little bottle of olive oil, such a necessary accoutrement to the fisherman, for should a slight wind blow up and ruffle the waters, a sprinkling of oil would have a magically calming effect on the pleated surface of the sea. Slowly and steadily we crept out towards the black triangular silhouette of Pondikonissi to where the reefs lay. When we neared them Taki rested on his oars for a moment and looked at me.

"We'll go round and round for five minutes," he said, "so that I may catch what there is. Then after that I will take you round to catch the things that you want."

I readily agreed to this, for I was anxious to see how Taki fished with his massive trident. Very slowly we edged our way round the biggest of the reefs, the light illuminating the strange submarine cliffs covered with pink and purple seaweeds that looked like fluffy oak trees. Peering down into the water, one felt as though one were a kestrel, floating smoothly on outstretched wings over a multi-coloured autumn forest.

Suddenly Taki stopped rowing and dug his oars gently into the water to act as a brake. The boat came to an almost complete standstill as he picked up the trident.

"Look," he said, pointing to the sandy bottom under a great bulwark of submarine cliff. "Scorpios."

At first glance I could see nothing, then suddenly I saw what he meant. Lying on the sand was a fish some two feet long with a great filigree of sharp spines like a dragon's crest along its back, and enormous petrel fins spread out on the sand. It had a tremendously wide head with golden eyes and a sulky, pouting mouth. But it was the colours that astonished me, for it was decked out in a series of reds ranging from scarlet to wine, pricked out and accentuated here and there with white. It looked immensely sure of itself as it lay there, flamboyant, on the sand, and immensely dangerous, too.

"This is good eating," whispered Taki to my surprise, for the fish, if anything, looked highly poisonous.

Slowly and delicately he lowered the trident into the water, easing the barbed fork inch by inch towards the fish. There was no sound except the peevish hissing of the lamp. Slowly, inexorably, the trident got closer and closer. I held my breath. Surely that great fish with its gold-flecked eyes must notice its approaching doom? A sudden flip of the tail, I thought, and a swirl of sand and it would be gone. But no. It just lay there gulping methodically and pompously to itself. When the trident was within a foot of it, Taki paused. I saw him gently shift his grip on the haft. He stood immobile for a second, although it seemed an interminable time to me, and then suddenly, so speedily that I did not actually see the movement, he drove the five prongs swiftly and neatly through the back of the great fish's head. There was a swirl of sand and blood and the fish twisted and writhed on the prongs, curling its body so that the spines along its back jabbed at the trident. But Taki had driven the trident home too skilfully and it could not escape. Quickly, hand over hand, he pulled in the pole, and the fish came over the side and into the boat, flapping and writhing. I came forward to help him get it off the prongs, but he pushed me back roughly.

"Take care," he said, "the scorpios is a bad fish."

I watched while, with the aid of the oar blade, he got the fish off the trident, and although to all intents and purposes it must have been dead, it still wriggled and flapped and tried to drive the spines on its back into the side of the boat.

"Look, look," said Taki. "You see now why we call it scorpios. If he can stab you with those spines, Saint Spiridion, what pain you would have! You would have to go to the hospital quickly."

With the aid of the oar and the trident, and a dexterous bit of juggling, he managed to lift the scorpion fish up and drop it into an empty kerosene tin where it could do no harm. I wanted to know why, if it was poisonous, it was supposed to be good eating.

"Ah," said Taki, "it's only the spines. You cut those off. The flesh is sweet, as sweet as honey. I will give it to you to take home with you."

He bent over his oars once more and we proceeded to squeak our way along the edge of the reef again. Presently he paused once more. Here the seabed was sandy with just a few scattered tufts of young green ribbon-weed. Again, he slowed the boat to a standstill and picked up his trident.

"Look," he said. "Octopus."

My stomach gave a clutch of excitement, for the only octopuses I had seen had been the dead ones on sale in the town, and these, I felt sure, bore no resemblance to the living creature. But peer as hard as I could, the sandy bottom appeared to be completely devoid of life.

"There, *there*," said Taki, lowering the trident gently into the water and pointing. "Can't you see it? Did you leave your eyes behind? There, *there*. Look, I am almost touching it."

Still I could not see it. He lowered the trident another foot. "Now can you see it, foolish one?" he chuckled. "Just at the end of the prongs."

And suddenly I could see it. I had been looking at it all the time, but it was so grey and sandlike that I had mistaken it for part of the seabed. It squatted on the sand in a nest of tentacles, and there under its bald, domed head its eyes, uncannily human, peered up at us forlornly.

"It's a big one," said Taki.

He shifted the trident slightly in his grasp, but the movement was incautious. Suddenly the octopus turned from a drab sandy colour to a bright and startling iridescent green. It squirted a jet

50

of water out of its syphon, and projected by this, in a swirl of sand, it shot off the seabed. Its tentacles trailed out behind it, and as it sped through the water, it looked like a runaway balloon.

"Ah, *gammoto*," said Taki.

He threw the trident down and seizing the oars he rowed swiftly in the wake of the octopus. The octopus obviously possessed a touching faith in its camouflage, for it had come to rest on the seabed some thirty-five feet away.

Once again, Taki eased the boat up to it and once again he lowered the trident carefully into the water. This time he took no risks and made no incautious movements. When the pronged fork was within a foot of the octopus's domed head, Taki strengthened his grip on the pole and plunged it home. Immediately the silver sand boiled up in a cloud as the octopus's tentacles threshed and writhed and wound themselves round the trident. Ink spurted from its body and hung like a trembling curtain of black lace or coiled like smoke across the sand. Taki was chuckling now with pleasure. He hauled the trident up swiftly, and as the octopus came into the boat, two of its tentacles seized and adhered to the side. Taki gave a sharp tug and the tentacles were pulled free with a ripping, rasping noise that was like the sound of sticking plaster being removed, a thousand times magnified. Swiftly, Taki grabbed the round, slimy body of the octopus and deftly removed it from the prongs and then, to my astonishment, he lifted this writhing Medusa head and put it to his face so that the tentacles wound round his forehead, his cheeks, and his neck, the suckers leaving white impressions against his dark skin. Then, choosing his spot carefully, he suddenly buried his teeth in the very core of the

51

creature with a snap and a sideways jerk, reminiscent of a terrier breaking the back of a rat. He had obviously bitten through some vital nerve-centre, for immediately the tentacles released their grip on his head and fell limply, only their very extremities twitching and curling slightly. Taki threw the octopus into the tin with the scorpion fish and spat over the side of the boat and then, reaching over, cupped a handful of seawater and swilled his mouth out with it.

"You have brought me luck," he said, grinning and wiping his mouth. "It is not many nights that I get an octopus and a scorpios."

But apparently Taki's luck stopped short at the octopus, for although we circled the reef several times, we caught nothing more. We did see the head of a moray eel sticking out of its hole in the reef, an extremely vicious-looking head the size of a small dog's. But when Taki lowered the trident, the moray eel, very smoothly and with much dignity, retreated with fluid grace into the depths of the reef and we did not see him again. For myself, I was quite glad, for I imagined he must have been about six feet long, and to wrestle about in a dimly lit boat with a six-foot moray eel was an experience that even I, ardent naturalist though I was, felt I could do without.

"Ah, well," said Taki philosophically. "Now let's go and do your fishing."

He rowed me out to the largest of the reefs and landed me with my gear on its flat top. Armed with my net, I prowled along the edge of the reef while Taki rowed the boat some six feet behind me, illuminating the smouldering beauty of the rocks. There was so much life that I despaired of being able to capture it all.

There were fragile blennies, decked out in gold and scarlet; tiny fish half the size of a matchstick with great black eyes and pillar-box red bodies; and others, the same size, whose colouring was a combination of deep Prussian- and pale powder-blue. There were blood-red starfish and purple, brittle starfish, their long, slender, spiky arms forever coiling and uncoiling. These had to be lifted in the net with the utmost delicacy, for the slightest shock and they would, with gay abandon, shed all their arms lavishly. There were slipper limpets that, when you turned them over, you found had half the underside covered by a neat flange of shell, so that the whole thing *did* look rather like a baggy, shapeless carpet slipper designed for a gouty foot. Then there were cowries, some as white as snow and delicately ribbed, others a pale cream, heavily blotched and smudged with purple-black markings. Then there were the coat-of-mail shells, or chitons, some two and a half inches long, that clung to crannies in the rocks, looking like gigantic woodlice. I saw a baby cuttlefish the size of a match-box and almost fell off the edge of the reef in my efforts to capture him, but to my immense chagrin, he escaped. After only half an hour's collecting I found that my jars, tins, and boxes were crammed to overflowing with life, and I know that, albeit reluctantly, I would have to stop.

Taki, very good-humouredly, rowed me over to my favourite bay and stood watching with amusement while I carefully emptied my jars of specimens into my rock pool. Then he rowed me back to the jetty below Menelaos'. Here he strung a cord through the gills of the now dead scorpion fish and handed it to me.

"Tell your mother," he said, "to cook it with hot paprika and oil and potatoes and little marrows. It is very sweet."

I thanked him for this and for the fact that he had been so patient with me.

"Come fishing again," he said. "I shall be up here next week. Probably Wednesday or Thursday. I'll send a message to you when I arrive."

I thanked him and said I would look forward to it. He pushed the boat off and poled his way through the shallow waters heading in the direction of Benitses.

I shouted "Be happy" after him.

"*Pasto calo*," he answered. "Go to the good."

I turned and trudged my way wearily up the hill. I discovered to my horror that it was half past two and I knew Mother would by now have convinced herself that I had been drowned or eaten by a shark or overtaken by some similar fate. However, I hoped that the scorpion fish would placate her.

3

THE MYRTLE FORESTS

About half a mile north of the villa the olive grove thinned out and there was a great flat basin, fifty or sixty acres in extent, on which no olives grew. Here was only a great green forest of myrtle bushes, interspersed with dry, stony grassland, decorated with the strange candelabras of the thistles, glowing a vivid electric blue, and the huge flaky bulb of squills. This was one of my favourite hunting grounds, for it contained a remarkable selection of insect life. Roger and I would squat in the heavily scented shade of the myrtle bushes and watch the array of creatures that passed us; at certain times of the day the branches were as busy as the main street of a town.

The myrtle forests were full of mantises some three inches long, with vivid green wings. They would sway through the myrtle branches on their slender legs, their wickedly barbed front arms held up in an attitude of hypocritical prayer, their little pointed faces with their bulbous straw-coloured eyes turning this way and that, missing nothing, like angular, embittered spinsters at a cocktail party. Should a cabbage white or a fritillary land on the glossy myrtle leaves, the mantises

55

BIRDS, BEASTS AND RELATIVES

would approach them with the utmost caution, moving almost imperceptibly, pausing now and then to sway gently to and fro on their legs, beseeching the butterfly to believe they were really wind-ruffled leaves.

I once saw a mantis stalk and finally launch himself at a large swallow-tail which was sitting in the sun gently moving its wings and meditating. At the last minute, however, the mantis missed its footing and instead of catching the swallow-tail by the body, as it had intended to do, caught it by one wing. The swallow-tail came out of its trance with a start and flapped its wings so vigorously that it succeeded in lifting the forequarters of the mantis off the leaves. A few more vigorous flappings and, to the mantis' annoyance, the swallow-tail flew lopsidedly away with a large section missing from one wing. The mantis philosophically sat down and ate the piece of wing that it had retained in its claws.

Under the rocks that littered the ground among the thistles there lived a surprising variety of creatures, in spite of the fact that the earth was baked rock-hard by the sun and was almost hot enough to poach an egg. Here lived a beast that always gave me the creeps. It was a flattened centipede some two inches long, with a thick fringe of long spiky legs along each side of its body. It was so flat that it could get into the most minute crevice and it moved with tremendous speed, seeming more to glide over the ground than run, as smoothly as a flat pebble skims across ice. These creatures were called Scutigeridae, and I could think of no other name which would be so apt in conjuring up their particularly obnoxious form of locomotion.

Scattered among the rocks, you would find holes that had been driven into the hard ground, each the size of a half-crown or larger. They were silk-lined and with a web spread to a three-inch circle around the mouth of the burrow. These were the lairs of the tarantulas, great, fat, chocolate-coloured spiders with fawn-and-cinnamon markings. With their legs spread out, they covered an area perhaps the size of a coffee saucer and their bodies were about the size of half a small walnut. They were immensely powerful spiders, quick and cruel in their hunting, and displaying a remarkable sort of inimical intelligence. For the most part, they hunted at night, but occasionally you would see them during the day, striding swiftly through the thistles on their long legs, in search of their prey. Generally, as soon as they saw you, they would scuttle off and soon be lost among the myrtles, but one day I saw one who was so completely absorbed that he let me approach quite close.

He was some six or seven feet away from his burrow, and he was standing halfway up a blue thistle, waving his front legs and peering about him, reminding me irresistibly of a hunter who had climbed up a tree in order to see if there is any game about. He continued to do this for about five minutes while I squatted on my haunches and watched him. Presently he climbed carefully down the thistle and set off in a very determined manner. It was almost as though he had seen something from his lofty perch, but searching the ground around, I could see no sign of life, and in any case I was not at all sure that a tarantula's eyesight was as good as all that. But he marched along in a determined fashion until he came to a large clump of Job's tears, a fine trembling grass whose seed-heads look like little white plaited rolls of bread. Going closer to this, I suddenly realized what the tarantula appeared to be after, for under the delicate fountain of white grass there was a lark's nest. It had four eggs in it and one of them had just hatched, and the tiny, pink, downy offspring was still struggling feebly in the remains of the shell.

Before I could do anything sensible to save it, the tarantula had marched up over the edge of the nest. He loomed there for a moment, monstrous and terrifying, and then swiftly he drew the quivering baby to him and sank his long, curved mandibles into its back. The baby gave two minute, almost inaudible squeaks and opened its mouth wide as it writhed briefly in the hairy embrace of the spider. The poison took effect and it went rigid for a brief moment and then hung limply. The spider waited, immobile, till he was certain the poison had done its work, and then he turned and marched off, the baby hanging limply from his jaws. He looked like some strange, leggy retriever, bringing in his first grouse of the season. Without a pause, he hurried back to his burrow and disappeared inside it, carrying the limp, pathetic little body of the fledgling.

I was amazed by this encounter, for two reasons: firstly, because I did not realize that tarantulas would tackle anything the size of a baby bird, and secondly, because I could not see how he knew the nest was there – and he obviously did know, for he walked, unhesitatingly, straight to it. The distance from the thistle he had climbed to the nest was about thirty-five feet, as I found out by pacing it, and I was positive that no spider had the eyesight to be able to spot such a well camouflaged nest and the fledgling from that distance. This left only smell, and here again, although I knew animals could smell subtle scents which our blunted nostrils could not pick up, I felt that on a breathlessly still day at thirty-five feet it would take a remarkable olfactory sense to be able to pinpoint the baby lark. The only solution I could come to was that the spider had, during his perambulations, discovered the nest and kept checking on it periodically to see whether the young had hatched. But this did not satisfy me as an explanation, for it attributed a thought process to an insect which I was pretty certain it did not possess. Even my oracle, Theodore, could not explain this puzzle satisfactorily. All I knew was that that particular pair of larks did not succeed in rearing a single young one that year.

Other creatures that fascinated me greatly in the myrtle forests were the ant-lion larvae. Adult ant-lions come in a variety of sizes and, for the most part, rather drab colouring. They look like extremely untidy and demented dragonflies. They have wings that seem to be out of all proportion to their bodies and these they flap with a desperate air, as though it required the maximum amount of energy to prevent them from crashing to the earth. They were a good-natured, bumbling sort of beast, and did no harm to anybody. But the same could not be said of their larvae. What the rapacious dragonfly larvae were to the pond, the ant-lion larvae were to the dry, sandy areas that lay between the myrtle bushes. The only sign that there were ant-lion larvae about was a series of curious, cone-shaped depressions in areas where the soil was fine and soft enough to be dug. The first time I discovered these cones, I was greatly puzzled as to what had made them. I wondered if perhaps some mice had been excavating for roots or something similar; I was unaware that at the base of each cone was the architect, waiting taut and ready in the sand, as dangerous as a hidden mantrap. Then I saw one of these cones in action and realized for the first time that it was not only the larva's home, but also a gigantic trap.

An ant would come trotting along (I always felt they hummed to themselves as they went about their work); it might be one of the little, busy, black variety or one of the large, red, solitary ants that staggered about the countryside with their red abdomens pointing to the sky, for some obscure reason, like anti-aircraft guns. Whichever species it was, if it happened to walk over the edge of one of the little pits, it immediately found that the sloping sides shifted so that it very soon started to slide down towards the base of the cone. It would then turn and try to climb out of the pit, but the earth or sand would shift in little avalanches under its feet. As soon as one of these avalanches had trickled down to the base of the cone, it would be the signal for the larva to come into action. Suddenly the ant would find itself bombarded with a rapid machine-gun fire of sand or earth, projected up from the bottom of the pit with incredible speed by the head of the larva. With the shifting ground underfoot and being bombarded with earth or sand, the ant would miss its foothold and roll ignominiously down to the bottom of the pit. Out of the sand, with utmost speed, would appear the head of the ant-lion larva, a flattened, ant-like head, with a pair of enormous curved jaws, like sickles. These would be plunged into the unfortunate ant's body and the larva would sink back beneath the sand, dragging the kicking and struggling ant with it to its grave. As I felt the ant-lion larvae took an unfair advantage over the dim-witted and rather earnest ants, I had no compunction in digging them up when I found them, taking them home, and making them hatch out eventually in little muslin cages, so that if they were a species new to me, I could add them to my collection.

One day we had one of those freak storms when the sky turned blue-black and the lightning fretted a silver filigree across it. And then had come the rain – great, fat, heavy drops, as warm as blood. When the storm had passed, the sky had been washed to the clear blue of a hedge-sparrow's egg and the damp earth sent out wonderfully rich, almost gastronomic smells as of fruit cake or plum pudding; and the olive trunks steamed as the rain was dried off them by the sun, each trunk looking as though it were on fire. Roger and I liked these summer storms. It was fun to be able to splash through the puddles and feel one's clothes getting wetter and wetter in the warm rain. In addition to this, Roger derived considerable amusement by barking at the lightning. When the rain ceased we were passing the myrtle forests, and I went in on the off-chance that the storm might have brought out some creatures that would normally be sheltering from the heat of the day. Sure enough, on a myrtle branch there were two fat, honey- and amber-coloured snails gliding smoothly towards each other, their horns waving provocatively. Normally, I knew, in the height of the summer, these snails would aestivate. They would attach themselves to a convenient branch, construct a thin, paper-like front door over the mouth of the shell, and then retreat deep into its convolutions in order to husband the moisture in their bodies from the fierce heat of the sun. This freak storm had obviously awakened them and made them feel gay and romantic. As I watched them they glided up to each other until their horns touched. Then they paused and gazed long and earnestly into each other's eyes. One of them then shifted his position slightly so that he could glide alongside the other one. When he was alongside, something happened that made me doubt the evidence of my own eyes. From his side, and almost simultaneously from the side of the other snail, there shot what appeared to be two minute, fragile white darts, each attached to a slender white cord. The dart from snail one pierced the side of snail two and disappeared, and the dart from snail two performed a similar function on snail one. So, there they were, side by side attached to each other by the two little white cords. And there they sat like two curious sailing ships roped together. This was amazing enough, but stranger things were to follow. The cords gradually appeared to get shorter and shorter and drew the two snails together. Peering at them so closely that my nose was almost touching them, I came to the incredulous conclusion that each snail, by some incredible mechanism in its body, was winching its rope in, thus hauling the other until presently their bodies were pressed tightly together. I knew they must be mating, but their bodies had become so amalgamated that I could not see the precise nature of the act. They stayed rapturously side by side for some fifteen minutes and then, without so much as a nod or a thank you, they glided away in opposite directions, neither one displaying any signs of darts or ropes, or indeed any sign of enthusiasm at having culminated their love affair successfully.

I was so intrigued by this piece of behaviour that I could hardly wait until the following Thursday, when Theodore came to tea, to tell him about it. Theodore listened, rocking gently on his toes and nodding gravely while I graphically described what I had witnessed.

"Aha, yes," he said when I had finished. "You were…um…you know…um…extremely lucky to see that. I have watched any number of snails and I have never seen it."

I asked whether I had imagined the little darts and the ropes.

"No, no," said Theodore. "That's quite correct. The darts are formed of a sort of…um…calcium–like substance and once they have penetrated the snail, they, you know, disappear…dissolve. It seems there is some evidence to think that the darts cause a *tingling* sensation which the snails…um…apparently find pleasant."

I asked whether I was right in assuming that each snail had winched its rope in.

"Yes, yes, that's quite correct," said Theodore. "They apparently have some…um…sort of mechanism inside which can pull the rope back again."

I said I thought it was one of the most remarkable things I had ever seen.

"Yes, indeed. Extremely curious," said Theodore, and then added a bombshell that took my breath away. "Once they are alongside, the…um…male half of one snail mates with the, um…female half of the other snail and…um, *vice versa*, as it were."

It took me a moment or so to absorb this astonishing information. Was I correct in assuming, I inquired cautiously, that each snail was both male *and* female?

"Um. Yes," said Theodore, "hermaphrodite."

His eyes twinkled at me and he rasped the side of his beard with his thumb. Larry, who had been wearing the pained expression he normally wore when Theodore and I discussed natural history, was equally astonished by this amazing revelation of the snails' sex life.

"Surely you're joking, Theodore?" he protested. "You mean to say that each snail is both a male and a female?"

"Yes, indeed," said Theodore, adding with masterly understatement, "it's very curious."

"Good God," cried Larry. "I think it's unfair. All those damned slimy things wandering about seducing each other like mad all over the bushes, and having the pleasures of both sensations. Why couldn't such a gift be given to the human race? That's what I want to know."

"Aha, yes. But then you would have to lay eggs," Theodore pointed out.

"True," said Larry, "but what a marvellous way of getting out of cocktail parties – 'I'm terribly sorry I can't come,' you would say. 'I've got to sit on my eggs.'"

Theodore gave a little snort of laughter.

"But snails don't sit on their eggs," he explained. "They bury them in damp earth and leave them."

"The ideal way of bringing up a family," said Mother, unexpectedly but with immense conviction. "I wish I'd been able to bury you all in some damp earth and leave you."

"That's an extremely harsh and ungrateful thing to say," said Larry. "You've probably given Gerry a complex for the rest of his life."

But if the conversation had given me a complex, it was one about snails, for I was already planning vast snail-hunting expeditions with Roger, so that I could bring dozens of them back to the villa and keep them in tins, where I could observe them shooting their love-darts at each other to my heart's content. But, in spite of the fact that I caught hundreds of snails during the next few weeks, kept them incarcerated in tins and lavished every care and attention on them (even gave them simulated thunderstorms with the aid of a watering can), I could not get them to mate.

The only other time I saw snails indulging in this curious love-play was when I succeeded in obtaining a pair of the giant Roman, or apple, snails that lived on the stony outcrops of the Mountain of the Ten Saints, and the only reason I was able to get up there and capture these snails was because, on my birthday, Mother had purchased for me my heart's desire, a sturdy baby donkey.

Although, ever since we arrived in Corfu, I had been aware that there were vast quantities of donkeys there – indeed the entire agricultural economy of the island depended on them – I had not really concentrated on them until we had gone to Katerina's wedding. Here a great number of the donkeys had brought with them their babies, many of them only a few days old. I was enchanted by their bulbous knees, their great ears, and their wobbling, uncertain walk and I had determined then, come what might, that I would possess a donkey of my own.

As I explained to Mother, while trying to argue her into agreeing to this, if I had a donkey to carry me and my equipment, I could go so much farther afield. Why couldn't I have it for Christmas, I asked? Because, Mother replied, firstly, they were too expensive, and secondly, there were not any babies available at that precise time. But if they were too expensive, I argued, why couldn't I have one as a Christmas and birthday present? I would willingly forgo all other presents in lieu of a donkey. Mother said she would see, which I knew from bitter experience generally meant that she would forget about the matter as rapidly and as comprehensively as possible. As it got near to my birthday, I once again reiterated all the arguments in favour of having a donkey. Mother just repeated that we would see.

Then one day, Costas, the brother of our maid, made his appearance in the olive grove just outside our little garden carrying on his shoulders a great bundle of tall bamboos. Whistling happily to himself he proceeded to dig holes in the ground and to set the bamboos upright so that they formed a small square. Peering at him through the fuchsia hedge, I wondered what on earth he was doing, so, whistling Roger, I went round to see.

"I am building," said Costas, "a house for your mother." I was astonished. What on earth could Mother want a bamboo house for? Had she, perhaps, decided to sleep out of doors? I felt this was unlikely. What, I inquired of Costas, did Mother want with a bamboo house?

He gazed at me wall-eyed.

"Who knows?" he said shrugging. "Perhaps she wants to keep plants in it or store sweet potatoes for the winter."

I thought this was extremely unlikely as well, but having watched Costas for half an hour I grew bored and went off for a walk with Roger.

By the next day the framework of the bamboo hut had been finished and Costas was now busy twining bundles of reeds between the bamboos to form solid walls and the roof. By the next day it was completed and looked exactly like one of Robinson Crusoe's earlier attempts at house-building. When I inquired of Mother what she intended to use the house for, she said that she was not quite sure, but she felt it would come in useful. With that vague information I had to be content.

The day before my birthday, everybody started acting in a slightly more eccentric manner than usual. Larry, for some reason best known to himself, went about the house shouting "Tantivy!" and "Tally-ho" and similar hunting slogans. As he was fairly frequently afflicted in this way, I did not take much notice.

Margo kept dodging about the house carrying mysterious bundles under her arms, and at one point I came face to face with her in the hall and noted, with astonishment, that her arms were full of multi-coloured decorations left over from Christmas. On seeing me she uttered a squeak of dismay and rushed into her bedroom in such a guilty and furtive manner that I was left staring after her with open mouth.

Even Leslie and Spiro were afflicted, it seemed, and they kept going into mysterious huddles in the garden. From the snippets of their conversation that I heard, I could not make head or tail of what they were planning.

"In the backs seats," Spiro said, scowling. "Honest to Gods, Masters Leslies, I have dones it befores."

"Well, if you're sure, Spiro," Leslie replied doubtfully, "but we don't want any broken legs or anything."

Then Leslie saw me undisguisedly eavesdropping and asked me truculently what the hell I thought I was doing, eavesdropping on people's private conversations? Why didn't I go down to the nearest cliff and jump off? Feeling that the family were in no mood to be amicable, I took Roger off into the olive groves and for the rest of the day we ineffectually chased green lizards.

That night I had just turned down the lamp and snuggled down in bed when I heard sounds of raucous singing, accompanied by gales of laughter, coming through the olive groves. As the uproar got closer, I could recognize Leslie's and Larry's voices, combined with Spiro's, each of them appearing to be singing a different song. It seemed as though they had been somewhere and celebrated too well. From the indignant whispering and shuffling going on in the corridor, I could tell that Margo and Mother had reached the same conclusion.

They burst into the villa, laughing hysterically at some witticism that Larry had produced, and were shushed fiercely by Margo and Mother.

"Do be quiet," said Mother. "You'll wake Gerry. What have you been drinking?"

"Wine," said Larry in a dignified voice. He hiccupped.

"Wine," said Leslie. "And then we danced, and Spiro danced, and I danced, and Larry danced. And Spiro danced and then Larry danced and then I danced."

"I think you had better go to bed," said Mother.

"And then Spiro danced again," said Leslie, "and then Larry danced."

"All right, dear, all right," said Mother. "Go to *bed*, for heaven's sake. Really, Spiro, I do feel that you shouldn't have let them drink so much."

"Spiro danced," said Leslie, driving the point home.

"I'll take him to bed," said Larry. "I'm the only sober member of the party."

There was the sound of lurching feet on the tiles as Leslie and Larry, clasped in each other's arms, staggered down the corridor.

"I'm now dancing with *you*," came Leslie's voice as Larry dragged him into his bedroom and put him to bed.

"I'm sorrys, Mrs Durrells," said Spiro, his deep voice thickened with wine, "but I couldn't stops thems."

"Did you get it?" said Margo.

"Yes, Missy Margos. Don'ts you worrys," said Spiro. "It's down with Costas."

Eventually Spiro left and I heard Mother and Margaret going to bed. It made a fittingly mysterious end to what had been a highly confusing day as far as I was concerned. But I soon forgot about the family's behaviour, as, lying in the dark wondering what my presents were going to be the following day, I drifted off to sleep.

The following morning I woke and lay for a moment wondering what was so special about that day, and then I remembered. It was my birthday. I lay there savouring the feeling of having a whole day to myself when people would give me presents and the family would be forced to accede to any reasonable requests. I was just about to get out of bed and go and see what my presents were, when a curious uproar broke out in the hall.

"Hold its head. Hold its *head*," came Leslie's voice.

"Look out, you're spoiling the decorations," wailed Margo.

"Damn the bloody decorations," said Leslie. "Hold its *head*."

"Now, now, dears," said Mother, "don't quarrel."

"Dear God," said Larry in disgust, "dung all over the floor."

The whole of this mysterious conversation was accompanied by a strange pitter-pattering noise, as though someone were bouncing ping-pong balls on the tile floor of the hall. What on earth, I wondered, was the family up to now? Normally at this time they were still lying, semi-conscious, groping bleary-eyed for their early morning cups of tea. I sat up in bed, preparatory to going into the hall to join in whatever fun was afoot, when my bedroom door burst open and a donkey, clad in festoons of coloured crepe paper, Christmas decorations, and with three enormous feathers attached skilfully between its large ears, came galloping into the bedroom, Leslie hanging grimly on to its tail, shouting, "Woa, you bastard!"

"Language, dear," said Mother, looking flustered in the doorway.

"You're spoiling the decorations," screamed Margo.

"The sooner that animal gets out of here," said Larry, "the better. There's dung all over the hall now."

"You frightened it," said Margo.

"I didn't do anything," said Larry indignantly. "I just gave it a little push."

The donkey skidded to a halt by my bedside and gazed at me out of enormous brown eyes. It seemed rather surprised. It shook itself vigorously so that the feathers between its ears fell off and then very dexterously it hacked Leslie on the shin with its hind leg.

"Jesus!" roared Leslie, hopping around on one leg. "It's broken my bloody leg."

"Leslie, dear, there is no need to swear so much," said Mother. "Remember Gerry."

"The sooner you get it out of that bedroom the better," said Larry. "Otherwise the whole place will smell like a midden."

"You've simply *ruined* its decorations," said Margo, "and it took me hours to put them on."

But I was taking no notice of the family. The donkey had approached the edge of my bed and stared at me inquisitively for a moment and then had given a little throaty chuckle and thrust in my outstretched hands a grey muzzle as soft as everything soft I could think of – silkworm cocoons, newly born puppies, sea pebbles, or the velvety feel of a tree frog. Leslie had now removed his trousers and was examining the bruise on his shin, cursing fluently.

"Do you like it dear?" asked Mother.

Like it! I was speechless.

The donkey was a rich dark brown, almost a plum colour, with enormous ears like arum lilies, white socks over tiny polished hooves as neat as a tap-dancer's shoes. Running along her back was the broad black cross that denotes so proudly that her race carried Christ into Jerusalem (and has since continued to be one of the most maligned domestic animals ever), and round each great shining eye she had a neat white circle which denoted that she came from the village of Gastouri.

"You remember Katerina's donkey that you liked so much?" said Margo. "Well, this is her baby."

This, of course, made the donkey even more special. The donkey stood there looking like a refugee from a circus, chewing a piece of tinsel meditatively, while I scrambled out of bed and flung on my clothes. Where, I inquired breathlessly of Mother, was I to keep her? Obviously I couldn't keep her in the villa in view of the fact that Larry had just pointed out to Mother that she could, if she so wished, grow a good crop of potatoes in the hall.

"That's what that house Costas built is for," said Mother.

I was beside myself with delight. What a noble, kindly, benevolent family I had! How cunningly they had kept the secret from me! How hard they had worked to deck the donkey out in its finery! Slowly and gently, as though she were some fragile piece of china, I led my steed out through the garden and round into the olive grove, opened the door of the little bamboo hut, and took her inside. I thought I ought to just try her for size, because Costas was a notoriously bad workman. The little house was splendid. Just big enough for her. I took her out again and tethered her to an olive tree on a long length of rope, then I stayed for half an hour in a dreamlike trance admiring her from every angle while she grazed placidly. Eventually I heard Mother calling me in to breakfast and I sighed with satisfaction. I had decided that, without any doubt whatsoever, and without wishing in any way to be partisan, this donkey was the finest donkey in the whole of the island of Corfu. For no reason that I could think of, I decided to call her

Sally. I gave her a quick kiss on her silken muzzle and then went in to breakfast.

After breakfast, to my astonishment, Larry, with a magnanimous air, said that if I liked he would teach me to ride. I said that I didn't know he could ride.

"Of course," said Larry airily. "When we were in India I was always galloping about on ponies and things. I used to groom them and feed them and so forth. Have to know what you're doing, of course."

So, armed with a blanket and a large piece of webbing, we went out into the olive grove, placed the blanket on Sally's back, and tied it in position. She viewed these preparations with interest but a lack of enthusiasm. With a certain amount of difficulty, for Sally would persist in walking round and round in a tight circle, Larry succeeded in getting me onto her back. He then exchanged her tether for a rope halter and rope reins.

"Now," he said, "you just steer her as though she's a boat. When you want her to go faster, just simply kick her in the ribs with your heels."

If that was all there was to riding, I felt, it was going to be simplicity itself. I jerked on the reins and dug my heels into Sally's ribs. It was unfortunate that my fall was broken by a large and exceptionally luxuriant bramble bush. Sally peered at me as I extricated myself, with a look of astonishment on her face.

"Perhaps," said Larry, "you ought to have a stick so then you can use your legs for gripping on to her and you won't fall off."

He cut me a short stick and once again I mounted Sally. This time I wrapped my legs tightly round her barrel body and gave her a sharp tap with my switch. She bucked several times, indignantly, but I clung on like a limpet, and to my delight, within half an hour, I had her trotting to and fro between the olive trees, responding neatly to tugs on the rein. Larry had been lying under the olives smoking and watching my progress. Now, as I appeared to have mastered the equestrian art, he rose to his feet and took a penknife out of his pocket.

"Now," he said, as I dismounted, "I'll show you how to look after her. First of all, you must brush her down every morning. We'll get a brush for you in town. Then you must make sure her hooves are clean. You must do that every day."

I inquired, puzzled, how did one clean donkeys' hooves?

"I'll show you," said Larry nonchalantly.

He walked up to Sally, bent down, and picked up her hind leg.

"In here," he said, pointing with the blade of the knife at Sally's hoof, "an awful lot of muck gets trapped. This can lead to all sorts of things. Foot-rot and so forth, and it's very important to keep them clean."

So saying, he dug his penknife blade into Sally's hoof. What Larry had not realized was that donkeys in Corfu were unshod and that a baby donkey's hoof is still, comparatively speaking, soft and very delicate. So, not unnaturally, Sally reacted as though Larry had jabbed her with a red-hot skewer. She wrenched her hoof out of his hands and as he straightened up and turned in astonishment, she did a pretty pirouette and kicked him neatly in the pit of the stomach with both hind legs. Larry sat down heavily, his face went white, and he doubled up, clasping his stomach and making strange rattling noises. The alarm I felt was not for Larry but for Sally, for I was quite sure that he would extract the most terrible retribution when he recovered. Hastily I undid Sally's rope and flicked her on the rump with the stick and watched her canter off into the olives. Then I ran into the house and informed Mother that Larry had had an accident. The entire family, including Spiro, who had just arrived, came running out into the olive grove where Larry was still writhing about uttering great sobbing, wheezing noises.

"Larry, dear," said Mother distraught, "what *have* you been doing?"

"Attacked," gasped Larry between wheezes. "Unprovoked... Creature mad... Probably rabies... Ruptured appendix."

With Leslie on one side of him and Spiro on the other they carted Larry slowly back to the villa, with Mother and Margo fluttering commiseratingly and ineffectually around him. In a crisis of this magnitude, involving my family, one had to keep one's wits about one or all was lost. I ran swiftly round to the kitchen door where, panting but innocent, I informed our maid that I was going to spend the day out and could she give me some food to eat. She put half a loaf of bread, some onions, some olives, and a hunk of cold meat into a paper bag and gave it to me. Fruit I knew I could obtain from any of my peasant friends. Then I raced through the olive groves, carrying this provender, in search of Sally.

I eventually found her half a mile away, grazing on a succulent patch of grass. After several ineffectual attempts, I managed to scramble up onto her back and then, belabouring her behind with a stick, I urged her to a brisk trot as far away from the villa as possible.

I had to return to the villa for tea because Theodore was coming. When I got back I found Larry, swathed in blankets, lying on the sofa giving Theodore a graphic description of the incident.

"And then, absolutely unprovoked, it suddenly turned on me with slavering jaws, like the charge of the Light Brigade." He broke off to glare at me as I entered the room. "Oh, so you decided to come back. And what, may I inquire, have you done with that equine menace?"

I replied that Sally was safely bedded down in her stable and had, fortunately, suffered no ill effects from the incident. Larry glared at me.

"Well, I'm delighted to hear that," he said caustically. "The fact that I am lying here with my spleen ruptured in three places is of apparently little or no moment."

"I have brought you...um...a little, you know...er...gift," said Theodore, and he presented me with a replica of his own collecting box, complete with tubes and a fine muslin net. I could not have asked for anything nicer and I thanked him volubly.

"You had better go and thank Katerina too, dear," said Mother. "She didn't really want to part with Sally, you know."

"I am surprised," said Larry. "I'd have thought she'd have been only too *glad* to get rid of her."

"You'd better not go and see Katerina now," said Margo. "She's getting near her time."

Intrigued by this unusual phrase, I asked what "getting near her time" meant.

"She's going to have a baby, dear," said Mother.

"The wonder of it is," said Larry, "as I thought when we went to the wedding, she didn't have it in the vestry."

"Larry, dear," said Mother. "Not in front of Gerry."

"Well, it's true," said Larry. "I've never seen such a pregnant bride in white."

I said I thought it would be a good idea if I went to thank Katerina *before* she had the baby because after she had it she would probably be very busy. Reluctantly, Mother agreed to this, and so the following morning I mounted Sally and rode off through the olive trees in the direction of Gastouri, Roger trotting behind and indulging in a game which he and Sally had invented between them, which consisted of Roger darting in at intervals and nibbling her heels gently, growling furiously, whereupon Sally would give a skittish little buck and attempt to kick him in the ribs.

Presently we came to the little low white house, with the flattened area outside its front door neatly ringed with old rusty cans filled with flowers. To my astonishment I saw that we were not the only visitors that day. There were several elderly gentlemen sitting round a small table, hunched over glasses of wine, their enormous, swooping, nicotine-stained moustaches flapping up and down as they talked to each other. Clustered in the doorway of the house and peering eagerly through the one small window that illuminated its interior, there was a solid wedge of female relatives, all chattering and gesticulating at once.

From inside the house came a series of piercing shrieks, interspersed with cries for help from the Almighty, the Virgin Mary, and St Spiridion. I gathered from all this uproar and activity that I had arrived in the middle of a family row. This interfamily warfare was quite a common thing among the peasants and something I always found very enjoyable, for any quarrel, however trivial, was carried on with grim determination until it was sucked dry of the very last juices of drama, with people shouting abuse at one another through the olive trees and the men periodically chasing each other with bamboos.

I tethered Sally and made my way to the front door of the house, wondering, as I did so, what this particular row was about. The last one in this area that I remembered had lasted for a prodigious length of time (three weeks) and had all been started by a small boy who told his cousin that his grandfather cheated at cards. I wriggled and pushed my way determinedly through the knot of people who blocked the doorway and finally got inside, only to find the entire room seemed to be filled with Katerina's relatives, packed shoulder to shoulder like a football crowd. I had, quite early in life, discovered that the only way of dealing with a situation like this was to get down on one's hands and knees and crawl. This I did and by this means successfully achieved the front row in the circle of relatives that surrounded the great double bed.

Now I could see that something much more interesting than a family row was taking place. Katerina was lying on the bed with her cheap print frock rolled right up above her great, swollen breasts. Her hands were tightly clasping the head of the big brass bedstead, her white mound of a stomach quivered and strained with what appeared to be a life of its own, and she kept drawing her legs up and screaming, rolling her head from side to side, the sweat pouring down her face. Near her by the bedside, and obviously in charge of the proceedings, was a tiny, dirty, wizened little witch of a woman holding a bucket in one hand full of well water. Periodically she would dip a bundle of filthy rags into this and mop Katerina's face and her thighs with it. On the table by the bedstead a jug full of wine and a glass stood, and every time the old crone had finished the ablutions, she would put a drop of wine in the glass and force it into Katerina's mouth; then she would fill the glass and drain it herself, for presumably, in her capacity as midwife, she needed to keep up her strength as much as Katerina.

I congratulated myself warmly on the fact that I had not been deviated on my ride up to Katerina's house by several interesting things I had seen. If, for example, I had stopped to climb up to what I was pretty certain was a magpie's nest, I would probably have missed this whole exciting scene. Curiously enough, I was so used to the shrill indignation of the peasants over the most trivial circumstances that I did not really, consciously, associate Katerina's falsetto screams with pain. It was obvious that she was in some pain. Her face was white, crumpled, and old-looking, but I automatically subtracted ninety per cent of the screaming as exaggeration. Now and then, when she uttered a particularly loud scream and implored St Spiridion for his aid, all the relatives would scream in sympathy and also implore the Saint's intervention. The resulting cacophony in that tiny space had to be heard to be believed.

Suddenly Katerina clasped the bed-head still more tightly, the muscles in her brown arms showing taut. She writhed, drew up her legs and spread them wide apart.

"It is coming. It is coming. Praised be Saint Spiridion," shouted all the relatives in chorus, and I noticed in the middle of the tangled, matted mass of Katerina's pubic hairs a round white object appear, rather like the top of an egg. There was a moment's pause and Katerina strained again and uttered a moaning gasp. Then, to my entranced delight, the baby's head suddenly popped out of her like a rabbit out of a hat, to be quickly followed by its pink, twitching body. Its face and its limbs were as crumpled and as delicate as a rose's petals. But it was its minuteness and the fact that it was so perfectly formed that intrigued me. The midwife shuffled forward shouting prayers and instructions to Katerina and seized the baby from between her blood-stained thighs. At that moment, to my intense annoyance, the ring of relatives all moved forward a pace in their eagerness to see the sex of the child, so that I missed the next piece of the drama, for all I could see were the large and extremely well-padded rumps of two of Katerina's larger aunts.

By the time I had burrowed between their legs and voluminous skirts and got to the front of the circle again, the midwife – at shouts of delight from everybody – declared the baby to be a boy and had severed the umbilical cord with a large and very ancient penknife she had extracted from a pocket in her skirt. One of the aunts surged forward and together she and the midwife tied the cord. Then, while the aunt held the squalling, twitching, pink blob of life, the midwife dipped her bundle of rags into the bucket and proceeded to swab the baby down. This done, she then filled a glass with wine and gave a couple of sips to Katerina and then filled her mouth with wine and proceeded to spit it from her toothless gums all over the baby's head, making the sign of the cross over its little body as she did so. Then she clasped the baby to her bosom and turned fiercely on the crowd of relatives.

"Come now, come now," she shrilled. "It is done. He has arrived. Go now, go now."

Laughing and chattering excitedly, the relatives poured out of the little house and immediately started drinking wine and congratulating each other as though they had all personally been responsible for the successful birth of the baby. In the airless little room, smelling so strongly of sweat and garlic, Katerina lay exhausted on the bed, making feeble attempts to pull her dress down to cover her nakedness. I went to the edge of the bed and looked down at her.

"*Yasu*, Gerry mine," she said and sketched a white travesty of her normal brilliant smile. She looked incredibly old, lying there. I congratulated her politely on the birth of her first son and then thanked her for the donkey. She smiled again.

"Go outside," she said. "They will give you some wine."

I left the little room and hurried after the midwife, for I was anxious to see what the next stage was in her treatment of the baby. Out at the back of the house she had spread a white linen cloth over a small table and placed the child on it. Then she picked up great rolls of previously prepared cloth, like very wide bandage, and with the aid of one of the more nimble and sober aunts, she proceeded to wind this round and round the baby's tiny body, pausing frequently to make sure its arms lay flat by its sides and its legs were together. Slowly and methodically she bound it up as straight as a guardsman. It lay there with only its head sticking out from this cocoon of webbing. Greatly intrigued by this, I asked the midwife why she was binding the baby up.

"Why? Why?" she said, her grizzled grey eyebrows flapping over her eyes, milky with cataracts, that peered at me fiercely. "Because, if you don't bind up the baby, its limbs won't grow straight. Its bones are as soft as an egg. If you don't bind it up, its limbs will grow crooked or when it kicks and waves its arms about, it will break its bones, like little sticks of charcoal."

I knew that babies in England were not bound up in this way, and I wondered whether this was because the British were in some way tougher-boned. Otherwise, it seemed to me, there would have been an awful lot of deformities inhabiting the British Isles. I made a mental note to discuss this medical problem with Theodore at the first opportunity.

After I had drunk several glasses of wine to honour the baby and eaten a large bunch of grapes, I got on Sally's back and rode slowly home. I would not have missed that morning for anything, I decided. But, thinking about it as we jogged through the dappled shade of the olives, the thing that amazed me was that anything so perfect and so beautiful should have matured and come forth from the interior of what, to me, was an old woman. It was like, I reflected, breaking open the old, brown, prickly husk of a chestnut and finding the lovely gleaming trophy inside.

PART TWO

Kontokali

Hospitality is, indeed, now no less than in classical times, a sacred duty in these islands, and it is a duty most conscientiously performed.

— Professor Anstead

4

THE PYGMY JUNGLE

It was a warm spring day, as blue as a jay's wing, and I waited impatiently for Theodore to arrive, for we were going to take a picnic lunch and walk two or three miles to a small lake that was one of our happiest hunting-grounds. These days spent with Theodore, these "excursions" as he called them, were of absorbing interest to me, but they must have been very exhausting for Theodore, for, from the moment of his arrival till his departure, I would ply him with a ceaseless string of questions.

Eventually, Theodore's cab clopped and tinkled its way up the drive and Theodore dismounted, clad, as always, in the most unsuitable attire for collecting: a neat tweed suit, respectable, highly polished boots, and a grey Homburg perched squarely on his head. The only ungracious note in this city gentleman's outfit was his collecting box, full of tubes and bottles, slung over one shoulder, and a small net with a bottle dangling from the end, attached to the end of his walking-stick.

"Ah, um," he said, shaking me gravely by the hand. "How are you? I see that we have got, um…a nice day for our excursion."

As at that time of year one got weeks on end of nice days, this was scarcely surprising, but Theodore always insisted on mentioning it as though it was some special privilege that had been granted us by the gods of collecting. Quickly we gathered up the bag of food and the little stone bottles of ginger beer Mother had prepared for us, and slung these on our backs, together with my collecting equipment, which was slightly more extensive than Theodore's, since everything was grist to my mill and I had to be prepared for any eventuality.

Then, whistling for Roger, we went off through the sunlit olive groves, striped with shade, the whole island, spring fresh and brilliant, lying before us. At this time of the year the olive groves would be full of flowers. Pale anemones with the tips of their petals dyed red as though they had been sipping wine, pyramid orchids that looked as though they had been made of pink icing, and yellow crocuses so fat, glossy, and waxy-looking you felt they would light like a candle if you set a match to their stamens. We would tramp through the rough stone paths among the olives, then for a mile or so follow the road lined with tall and ancient cypresses, each covered in a layer of white dust, like a hundred dark paint brushes loaded with chalk white. Presently we would strike off from the road and make our way over the crest of a small hill and there, lying below us, would be the lake, perhaps four acres in extent, its rim shaggy with reeds and its water green with plants.

On this particular day, as we made our way down the hillside towards the lake, I was walking a little ahead of Theodore and I suddenly came to an abrupt halt and stared with amazement at the path ahead of me. Alongside the edge of the path was the bed of a tiny stream which meandered its way down to join the lake. The stream was such a tiny one that even the early spring sun had succeeded in drying it up, so that there was only the smallest trickle of water. Through the bed of the stream and then up across the path and into the stream again lay what at first sight appeared to be a thick cable which seemed to be mysteriously possessed of a life of its own. When I looked closely I could see that the cable was made up of what looked like hundreds of small, dusty snakes. I shouted eagerly to Theodore and when he came I pointed this phenomenon out to him.

"Aha!" he said, his beard bristling and a keen light of interest in his eyes. "Um, yes. Very interesting. Elvers."

What kind of snake was an elver, I inquired, and why were they all travelling in a procession?

"No, no," said Theodore. "They are not snakes. They are baby eels and they appear to be, um…you know, making their way down to the lake."

Fascinated, I crouched over the long column of baby eels, wriggling determinedly through the stone and grass and prickly thistles, their skins dry and dusty. There seemed to be millions of them. Who, in this dry, dusty place, would expect to find eels wriggling about?

"The whole, um…history of the eel," said Theodore, putting his collecting box on the ground and seating himself on a convenient rock, "is very curious. You see, at certain times the adult eels leave the ponds or rivers where they have been living and, er…make their way down to the sea. All the European eels do this and so do the North American eels. Where they went to was, for a long time, a mystery. The only thing, um…you know…scientists knew was that they never came *back*, but that eventually these baby eels would return and repopulate the same rivers and streams. It was not until after quite a number of years that people discovered what really happened."

He paused and scratched his beard thoughtfully.

"All the eels made their way down to the sea and then swam through the Mediterranean, across the Atlantic, until they reached the Sargasso Sea, which is, as you know, off the north-eastern coast of South America. The…um…North American eels, of course, didn't have so far to travel, but they made their way to the same place. Here they mated, laid their eggs, and died. The eel larvae, when it hatches out, is a very curious, um…you know…leaf-shaped creature and transparent, so unlike the adult eel that for a long time it was classified in a separate genera. Well, these larvae make their way slowly backwards to the place where their parents have come from and by the time they reach the Mediterranean or the North American shore, they look like these."

Here Theodore paused and rasped his beard again and delicately inserted the end of his cane into the moving column of elvers so that they writhed indignantly.

"They seem to have a very um…you know…strong homing instinct," said Theodore. "We must be some two miles from the sea, I suppose, and yet all these little elvers are making their way across this countryside in order to get back to the same lake that their parents left."

He paused and glanced about him keenly and then pointed with his stick.

"It's quite a hazardous journey," he observed, and I saw what he meant, for a kestrel was flying like a little black cross just above the line of baby eels, and as we watched he swooped and flew away with his claws firmly gripping a writhing mass of them.

As we walked on, following the line of eels, since they were going in the same direction, we saw other predators at work. Groups of magpies and jackdaws and a couple of jays flew up at our approach and we caught, out of the corner of our eye, the red glint of a fox disappearing into the myrtle bushes.

When we reached the lakeside, we had a set pattern of behaviour. First we would have a prolonged discussion as to which olive tree would be the best to put some of our equipment and our food under – which one would cast the deepest and the best shade at noon. Having decided on this, we would make a little pile of our possessions under it and then, armed with our nets and collecting boxes, we would approach the lake. Here we would potter happily for the rest of the morning, pacing with the slow concentration of a pair of fishing herons, dipping our nets into the weed-filigreed water. Here Theodore came into his own more than anywhere else. From the depths of the lake, as he stood there with the big scarlet dragonflies zooming like arrows round him, he would extract magic that Merlin would have envied.

Here in the still, wine-gold waters, lay a pygmy jungle. On the lake bottom prowled the deadly dragonfly larvae, as cunning a predator as the tiger, inching its way through the debris of a million last year's leaves. Here the black tadpoles, sleek and shiny as liquorice drops, disported in the shallows like plump herds of hippo in some African river. Through green forests of weed the multi-coloured swarms of microscopic creatures twitched and fluttered like flocks of exotic birds, while among the roots of the forests the newts, the leeches uncoiled like great snakes in the gloom, stretching out beseechingly, ever hungry. And here the caddis larvae, in their shaggy coats of twigs and debris, crawled dimly like bears fresh from hibernation across the sun-ringed hills and valleys of soft black mud.

"Aha, now, this is rather interesting. You see this, um…little maggot-like thing? Now this is the larvae of the China-mark moth. I think, as a matter of fact, you have got one in your collection. What? Well, they're called China-mark moths because of the markings on the wing, which are said to resemble very closely marks that potters put on the base of, er…you know, very *good* china. Spode and so forth. Now the China-mark is interesting because it is one of the few moths that have aquatic larvae. The larvae live under water until they are…um…ready to pupate. The interesting things about this particular species is that they have, er…um…you know, two forms of female. The male, of course, is fully winged and flies about when it hatches and er…so does one of the females. But the other female when it hatches out has, um…no wings and continues to live under the water, using its legs to swim with."

Theodore paced a little farther along the bank on the mud that was already dried and jigsawed by the spring sun. A kingfisher exploded like a blue firework from the small willow, and out on the centre of the lake a tern swooped and glided on graceful, sickle-shaped wings. Theodore dipped his net into the weedy water, sweeping it to and fro gently, as though he were stroking a cat. Then the net was lifted and held aloft, while the tiny bottle that dangled from it would be subjected to a minute scrutiny through a magnifying glass. "Um, yes. Some cyclopes. Two mosquito larvae. Aha, that's interesting. You see this caddis larva has made his case entirely out of baby ram's-horn snail shells. It is...you know...remarkably pretty. Ah now! Here we have, I think, yes, yes, here we have some rotifers."

In a desperate attempt to keep pace with this flood of knowledge, I asked what rotifers were and peered into the little bottle through the magnifying glass at the twitching, wriggling creatures, as Theodore told me.

"The early naturalists used to call them wheel animalcules, because of their curious limbs, you know. They wave them about in a very curious fashion, so that they almost look like, um...you know, um...er...like the *wheels* of a watch. When you next come to see me I'll put some of these under the microscope for you. They are really extraordinarily beautiful creatures. These are, of course, all females."

I asked why, of course, they should be females?

"This is one of the interesting things about the rotifer. The females produce virgin eggs. Um...that is to say, they produce eggs without having come into contact with a male. Um...er...somewhat like a chicken, you know. But the difference is that the *rotifer* eggs hatch out into other females which in turn are capable of laying more eggs which...um... again hatch out into females. But at certain times, the females lay *smaller* eggs, which hatch out into males. Now, as you will see when I put these under the microscope, the female has a −

how shall one say? – a quite *complex* body, an alimentary tract, and so on. The male has nothing at all. He is really just, er... um...a swimming bag of sperm."

I was bereft of speech at the complexities of the private life of the rotifer.

"Another curious thing about them," Theodore continued, happily piling miracle upon miracle, "is that at certain times, er...you know, if it is a hot summer or something like that and the pond is liable to dry up, they go down to the bottom and form a sort of hard shell round themselves. It's a sort of *suspended animation*, for the pond can dry up for, er...um...let us say seven or eight years, and they will just lie there in the dust. But as soon as the first rain falls and fills the pond, they come to life again."

Again we moved forward, sweeping our nets through the balloon-like masses of frogs' spawn and the trailing necklace-like strings of the toad spawn.

"Here is, er...if you just take the glass a minute and look...an exceptionally fine hydra."

Through the glass there sprang to life a tiny fragment of weed to which was attached a long slender coffee-coloured column, at the top of which was a writhing mass of elegant tentacles. As I watched, a rotund and earnest cyclops, carrying two large and apparently heavy sacks containing pink eggs, swam in a series of breathless jerks too close to the writhing arms of the hydra. In a moment it was engulfed. It gave a couple of violent twitches before it was stung to death. I knew, if you watched long enough, you could watch the cyclops being slowly and steadily engulfed and passing, in the shape of a bulge, down the column of the hydra.

Presently the height and the heat of the sun would tell us that it was lunch-time, and we would make our way back to our olive trees and sit there eating our food and drinking our ginger beer to the accompaniment of the sleepy zithering of the first-hatched cicadas of the year and the gentle, questioning coos of the collared doves.

"In Greek," Theodore said, munching his sandwich methodically, "the name for collared dove is *dekaoctur* – 'eighteener,' you know. The story goes that when Christ was... um...carrying the cross to Calvary, a Roman soldier, seeing that He was exhausted, took pity on Him. By the side of the road there was an old woman selling...um...you know...*milk*, and so the Roman soldier went to her and asked her how much a cupful would cost. She replied that it would cost eighteen coins. But the soldier had only seventeen. He...er...you know...pleaded with the woman to let him have a cupful of milk for Christ for seventeen coins, but the woman avariciously held out for eighteen. So, when Christ was crucified, the old woman was turned into a turtle-dove and condemned to go about for the rest of her days repeating *dekaocto, dekaocto* – 'eighteen, eighteen.' If ever she agrees to say *deka-epta*, seventeen, she will regain her human form. If, out of obstinacy, she says *deka-ennaea*, nineteen, the world will come to an end."

In the cool olive shade the tiny ants, black and shiny as caviare, would be foraging for our leftovers among last year's discarded olive leaves that the past summer's sun had dried and coloured a nut-brown and banana-yellow. They lay there as curled and as crisp as brandy-snaps. On the hillside behind us a herd of goats passed, the leader's bell clonking mournfully. We could hear the tearing sound of their jaws as they ate, indiscriminately, any foliage that came within their reach. The leader paced up to us and gazed for a minute with baleful, yellow eyes, snorting clouds of thyme-laden breath at us.

"They should not, er...you know, be left unattended," said Theodore, prodding the goat gently with his stick. "Goats do more damage to the countryside than practically anything else."

The leader uttered a short sardonic "bah" and then moved away, with his destructive troop following him.

We would lie for an hour or so, drowsing, and digesting our food, staring up through the tangled olive branches at a sky that was patterned with tiny white clouds like a child's fingerprints on a blue, frosty, winter window.

"Well," Theodore would say at last, getting to his feet, "I think perhaps we ought to...you know...just see what the *other* side of the lake has to offer."

So once more we would commence our slow pacing of the rim of the shore. Steadily our test tubes, bottles, and jars would fill with a shimmer of microscopic life, and my boxes and tins and bags would be stuffed with frogs, baby terrapins, and a host of beetles.

"I suppose," Theodore would say at last, reluctantly, glancing up at the sinking sun, "I suppose...you know...we ought to be getting along home."

And so we would laboriously hoist our now extremely heavy collecting boxes onto our shoulders and trudge homeward on weary feet, Roger, his tongue hanging out like a pink flag, trotting soberly ahead of us. Reaching the villa, our catches would be moved to more capacious quarters. Then Theodore and I would relax and discuss the day's work, drinking gallons of hot, stimulating tea and gorging ourselves on golden scones, bubbling with butter, fresh from Mother's oven.

It was when I paid a visit to this lake without Theodore that I caught, quite by chance, a creature that I had long wanted to meet. As I drew my net up out of the waters and examined the tangled weed mass it contained, I found crouching there, of all unlikely things, a spider. I was delighted, for I had read about this curious beast, which must be one of the most unusual species of spider in the world, for it lives a very strange aquatic existence. It was about half an inch long and marked in a rather vague sort of way with silver and brown. I put it triumphantly into one of my collecting tins and carried it home tenderly.

Here I set up an aquarium with a sandy floor and decorated it with some small dead branches and fronds of waterweed. Putting the spider on one of the twigs that stuck up above the water-level, I watched to see what it would do. It immediately ran down the twig and plunged into the water, where it turned a bright and beautiful silver, owing to the numerous minute air bubbles trapped in the hairs on its body. It spent five minutes or so running about below the surface of the water, investigating all the twigs and waterweed before it finally settled on a spot in which to construct its home.

Now the water spider was the original inventor of the diving-bell, and sitting absorbed in front of the aquarium, I watched how it was done. First the spider attached several lengthy strands of silk from the weeds to the twigs. These were to act as guy ropes. Then, taking up a position roughly in the centre of these guy ropes, it proceeded to spin an irregular oval-shaped flat web of a more or less conventional type, but of a finer mesh, so that it looked more like a cobweb. This occupied the greater part of two hours. Having got the structure of its home built to its satisfaction, it now had to give it an air supply. This it did by making numerous trips to the surface of the water and into the air. When it returned to the water its body would be silvery with air bubbles. It would then run down and take up its position underneath the web and, by stroking itself with its legs, rid itself of the air bubbles, which rose and were immediately trapped underneath the web. After it had done this five or six times, all the tiny bubbles under the web had amalgamated into one big bubble. As the spider added more and more air to this bubble and the bubble grew bigger and bigger, its strength started to push the web up until eventually the spider had achieved success. Firmly anchored by the guy ropes between the weed and the twigs was suspended a bell-shaped structure full of air. This was now the spider's home in which it could live quite comfortably without even having to pay frequent visits to the surface, for the air in the bell would, I knew, be replenished by the oxygen given up by the weeds, and the carbon monoxide given out by the spider would soak through the silky walls of its house.

Sitting and watching this miraculous piece of craftsmanship, I wondered how on earth the very first water spider (who wanted to *become* a water spider) had managed to work out this ingenious method of living below the surface. But the habit of living in its own home-made submarine is not the only peculiar thing about this spider. Unlike the greater majority of species, the male is about twice the size of the female, and once they have mated, the male is not devoured by his wife, as happens so frequently in the married life of the spider. I could tell from her size that my spider was a female and I thought that her abdomen looked rather swollen. It seemed to me she might be expecting a happy event, so I took great pains to make sure that she got plenty of good food. She liked fat green daphnia, which she was extraordinarily adept at catching as they swam past; but probably her favourite food of all was the tiny, newly hatched newt efts which, although they were a bulky prey for her, she never hesitated to tackle. Having captured whatever titbit happened to be passing, she would then carry it up into her bell and eat it there in comfort.

Then came the great day when I saw that she was adding an extension to the bell. She did not hurry over this and it took her two days to complete. Then one morning, on peering into her tank, I saw to my delight that the nursery contained a round ball of eggs. In due course these hatched out into miniature replicas of the mother. I soon had more water spiders than I knew what to do with and I found, to my annoyance, that the mother, with complete lack of parental feeling, was happily feeding off her own progeny. So I was forced to move the babies into another aquarium, but as they grew they took to feeding upon each other and so in the end I just kept the two most intelligent-looking ones and took all the rest down to the lake and let them go.

It was at this time, when I was deeply involved with the water spiders, that Sven Olson at last turned up. Larry, to

Mother's consternation, had developed the habit of inviting hordes of painters, poets, and authors to stay without any reference to her. Sven Olson was a sculptor, and we had had some warning of his impending arrival, for he had been bombarding us for several weeks with contradictory telegrams about his movements, which had driven Mother to distraction because she kept having to make and unmake his bed. Mother and I were having a quiet cup of tea on the veranda when a cab made its appearance, wound its way up the drive, and came to a stop in front of the house. In the back was seated an enormous man who bore a remarkable facial resemblance to the reconstructions of Neanderthal man. He was clad in a white singlet, a pair of voluminous brightly checked plus-fours, and sandals. On his massive head was a broad-brimmed straw hat. The two holes situated one each side of the crown argued that this hat had been designed for the use of a horse. He got ponderously out of the cab, carrying a very large and battered Gladstone bag and an accordion. Mother and I went down to greet him. As he saw us approaching, he swept off his hat and bowed, revealing that his enormous cranium was completely devoid of hair except for a strange, grey, tattered duck's tail on the nape of his neck.

"Mrs Durrell?" he inquired, fixing Mother with large and childlike blue eyes. "I am enchanted to meet you. My name is Sven."

His English was impeccable, with scarcely any trace of an accent, but his voice was quite extraordinary, for it wavered between a deep rich baritone and a quavering falsetto, as though, in spite of his age, his voice was only just breaking. He extended a very large, white, spade-shaped hand to Mother and bowed once again.

"Well, I am glad you have managed to get here at last," said Mother, brightly and untruthfully. "Do come in and have some tea."

I carried his accordion and his Gladstone bag and we all went and sat on the balcony and drank tea and stared at each other. There was a long, long silence while Sven munched on a piece of toast and occasionally smiled lovingly at Mother, while she smiled back and desperately searched her mind for suitable intellectual topics of conversation. Sven swallowed a piece of toast and coughed violently. His eyes filled with tears.

"I love toast," he gasped. "I simply love it. But it always does this to me."

We plied him with more tea and presently his paroxysms of coughing died away. He sat forward, his huge hands folded in his lap, showing white as marble against the hideous pattern of his plus-fours, and fixed Mother with an inquiring eye.

"Are you," he inquired wistfully, "are you, by any chance, musically inclined?"

"Well," said Mother, startled, and obviously suffering from the hideous suspicion that if she said "Yes" Sven might ask her to sing, "I like music, of course, but I...can't play anything."

"I suppose," said Sven diffidently, "you wouldn't like me to play something for you?"

"Oh, er, yes, by all means," said Mother. "That would be delightful."

Sven beamed lovingly at her, picked up his accordion and unstrapped it. He extended it like a caterpillar and it produced noise like the tail-end of a donkey's bray.

"She," said Sven, lovingly patting the accordion, "has got some sea air in her."

He settled his accordion more comfortably against his broad chest, arranged his sausage-like fingers carefully on the keys, closed his eyes, and began to play. It was a very complicated and extraordinary tune. Sven was wearing such an expression of rapture upon his ugly face that I was dying to laugh and was having to bite the insides of my cheeks to prevent it. Mother sat there with a face of frozen politeness like a world-famous conductor being forced to listen to somebody giving a recital on a penny whistle. Eventually the tune came to a harsh, discordant end. Sven heaved a sigh of pure delight, opened his eyes, and smiled at Mother.

"Bach is so beautiful," he said.

"Oh, yes," said Mother with well-simulated enthusiasm.

"I'm glad you like it," said Sven. "I'll play you some more." So for the next hour Mother and I sat there, trapped, while Sven played piece after piece. Every time Mother made some move to seek an escape, Sven would hold up one of his huge hands, as though arresting a line of imaginary traffic, and say, "Just one more," archly, and Mother, with a tremulous smile, would sit back in her chair.

It was with considerable relief that we greeted the rest of the family when they arrived back from town. Larry and Sven danced round each other, roaring like a couple of bulls and exchanging passionate embraces, and then Larry dragged Sven off to his room and they were closeted there for hours, the sound of gales of laughter occasionally drifting down to us.

"What's he like?" asked Margo.

"Well, I don't really know, dear," said Mother. "He's been playing to us ever since he arrived."

"Playing?" said Leslie. "Playing what?"

"His barrel-organ, or whatever you call it," said Mother.

"My God," said Leslie. "I can't stand those things. I hope he isn't going to play it all over the house."

"No, no, dear. I'm sure he won't," said Mother hastily, but her tone lacked conviction.

Just at that moment Larry appeared on the veranda again. "Where's Sven's accordion?" he asked. "He wants to play me something."

"Oh, God," said Leslie. "There you are. I told you."

"I hope he isn't going to play that accordion all the time, dear," said Mother. "We've already had an hour of it and it's given me a splitting headache."

"Of course he won't play it all the time," said Larry irritably, picking up the accordion. "He just wants to play me one tune. What was he playing to you, anyway?"

"The most weird music," said Mother. "By some man – you know the one – something to do with trees."

The rest of the day was, to say the least, harrying. Sven's repertoire was apparently inexhaustible and when, during dinner, he insisted on giving us an impression of mealtime in a Scottish fortress by marching round and round the table playing one of the more untuneful Scottish reels, I could see the defences of the family crumbling. Even Larry was beginning to look a little pensive. Roger, who was uninhibited and straightforward in his dealings with human beings, summed up his opinion of Sven's performance by throwing back his head and howling dismally, a thing he only did normally when he heard the national anthem.

But by the time Sven had been with us three days, we had become more or less inured to his accordion, and Sven himself charmed us all. He exuded a sort of innocent goodness, so that whatever he did one could not be annoyed with him, any more than you can be annoyed with a baby for wetting its nappy. He quickly endeared himself to Mother, for, she discovered, he was an ardent cook himself and carried round an enormous leather-bound notebook in which he jotted down recipes. He and Mother spent hours in the kitchen, teaching each other how to cook their favourite dishes, and the results were meals of such bulk and splendour that all of us began to feel liverish and out of sorts.

It was about a week after his arrival that Sven wandered one morning into the room I proudly called my study. In that massive villa we had such a superfluity of rooms that I had succeeded in getting Mother to give me a special room of my own in which I could keep all my creatures.

My menagerie at this time was pretty extensive. There was Ulysses, the scop's owl, who spent all day sitting on the pelmet above the window, imitating a decaying olive stump, and occasionally, with a look of great disdain, regurgitating a pellet onto the newspaper spread below him. The dog contingent had been increased to three by a couple of young mongrels who had been given to me for my birthday by a peasant family and who, because of their completely undisciplined behaviour, had been christened Widdle and Puke. There were rows and rows of jam-jars, some containing specimens in methylated spirits, others containing microscopic life. And then there were six aquariums that housed a variety of newts, frogs, snakes, and toads. Piles of glass-topped boxes contained my collections of butterflies, beetles, and dragonflies. Sven, to my astonishment, displayed a deep and almost reverent interest in my collection. Delighted to have somebody displaying enthusiasm for my cherished menagerie, I took him on a carefully conducted tour and showed him everything, even, after swearing him to secrecy, my family of tiny, chocolate-coloured scorpions that I had smuggled into the house unbeknownst to the family. One of the things that impressed Sven most was the underwater bell of the spider, and he stood quite silently in front of it, his great blue eyes fixed on it intensely, watching the spider as she caught her food and carried it up into the little dome. Sven displayed such enthusiasm that I suggested to him, rather tentatively, that he might like to spend a little time in the olive groves with me, so that I could show him some of these creatures in their natural haunts.

"But how kind of you," he said, his great, ugly face lighting up delightedly. "Are you sure I won't be interfering?"

No, I assured him he would not be interfering.

"Then I would be delighted," said Sven. "Absolutely delighted."

So, for the rest of his stay, we would disappear from the villa after breakfast and spend a couple of hours in the olive groves.

On Sven's last day – he was leaving on the evening boat – we held a little farewell lunch party for him and invited Theodore. Delighted at having a new audience, Sven immediately gave Theodore a half-hour recital of Bach on his accordion.

"Um," said Theodore, when Sven had finished, "do you, you know, er… know any other tunes?"

"Just name it, Doctor," said Sven, spreading out his hands expansively. "I will play it for you."

Theodore rocked thoughtfully for a moment on his toes.

"You don't by any chance, I suppose, er…happen to know a song called 'There Is a Tavern in the Town'?" he inquired shyly.

"Of course!" said Sven and immediately crashed into the opening bars of the song.

Theodore sang vigorously, his beard bristling, his eyes bright, and when he had come to the end, Sven, without pause, switched into "Clementine". Emboldened by Theodore's Philistine attitude towards Bach, Mother asked Sven whether he could play "If I Were a Blackbird" and "The Spinning Wheel Song", which he promptly executed in a masterly fashion.

Then the cab arrived to take him down to the docks, and he embraced each one of us fondly, his eyes full of tears. He climbed into the back of the cab with his Gladstone bag beside him and his precious accordion on his lap, and he waved to us extravagantly as the cab disappeared down the drive.

"Such a *manly* man," said Mother with satisfaction, as we went inside. "Quite one of the old school."

"You should have told him that," said Larry, stretching himself out on the sofa and picking up his book. "There's nothing homos like better than to be told they are virile and manly."

"Whatever do you mean?" asked Mother, putting on her spectacles and glaring at Larry suspiciously.

Larry lowered his book and looked at her, puzzled.

"Homosexuals like to be told they are virile and manly," he said at length, patiently, and with the air of one explaining a simple problem to a backward child.

Mother continued to glare at him, trying to assess whether or not it was one of Larry's elaborate leg-pulls.

"You are not trying to tell me," she said at last, "that that man is a – is a – is one of *those?*"

"Dear God, Mother, of course he is," said Larry, irritably. "He's a rampaging old queer – the only reason he's gone rushing back to Athens is because he's living with a ravishing seventeen-year-old Cypriot boy and he doesn't trust him."

"Do you mean to say," asked Margo, her eyes wide, "that they get *jealous* of each other?"

"Of course they do," said Larry, and dismissing the subject, he returned to his book.

"How extraordinary," said Margo. "Did you hear that, Mother? They actually get jealous – "

"Margo!" said Mother quellingly. "We won't go into that. What *I* want to know, Larry, is why you invited him here if you knew he was, er, that way inclined?"

"Why not?" Larry inquired.

"Well, you might at least have thought of *Gerry*," said Mother, bristling.

"Gerry?" asked Larry in surprise. "Gerry? What's he got to do with it?"

"What's he got to *do* with it? Really, Larry, you do make me cross. That man could have been a bad influence on the boy if he had had much to do with him."

Larry sat back on the sofa and looked at Mother. He gave a small exasperated sigh and put his book down.

"For the last three mornings," he said, "Gerry's been giving Sven natural history lessons in the olive groves. It doesn't appear to have done either of them irretrievable harm."

"What?" squeaked Mother. "What?"

I felt it was time to intervene. After all, I liked Sven. I explained how, early in his stay, he had wandered into my room and had become immediately absorbed and fascinated by my collection of creatures. Feeling that one convert was worth half a dozen saints, I had offered to take him into the olive groves and show him all my favourite haunts. So every morning we would set off into the olives and Sven would spend hours lying on his stomach peering at the busy lines of ants carrying their grass seeds or watching the bulbous-bodied female mantis laying her frothy egg case on a stone, or peering down the burrows of trapdoor spiders, murmuring, "Wonderful! Wonderful!" to himself, in such an ecstatic tone of voice that it warmed my heart.

"Well, dear," said Mother, "I think, in future, if you want to take one of Larry's friends for walks you should tell me first."

5

CUTTLEFISH AND CRABS

Each morning when I awoke the bedroom would be tiger-striped by the sun peering through the shutters. As usual, I would find that the dogs had managed to crawl onto the bed without my realizing it and would now be occupying more than their fair share, sleeping deeply and peacefully. Ulysses would be sitting by the window staring at the bars of golden sunlight, his eyes slit into malevolent disapproval. Outside, one could hear the hoarse, jeering crow of a cockerel and the soft murmuring of the hens (a sound soothing as bubbling porridge) as they fed under the orange and lemon trees, the distant clonk of goat bells, sharp chittering of sparrows in the eaves, and the sudden outburst of wheezing, imploring cries that denoted one of the parent swallows had brought a mouthful of food to their brood in the nest beneath my window. I would throw back the sheet and turf the dogs out onto the floor, where they would shake and stretch and yawn, their pink tongues curled like exotic leaves, and then I would go over to the window and throw back the shutters. Leaning out over the sill, the morning sun warm on my naked body, I would scratch thoughtfully at the little pink seals the dogs' fleas had left on my skin, while I got my eyes adjusted to the light. Then I would peer down over the silver olive tops to the beach and the blue sea which lay half a mile away. It was on this beach that, periodically, the fishermen would pull in their nets, and when they did so this was always a special occasion for me, since the net dragged to shore from the depths of the blue bay would contain a host of fascinating sea life which was otherwise beyond my reach.

If I saw the little fishing boats bobbing on the water I would get dressed hurriedly, and taking my collecting gear I would run through the olive trees down to the road and along it until I reached the beach. I knew most of the fishermen by name, but there was one who was my special friend, a tall, powerful young man with a mop of auburn hair. Inevitably, he was called Spiro after Spiridion, so in order to distinguish him from all the other Spiros I knew, I called him Kokino, or red. Kokino took a great delight in obtaining specimens for me, and although he was not a bit interested in the creatures himself, he got considerable pleasure from my obvious happiness.

One day I went down to the beach and the net was halfway in. The fishermen, brown as walnuts, were hauling on the dripping lines, their toes spreading wide in the sand as they pulled the massive bag of the net nearer and nearer to the shore.

"Your health, *kyrié* Gerry," Kokino cried to me, waving a large freckled hand in greeting, his mop of hair glinting in the sun like a bonfire. "Today we should get some fine animals for you, for we put the net down in a new place."

I squatted on the sand and waited patiently while the fishermen, chattering and joking, hauled away steadily. Presently the top of the net was visible in the shallow waters, and as it broke surface you could see the glitter and wink of the trapped fish inside it. Hauled out onto the sand, it seemed as though the net were alive, pulsating with the fish inside it, and there was the steady, staccato purring noise of their tails, flapping futilely against each other. The baskets were fetched and the fish were picked out of the net and cast into them. Red fish, white fish, fish with wine-coloured stripes, scorpion fish like flamboyant tapestries. Sometimes there would be an octopus or a cuttlefish leering up from inside the net with a look of alarm in its human-looking eyes. Once all the edible contents of the net had been safely stowed away in the baskets, it was my turn.

In the bottom of the net would be a great heap of stones and seaweed and it was among these that I found my trophies: once a round flat stone from which grew a perfect coraline tree, pure white. It looked like a young beech tree in winter, its branches bare of leaves and covered with a layer of snow. Sometimes there would be cushion starfish, almost as thick as a sponge-cake and almost as large, the edges not forming pointed arms as with normal starfish, but rounded scallops. These starfish would be of a pale fawn colour, with a bright pattern of scarlet blotches. Once I got two incredible crabs, whose pincers and legs when pulled in tight fitted with immaculate precision the sides of their oval shells. These crabs were white with a rusty-red pattern on the back that looked not unlike an Oriental face. It was hardly what I would call protective colouration, and I imagine they must have had few enemies to be able to move about the seabed wearing such a conspicuous livery.

On this particular morning I was picking over a great pile of weed, and Kokino, having stowed away the last of the fish in the baskets, came over to help me. There was the usual assortment of tiny squids, the size of a matchbox, pipefish, spider crabs, and a variety of tiny fish which, in spite of their small size, had been unable to escape through the mesh of the net. Suddenly Kokino gave a little grunt, half surprise and half amusement, and picked something out of a tangled skein of seaweed and held it out to me on the calloused palm of his hand. I could hardly believe my eyes, for it was a sea horse. Browny-green, carefully jointed, looking like some weird chessman, it lay on Kokino's hand, its strange protruded mouth gasping and its tail coiling and uncoiling frantically. Hurriedly I snatched it from him and plunged it into a jar full of seawater, uttering a mental prayer to St Spiridion that I was in time to save it. To my delight it righted itself, then hung suspended in the jar, the tiny fins on each side of its horse's head fluttering themselves into a blur. Pausing only to make sure that it really was all right, I scrabbled through the rest of the weed with the fervour of a gold prospector panning a river-bed where he had found a nugget. My diligence was rewarded, for in a few minutes I had six sea horses of various sizes hanging suspended in the jar. Enraptured by my good luck, I bid Kokino and the other fishermen a hasty farewell and raced back to the villa.

Here I unceremoniously foreclosed on fourteen slow-worms and usurped their aquarium to house my new catches. I knew that the oxygen in the jar in which the sea horses were imprisoned would not last for long and if I wanted to keep them alive I would have to move quickly. Carrying the aquarium, I raced down to the sea again, washed it out carefully, filled the bottom with sand and dashed back to the villa with it; then I had to run down to the sea again three times with buckets to fill it up with the required amount of water. By the time I had poured the last bucket into it, I was so hot and sweaty I began to wonder whether the sea horses were worth it. But as soon as I tipped them into the aquarium I knew that they were. I had placed a small, twiggy, dead olive branch in the aquarium, which I had anchored to the sand, and as the sea horses plopped out of the jar they righted themselves and then, like ponies freshly released in a field, they sped round and round the aquarium, their fins moving so fast that you could not see them and each one gave the appearance of being driven by some small internal motor. Having, as it were, galloped round their new territory, they all made for the olive branch, entwined their tails round it lovingly, and stood there gravely at attention.

The sea horses were an instant success. They were about the only animal that I had introduced to the villa that earned the family's unanimous approval. Even Larry used to pay furtive visits to my study in order to watch them zooming and bobbing to and fro in their tank. They took up a considerable amount of my time, for I found that the seawater soon grew rancid, and in order to keep it clear and fresh I had to go down to the sea with buckets four or five times a day. This was an exhausting process, but I was glad that I kept it up, for otherwise I would not have witnessed a very extraordinary sight.

One of the sea horses, obviously an old specimen since he was nearly black, had a very well-developed paunch. This I merely attributed to age; then I noticed one morning there was a line along the paunch, almost as though it had been slit with a razor-blade. I was watching this and wondering whether the sea horses had been fighting and if so what they used as a weapon (for they seemed so defenceless), when to my complete and utter astonishment the slit opened a little wider and out swam a minute and fragile replica of the sea horse. I could hardly believe my eyes, but as soon as the first baby was clear of the pouch and hanging in the clear water, another one joined it and then another and another until there were twenty microscopic sea horses floating round their giant parent like a little cloud of smoke. Terrified lest the other adult sea horses eat the babies, I hurriedly set up another aquarium and placed what I fondly imagined to be the mother and her offspring in it. Keeping two aquariums going with fresh water was an even more Herculean task and I began to feel like a pit pony; but I was determined to continue until Thursday, when Theodore came to tea, so that I could show him my acquisitions.

"Aha," he said, peering into the tanks with professional zeal, "these are really most interesting. Sea horses are, of course, according to the books, supposed to be found here, but I myself have er…you know…never seen them previously."

I showed Theodore the mother with her swarm of tiny babies.

"No, no," said Theodore. "That's not the mother, that's the father."

At first I thought that Theodore was pulling my leg, but he went on to explain that when the female laid the eggs and they had been fertilized by the male, they were taken into this special brood-pouch by the male and there they matured and hatched, so what I had thought was a proud mother was in reality a proud father.

Soon the strain of keeping my stable of sea horses with a supply of microscopic seafood and fresh water became too great, and so with the utmost reluctance I had to take them down to the sea and release them.

It was Kokino who, as well as contributing specimens from his nets to my collection, showed me one of the most novel fishing methods I had ever come across.

I met him one day down by the shore putting a kerosene tin full of seawater into his rickety little boat. Reposing in the bottom of the tin was a large and very soulful-looking cuttlefish. Kokino had tied a string round it where the head met the great egg-shaped body. I asked him where he was going and he said he was going to fish for cuttlefish. I was puzzled because his boat did not contain any lines or nets or even a trident. How then did he propose to catch cuttlefish?

"With love," said Kokino mysteriously.

I felt it was my duty, as a naturalist, to investigate every method of capturing animals, so I asked Kokino whether it was possible for me to accompany him in order to see this mysterious process. We rowed the boat out into the blue bay until it hung over a couple of fathoms of crystal clear water. Here Kokino took the end of the long string that was attached to the cuttlefish and tied it carefully round his big toe. Then he picked up the cuttlefish and dropped it over the side of the boat. It floated in the water for a brief moment, looking up at us with what seemed to be an incredulous expression, and then, squirting out jets of water, it shot off in a series of jerks, trailing the string behind it, and soon disappeared in the blue depths. The string trailed gradually over the side of the boat, then tautened against Kokino's toe. He lit a cigarette and rumpled his flaming hair.

"Now," he said, grinning at me, "we will see what love can do."

He bent to his oars and rowed the boat slowly and gently along the surface of the bay, with frequent pauses during which he stared with intense concentration at the string fastened to his toe. Suddenly he gave a little grunt, let the oars fold to the side of the boat like the wings of a moth, and grasping the line, he started to pull it in. I leaned over the side of the boat, staring down into the clear water, my eyes straining towards the end of the taut black line. Presently, in the depths, a dim blur appeared as Kokino hauled more quickly on the line and the cuttlefish came into sight. As it got closer, I saw, to my astonishment, it was not one cuttlefish but two, locked together in a passionate embrace. Swiftly Kokino hauled them alongside and with a quick flip of the line landed them in the bottom of the boat. So engrossed was the male cuttlefish with his lady-love that not even the sudden transition from his watery home to the open air seemed to worry him in the slightest. He was clasping the female so tightly that it took Kokino some time to prise him loose and then drop him into the tin of seawater.

The novelty of this form of fishing greatly appealed to me, although I had the sneaking feeling that perhaps it was a little unsporting. It was rather like catching dogs by walking around with a bitch in season on the end of a long leash. Within an hour we had caught five male cuttlefish in a comparatively small area of the bay and it amazed me that there should be such a dense population of them in such a small area, for they were a creature that you very rarely saw unless you went fishing at night. The female cuttlefish, throughout this time, played her part with a sort of stoical indifference, but even so I felt that she should be rewarded, so I prevailed upon Kokino to let her go, which he did with obvious reluctance.

I asked him how he knew that the female was ready to attract the males, and he shrugged.

"It is the time," he said.

Could you then at this time, I inquired, put any female on the end of a string and obtain results?

"Yes," said Kokino. "But of course, some females, like some women, are more attractive than others and so you get better results with those."

My mind boggled at the thought of having to work out the comparative merits between two female cuttlefish. I felt it was a great pity that this method could not be employed with other creatures. The idea, for example, of dropping a female sea horse over the side on a length of cotton and then pulling her up in a tangled entourage of passionate males was very appealing. Kokino was, as far as I knew, the only exponent of this peculiar brand of fishing, for I never saw any other fisherman employ it, and indeed, the ones I mentioned it to had never even heard of it and were inclined to treat my story with raucous disbelief.

This tattered coast-line near the villa was particularly rich in sea life, and as the water was comparatively shallow it made it easier for me to capture things. I had succeeded in inveigling Leslie into making me a boat, which greatly facilitated my investigations. This craft, almost circular, flat-bottomed, and with a heavy list to starboard, had been christened the *Bootle-Bumtrinket* and, next to my donkey, was my most cherished possession. Filling the bottom with jars, tins, and nets and taking a large parcel of food with me, I would set sail in the *Bootle-Bumtrinket* accompanied by my crew of Widdle, Puke, and Roger and, occasionally, Ulysses, my owl, should he feel so inclined. We would spend the hot, breathless days exploring remote little bays and rocky and weed-encrusted archipelagoes. We had many curious adventures on these expeditions. Once we found a whole acre of seabed covered with a great swarm of sea hares, their royal-purple, egg-shaped bodies with a neat pleated frill along the edge and two strange protuberances on the head looking, in fact, extraordinarily like the long ears of a hare. There were hundreds of them gliding over the rocks and across the sand, all heading towards the south of the island. They did not touch each other or display any interest in each other, so I assumed it was not a mating gathering, but some form of migration.

On another occasion, a group of languid, portly, and good-natured dolphins discovered us riding at anchor in a small bay, and presumably attracted by the friendly colour scheme of orange and white in which the *Bootle-Bumtrinket* was painted, they disported themselves around us, leaping and splashing, coming up alongside the boat with their grinning faces, and breathing deep, passionate sighs at us from their blow-holes. A young one, more daring than the adults, even dived under the boat and we felt his back scrape along its flat bottom. My attention was equally divided between enjoying this delightful sight and trying to quell mutiny on the part of my crew, who had all reacted to the arrival of the dolphins in their individual ways. Widdle, never a staunch warrior, had lived up to his name copiously and crouched shivering in the bows, whining to himself. Puke had decided that the only way to save his life was to abandon ship and swim for the shore; he had to be restrained forcibly, as did Roger, who was convinced that if he was only allowed to jump into the sea with the dolphins, he would be able to kill them all, single-handedly, in a matter of moments.

It was during one of these expeditions that I came across a magnificent trophy that was, indirectly, responsible for leading Leslie into court, although I did not know it at the time. The family had all gone into town, with the exception of Leslie, who was recovering from a very severe attack of dysentery. It was his first day's convalescence and he lay on the sofa in the drawing-room as weak as a kitten, sipping iced tea and reading a large manual on ballistics. He had informed me, in no uncertain terms, that he did not want me hanging around making a nuisance of myself and so, as I did not want to go into the town, I had taken the dogs out in *Bootle-Bumtrinket*.

As I rowed along, I noticed on the smooth waters of the bay what I took to be a large patch of yellow seaweed. Seaweed was always worth investigating, as it invariably contained a host of small life and sometimes, if you were lucky, quite large creatures; so I rowed towards it. But as I got closer, I saw that it was not seaweed, but what appeared to be a yellowish-coloured rock. But what sort of rock could it be that floated in some twenty feet of water? As I looked closer, I saw, to my incredulous delight, that it was a fairly large turtle. Shipping the oars and urging the dogs to silence, I poised myself in the bows and waited, tense with excitement as the *Bootle-Bumtrinket* drifted closer and closer. The turtle, outspread, appeared to be floating on the surface of the sea, sound asleep. My problem was to capture him before he woke up. The nets and various other equipment I had in the boat had not been designed for the capture of a turtle measuring some three feet in length, so the only way I felt I could achieve success was by diving in on him, grabbing him, and somehow getting him into the boat before he woke up. In my excitement it never occurred to me that the strength possessed by a turtle of this size was considerable and that it was unlikely he was going to give up without a struggle. When the boat was some six feet away I held my breath and dived. I decided to dive under him so as to cut off his retreat, as it were, and as I plunged into the lukewarm water I uttered a brief prayer that the splash I made would not awaken him and that, even if it did, he would still be too dozy to execute a rapid retreat. I had dived deep and now I turned on my back and there, suspended above me like an enormous golden guinea, was the turtle. I shot up under him and grabbed him firmly by his front flippers, which curved like horny sickles from out of his shell. To my surprise even this action did not wake him, and when I rose, gasping, to the surface, still retaining my grasp on his flippers, and shook the water from my eyes, I discovered the reason. The turtle had been dead for a fair length of time, as my nose and the host of tiny fish nibbling at his scaly limbs told me.

Disappointing though this was, a dead turtle was better than no turtle at all, and so I laboriously towed his body alongside the *Bootle-Bumtrinket* and made it fast by one flipper to the side of the boat. The dogs were greatly intrigued, under the impression that this was some exotic and edible delicacy I had procured for their special benefit. The *Bootle-Bumtrinket*, owing to her shape, had never been the easiest of craft to steer, and now, with the dead weight of the turtle lashed to one side of her, she showed a tendency to revolve in circles. However, after an hour's strenuous rowing, we arrived safely at the jetty, and having tied up the boat, I then hauled the turtle's carcass onto the shore where I could examine it. It was a hawksbill turtle, the kind whose shell is used for the manufacture of spectacle frames and whose stuffed carcass you occasionally see in opticians' windows. His head was massive, with a great wrinkled jowl of yellow skin and a swooping beak of a nose that did give him an extraordinarily hawk-like look. The shell was battered in places, presumably by ocean storms or by the snap of a passing shark, and here and there it was decorated with little snow-white clusters of baby barnacles. His underside of pale daffodil-yellow was soft and pliable like thick, damp cardboard.

I had recently conducted a long and fascinating dissection of a dead terrapin that I had found and I felt this would be an ideal opportunity to compare the turtle's internal anatomy with that of his freshwater brother, so I went up the hill, borrowed the gardener's wheelbarrow, and in it transported my prize up to the house and laid him out in state on the front veranda.

I knew there would be repercussions if I endeavoured to perform my dissection of the turtle inside the house, but I felt that nobody in his right mind would object to the dissection of the turtle on the front veranda. With my notebook at the ready and my row of saws, scalpels, and razor blades neatly laid out as though in an operating theatre, I set to work.

I found that the soft yellow plastern came away quite easily, compared with the underside of the terrapin, which had taken me three quarters of an hour to saw through. When the plastern was free, I lifted it off like a cover off a dish and there, underneath, were all the delicious mysteries of the turtle's internal organs displayed, multi-coloured and odoriferous to a degree. So consumed with curiosity was I that I did not even notice the smell. The dogs, however, who normally considered fresh cow dung to be the ideal scent to add piquancy to their love-life, disappeared in a disapproving body, sneezing violently. I discovered, to my delight, that the turtle was a female and had a large quantity of half-formed eggs in her. They were about the size of ping-pong balls, soft, round, and as orange as a nasturtium. There were fourteen of them, and I removed them carefully and laid them in a gleaming, glutinous row on the flagstones. The turtle appeared to have a prodigious quantity of gut, and I decided that I should enter the exact length of this astonishing apparatus in my already bloodstained notebook. With the aid of a scalpel I detached the gut from the rear exit of the turtle and then proceeded to pull it out. It seemed never-ending, but before long I had it all laid out carefully across the veranda in a series of loops and twists, like a rather drunken railway line. One section of it was composed of the stomach, a rather hideous greyish bag like a water-filled balloon. This obviously was full of the turtle's last meal and I felt, in the interests of science, that I ought to check on what it had been eating just prior to its demise. I stuck a scalpel in the great wobbling mound and slashed experimentally. Immediately the whole stomach bag deflated with a ghastly sighing noise and a stench arose from its interior which made all the other smells pale into insignificance. Even I, fascinated as I was by my investigations, reeled back and had to retreat coughing to wait for the smell to subside.

I knew I could get the veranda cleaned up before the family got back from town, but in my excitement with my new acquisition, I had completely overlooked the fact that Leslie was convalescing in the drawing-room. The scent of the turtle's interior, so pungent that it seemed almost solid, floated in through the French windows and enveloped the couch on which he lay. My first intimation of this catastrophe was a blood-curdling roar from inside the drawing-room. Before I could do anything sensible, Leslie, swathed in blankets, appeared in the French windows.

"What's that bloody awful stink?" he inquired throatily. Then, as his glance fell upon the dismembered turtle and its prettily arranged internal organs spread across the flagstones, his eyes bulged and his face took on a heliotrope tinge. "What the hell's *that?*"

I explained, somewhat diffidently, that it was a turtle that I was dissecting. It was a female, I went on hurriedly, hoping to distract Leslie by detail. Here he could see the fascinating eggs that I had extracted from her interior.

"Damn her eggs," shouted Leslie, making it sound like some strange medieval oath. "Get the bloody thing away from here. It's stinking the place out."

I said that I had almost reached the end of my dissection and that I had then planned to bury all the soft parts and merely keep the skeleton and shell to add to my collection.

"You're doing nothing of the sort," shouted Leslie. "You're to take the whole bloody thing and bury it. Then you can come back and scrub the veranda."

Lucretia, our cook, attracted by the uproar, appeared in the French window next to Leslie. She opened her mouth to inquire into the nature of this family quarrel when she was struck amidships by the smell of the turtle. Lucretia always had fifteen or sixteen ailments worrying her at any given moment, which she cherished with the same loving care that other people devote to window-boxes or Pekingese. At this particular time it was her stomach that was causing her the most trouble. In consequence she gasped two or three times, feebly, like a fish, uttered a strangled "Saint Spiridion!" and fell into Leslie's arms in a well-simulated faint.

Just at that moment, to my horror, the car containing the rest of the family swept up the drive and came to a halt below the veranda.

"Hello, dear," said Mother, getting out of the car and coming up to the steps. "Did you have a nice morning?"

Before I could say anything, the turtle, as it were, got in before me. Mother uttered a couple of strange hiccupping cries, pulled out her handkerchief and clapped it to her nose.

"What," she demanded indistinctly, "is that terrible smell?"

"It's that bloody boy," roared Leslie from the French windows, making ineffectual attempts to prop the moaning Lucretia against the door jamb.

Larry and Margo had now followed Mother up the steps and caught sight of the butchered turtle.

"What...?" began Larry and then he too was seized with a convulsive fit of coughing.

"It's that damned boy," he said, gasping.

"Yes, dear," said Mother through her handkerchief. "Leslie's just told me."

"It's disgusting," wailed Margo, fanning herself with her handkerchief. "It looks like a railway accident."

"What *is* it, dear?" Mother asked me.

I explained that it was an exceedingly interesting hawksbill turtle, female, containing eggs.

"Surely you don't have to chop it up on the veranda?" said Mother.

"The boy's mad," said Larry with conviction. "The whole place smells like a bloody whaling ship."

"I really think you'll have to take it somewhere else, dear," said Mother. "We can't have this smell on the front veranda."

"Tell him to bury the damned thing," said Leslie, clasping his blankets more firmly about him.

"Why don't you get him adopted by a family of Eskimos?" inquired Larry. "They like eating blubber and maggots and things."

"Larry, don't be disgusting," said Margaret. "They can't eat anything like this. The very thought of it makes me feel sick."

"I think we ought to go inside," said Mother faintly. "Perhaps it won't smell as much in there."

"If anything, it smells worse in here," shouted Leslie from the French windows.

"Gerry dear, you must clean this up," said Mother as she picked her way delicately over the turtle's entrails, "and disinfect the flagstones."

The family went inside and I set about the task of clearing up the turtle from the front veranda. Their voices arguing ferociously drifted out to me.

"Bloody menace," said Leslie. "Lying here peacefully reading, and I was suddenly seized by the throat."

"Disgusting," said Margo. "I don't wonder Lucretia fainted."

"High time he had another tutor," said Larry. "You leave the house for five minutes and come back and find him disembowelling Moby Dick on the front porch."

"I'm sure he didn't mean any harm," said Mother, "but it was rather silly of him to do it on the veranda."

"Silly!" said Larry caustically. "We'll be blundering round the house with gas masks for the next six months."

I piled the remains of the turtle into the wheelbarrow and took it up to the top of the hill behind the villa. Here I dug a hole and buried all the soft parts and then placed the shell and the bone structure near a nest of friendly ants, who had, on previous occasions, helped me considerably by picking skeletons clean. But the most they had ever tackled had been a very large green lizard, so I was interested to see whether they would tackle the turtle. They ran towards it, their antennae waving eagerly, and then stopped, thought about it for a bit, held a little consultation and then retreated in a body; apparently even the ants were against me, so I returned dispiritedly to the villa.

Here I found that a thin, whining little man, obviously made belligerent by wine, was arguing with Lucretia on the still-odoriferous veranda. I inquired what the man wanted.

"He says," said Lucretia, with fine scorn, "that Roger has been killing his chickens."

"Turkeys," corrected the man. "Turkeys."

"Well, turkeys then," said Lucretia, conceding the point.

My heart sank. One calamity was being succeeded by another. Roger, we knew, had the most reprehensible habit of killing chickens. He derived a lot of innocent amusement in the spring and summer by chasing swallows. They would drive him into an apoplectic fury by zooming past his nose and then flying along the ground just ahead of him while he chased them, bristling with rage, uttering roars of fury. The peasants' chickens used to hide in the myrtle bushes and then, just as Roger was passing, they would leap out with a great flutter of wings and insane hysterical cackling right into his path. Roger, I was sure, was convinced that these chickens were a sort of ungainly swallow that he could get to grips with and so, in spite of yells of protest on our part, he would leap on them and kill them with one swift bite, all his hatred of the teasing summer swallows showing in his action. No punishment had any effect on him. He was normally an extremely obedient dog, except about this one thing, and so, in desperation, all we could do was to recompense the owners, but only on condition that the corpse of the chicken was produced as evidence.

Reluctantly I went in to tell the family that Roger had been at it again.

"Christ!" said Leslie, getting laboriously to his feet. "You and your sodding animals."

"Now, now, dear," said Mother placatingly. "Gerry can't help it if Roger kills chickens."

"Turkeys," said Leslie, "I bet he'll want a hell of a lot for those."

"Have you cleaned up the veranda, dear?" inquired Mother.

Larry removed a large handkerchief, drenched in eau-de-Cologne, which he had spread over his face. "Does it smell as though he's cleaned up the veranda?" he inquired.

I said hastily that I was just about to do it and followed Leslie to see the outcome of his conversation with the turkey owner.

"Well," said Leslie belligerently, striding out onto the veranda, "what do you want?"

The man cringed, humble, servile, and altogether repulsive. "Be happy, *kyrié*, be happy," he said, greeting Leslie.

"Be happy," Leslie replied in a gruff tone of voice that implied he hoped the man would be anything but. "What do you wish to see me about?"

"My turkeys, *kyrié*," explained the man. "I apologize for troubling you, but your dog, you see, he's been killing my turkeys."

126

"Well," said Leslie, "how many has he killed?"

"Five, *kyrié*," said the man, shaking his head sorrowfully. "Five of my best turkeys. I am a poor man, *kyrié*, otherwise I wouldn't have dreamed..."

"Five!" said Leslie startled, and turned an inquiring eye on me.

I said I thought it was quite possible. If five hysterical turkeys had leaped out of a myrtle bush, I could well believe that Roger would kill them all. For such a benign and friendly dog, he was a very ruthless killer when he got started.

"Roger is a good dog," said Lucretia belligerently.

She had joined us on the veranda and she obviously viewed the turkey owner with the same dislike as I did. Apart from this, in her eyes Roger could do no wrong.

"Well," said Leslie, making the best of a bad job, "if he's killed five turkeys, he's killed five turkeys. Such is life. Where are the bodies?"

There was a moment of silence.

"The bodies, *kyrié*?" queried the turkey owner tentatively.

"The bodies, the bodies," said Leslie impatiently. "You know, the bodies of the turkeys. You know we can't pay until you produce the bodies."

"But that's not possible," said the turkey owner nervously.

"What do you mean, not possible?" inquired Leslie.

"Well, it's not possible to bring the bodies, *kyrié*," said the turkey owner with a flash of inspiration, "because your dog has eaten them."

The explosion that this statement provoked was considerable. We all knew that Roger was, if anything, slightly overfed, and that he was of a most fastidious nature. Though he would kill a chicken, nothing would induce him to feed upon the carcass.

"Lies! Lies!" shrilled Lucretia, her eyes swimming with tears of emotion. "He's a good dog."

"He's never eaten anything in his life that he's killed," shouted Leslie. "Never."

"But five of my turkeys!" said the little man. "Five of them he's eaten!"

"When did he kill them?" roared Leslie.

"This morning, *kyrié*, this morning," said the man, crossing himself. "I saw it myself, and he ate them all."

I interrupted to say that Roger had been out that morning in the *Bootle-Bumtrinket* with me and, intelligent dog though he was, I did not see how he could be consuming the prodigious quantity of five turkeys on this man's farm and be out in the boat with me at the same time.

Leslie had had a trying morning. All he had wanted was to lie peacefully on the sofa with his manual of ballistics, but first he had been almost asphyxiated by my investigations into the internal anatomy of the turtle and now he was being faced by a drunken little man, trying to swindle us for the price of five turkeys. His temper, never under the best of control, bubbled over.

"You're a two-faced liar and a cheat," he snarled. The little man backed away and his face went white.

"You are the liar and the cheat," he said with drunken belligerence. "You are the liar and the cheat. You let your dog kill everybody's chickens and turkeys and then when they come to you for payment, you refuse. You are the liar and the cheat."

Even at that stage, I think that sanity could have prevailed, but the little man made a fatal mistake. He spat copiously and wetly at Leslie's feet. Lucretia uttered a shrill wail of horror and grabbed hold of Leslie's arm. Knowing his temper, I grabbed hold of the other one, too. The little man, appalled into a moment of sobriety, backed away. Leslie quivered like a volcano and Lucretia and I hung on like grim death.

"*Excreta* of a pig," roared Leslie. "Illegitimate son of a diseased whore."

The fine Greek oaths rolled out, rich, vulgar, and biological, and the little man turned from white to pink and from pink to red. He had obviously been unaware of the fact that Leslie had such a command over the fruitier of the Greek insults.

"You'll be sorry," he quavered. "You'll be sorry."

He spat once more with a pathetic sort of defiance and then turned and scuttled down the drive.

It took the combined efforts of the family and Lucretia three quarters of an hour to calm Leslie down, with the aid of several large brandies.

"Don't you worry about him, *kyrié* Leslie," was Lucretia's final summing up. "He's well-known in the village as a bad character. Don't you worry about him."

But we were forced to worry about him, for the next thing we knew, he had sued Leslie for not paying his debts and for defamation of character.

Spiro, when told the news, was furious.

"Gollys, Mrs Durrells," he said, his face red with wrath. "Why don'ts yous lets Masters Leslies shoot the son of a bitch?"

"I don't think that would really solve anything, Spiro," said Mother. "What we want to know now is whether this man has any chance of winning his case."

"Winnings!" said Spiro with fine scorn. "That bastard won't wins anythings. You just leaves it to me. I'll fixes it."

"Now, don't go and do anything rash, Spiro," said Mother. "It'll only make matters worse."

"I won'ts do anything rash, Mrs Durrells. But I'll fixes that bastard."

For several days he went about with an air of conspiratorial gloom, his bushy eyebrows tangled in a frown of immense concentration, only answering our questions monosyllabically. Then, one day, a fortnight or so before the case was due to be heard, we were all in town on a shopping spree. Eventually, weighed down by our purchases, we made our way to the broad, tree-lined Esplanade and sat there having a drink and exchanging greetings with our numerous acquaintances who passed. Presently Spiro, who had been glaring furtively about him with the air of a man who had many enemies, suddenly stiffened. He hitched his great belly up and leaned across the table.

"Master Leslies, you sees that mans over there, that one with the white hair?"

He pointed a sausage-like finger at a small, neat little man who was placidly sipping a cup of coffee under the trees.

"Well, what about him?" inquired Leslie.

"He's the judges," said Spiro.

"What judge?" said Leslie, bewildered.

"The judges who is going to tries your case," said Spiro. "I wants you go to over there and talks to him."

"Do you think that's wise?" said Larry. "He might think I'm trying to muck about with the course of justice and give me ten years in prison or something."

"Gollys, nos," said Spiro, aghast at such a thought. "He wouldn't puts Master Leslies in prison. He knows better than to do thats while I ams here."

"But even so, Spiro, don't you think he'll think it a little funny if Leslie suddenly starts talking to him?" asked Mother.

"Gollys nos," said Spiro. He glanced about him to make sure that we weren't overheard, leaned forward, and whispered, "He collects stamps."

The family looked bewildered.

"You mean he's a philatelist?" said Larry at length.

"No, no, Master Larrys," said Spiro. "He's not one of them. He's a married man and he's gots two childrens."

The whole conversation seemed to be getting even more involved than the normal ones that we had with Spiro.

"What," said Leslie patiently, "has his collecting stamps got to do with it?"

"I will takes you over there," said Spiro, laying bare for the first time the Machiavellian intricacies of his plot, "and yous tells hims that you will get him some stamps from England."

"But that's bribery," said Margaret, shocked.

"It isn't bribery, Misses Margos," said Spiro. "He collects stamps. He *wants* stamps."

"I should think if you tried to bribe him with stamps he'd give you about five hundred years' penal servitude," said Larry to Leslie judiciously.

I asked eagerly whether, if Leslie was condemned, he would be sent to Vido, the convict settlement on a small island that lay in the sparkling sea half a mile or so from the town.

"No, no, dear," said Mother, getting increasingly flustered. "Leslie won't be sent to Vido."

I felt this was rather a pity. I already had one convict friend, serving a sentence for the murder of his wife, who lived on Vido. He was a "trusty" and so had been allowed to build his own boat and row home for the weekends. He had given me a monstrous black-backed gull which tyrannized all my pets and the family. I felt that, exciting though it was to have a real murderer as a friend, it would have been better to have Leslie incarcerated on Vido so that he too could come home for the weekends. To have a convict brother would, I felt, be rather exotic.

"I don't see that if I just go and *talk* to him it can do any harm," said Leslie.

"I wouldn't," said Margo. "Remember, there's many a slip without a stitch."

"I do think you ought to be careful, dear," said Mother.

"I can see it all," said Larry with relish. "Leslie with a ball and chain; Spiro too, probably, as an accessory. Margo knitting them warm socks for the winter, Mother sending them food parcels and anti-lice ointment."

"Oh, do stop it, Larry," said Mother crossly. "This is no laughing matter."

"All you've gots to dos is to talks to him, Master Leslies," said Spiro earnestly. "Honest to Gods you've got to, otherwise I can't fixes it."

Spiro had, prior to this, never let us down. His advice had always been sound, and even if it hadn't been legal, we had never so far come to grief.

"All right," said Leslie. "Let's give it a bash."

"Do be careful, dear," said Mother as Leslie and Spiro rose and walked over to where the judge was sitting.

The judge greeted them charmingly and for half an hour Leslie and Spiro sat at his table sipping coffee while Leslie talked to him in voluble, but inaccurate, Greek. Presently the judge rose and left them with much handshaking and bowing. They returned to our table where we waited agog for the news.

"Charming old boy," said Leslie. "Couldn't have been nicer. I promised to get him some stamps. Who do we know in England who collects them?"

"Well, your father used to," said Mother. "He was a very keen philatelist when he was alive."

"Gollys, don't says that Mrs Durrells," said Spiro, in genuine anguish.

A short pause ensued while the family explained to him the meaning of the word philatelist.

"I still don't see how this is going to help the case," said Larry, "even if you inundate him with penny blacks."

"Never yous minds, Masters Larrys," said Spiro darkly. "I said I'd fixes it and I will. You just leaves it to me."

For the next few days Leslie, convinced that Spiro could obstruct the course of justice, wrote to everybody he could think of in England and demanded stamps. The result was that our mail increased threefold and that practically every free space in the villa was taken up by piles of stamps which, whenever a wind blew, would drift like autumn leaves across the room, to the vociferous, snarling delight of the dogs. As a result of this, many of the stamps began to look slightly the worse for wear.

"You're not going to give him *those*, are you?" said Larry, disdainfully surveying a pile of mangled, semi-masticated stamps that Leslie had rescued from the jaws of Roger half an hour previously.

"Well, stamps are supposed to be old, aren't they?" said Leslie belligerently.

"Old, perhaps," said Larry, "but surely not covered with enough spittle to give him hydrophobia."

"Well, if you can think of a better bloody plan, why don't you suggest it?" inquired Leslie.

"My dear fellow, *I* don't mind," said Larry. "When the judge is running around biting all his colleagues and you are languishing in a Greek prison, don't blame me."

"All I ask is that you mind your own bloody business," cried Leslie.

"Now, now, dear, Larry's only trying to be helpful," said Mother.

"Helpful," snarled Leslie, making a grab at a group of stamps that were being blown off the table. "He's just interfering as usual."

"Well, dear," said Mother, adjusting her spectacles, "I do think he may be right, you know. After all, some of those stamps do look a little, well, you know, second-hand."

"He wants stamps and he's bloody well going to get stamps," said Leslie.

And stamps the poor judge got, in a bewildering variety of sizes, shapes, colours, and stages of disintegration.

Then another thing happened that increased Leslie's confidence in winning the case a hundredfold. We discovered that the turkey man, whom Larry constantly referred to as Crippenopoulos, had been unwise enough to subpoena Lucretia as a witness for the prosecution. Lucretia, furious, wanted to refuse, until it was explained to her that she could not.

"Imagine that man calling me as a witness to help him," she said. "Well, don't you worry, *kyrié* Leslie, I'll tell the court how he forced you to swear at him and call him…"

The family rose in a body and vociferously informed Lucretia that she was not to do anything of the sort. It took us half an hour to impress upon her what she should and should not say. At the end of it, since Lucretia, like most Corfiotes, was not very strong on logic, we felt somewhat jaded.

"Well, with her as witness for the prosecution," said Larry, "I should think you'll probably get the death sentence."

"Larry dear, don't say things like that," said Mother. "It's not funny even in a joke."

"I'm not joking," said Larry.

"Rubbish," said Leslie uneasily. "I'm sure she'll be all right."

"I think it would be much safer to disguise Margo as Lucretia," said Larry judicially. "With her sweeping command over the Greek language she would probably do you considerably less harm."

"Yes," said Margo excitedly, struck for the first time by Larry's perspicacity, "why can't I be a witness?"

"Don't be damned silly," said Leslie. "You weren't there. How can you be a witness?"

"I was almost there," said Margo. "I was in the kitchen."

"That's all you need," said Larry to Leslie. "Margo and Lucretia in the witness-box and you won't even need a judge. You'll probably be lynched by the mob."

When the day of the case dawned, Mother rallied the family.

"It's ridiculous for us all to go," said Larry. "If Leslie wants to get himself into prison, that's his affair. I don't see why we should be dragged into it. Besides, I wanted to do some writing this morning."

"It's our duty to go," said Mother firmly. "We must put on a bold front. After all, I don't want people to think that I'm rearing a family of jailbirds."

So we all put on our best clothes and sat waiting patiently until Spiro came to collect us.

"Now, don'ts yous worrys, Master Leslies," he scowled, with the air of a warder in the condemned cell. "Everything's going to be OKs."

But in spite of this prophecy, Larry insisted on reciting "The Ballad of Reading Gaol" as we drove into town, much to Leslie's annoyance.

The courtroom was a bustle of uncoordinated activity. People sipped little cups of coffee, other people shuffled through piles of papers in an aimless but dedicated way, and there was lots of chatter and laughter. Crippenopoulos was there in his best suit, but avoided our eye. Lucretia, for some reason best known to herself, was clad entirely in black. It was, as Larry pointed out, a premature move. Surely she should have reserved her mourning for after the trial.

"Now, Master Leslies," said Spiro, "you stands there, and I stands there and translates for you."

"What for?" inquired Leslie, bewildered.

"Because you don'ts speaks Greeks," said Spiro.

"Really, Spiro," protested Larry, "I admit his Greek is not Homeric, but it is surely perfectly adequate?"

"Masters Larrys," said Spiro, scowling earnestly, "Master Leslies mustn'ts speaks Greeks."

Before we could inquire more deeply into this, there was a general scuffling and the judge came in. He took his seat and his eyes roved round the court and then, catching sight of Leslie, he beamed and bowed.

"Hanging judges always smile like that," said Larry.

"Larry dear, do stop it," said Mother. "You're making me nervous."

There was a long pause while what was presumably the Clerk of the Court read out the indictment. Then Crippenopoulos was called to give his evidence. He put on a lovely performance, at once servile and indignant, placating but belligerent. The judge was obviously impressed and I began to get quite excited. Perhaps I would have a convict for a brother after all. Then it was Leslie's turn.

"You are accused," said the judge, "of having used defamatory and insulting language to this man and endeavouring to deprive him of rightful payment for the loss of five turkeys, killed by your dog."

Leslie stared blank-faced at the judge. "What's he say?" he inquired of Spiro. Spiro hitched his stomach up.

"He says, Masters Leslies," and his voice was so pitched that it rumbled through the courtroom like thunder, "he says that you insults this mans and that you tries to swindle him out of moneys for his turkeys."

"That's ridiculous," said Leslie firmly.

He was about to go on when Spiro held up a hand like a ham and stopped him. He turned to the judge.

"The *kyrios* denies the charge," he said. "It would be impossible for him to be guilty anyway, because he doesn't speak Greek."

"Christ!" groaned Larry sepulchrally. "I hope Spiro knows what he's doing."

"What's he saying? What's he doing?" said Mother nervously.

"As far as I can see, putting a noose round Leslie's neck," said Larry.

The judge, who had had so many coffees with Leslie, who had received so many stamps from him, and who had had so many conversations in Greek with him, stared at Leslie impassively. Even if the judge had not known Leslie personally, it would have been impossible for him not to know that Leslie had some command over the Greek language. Nothing anyone did in Corfu was sacrosanct, and if you were a foreigner, of course, the interest in and the knowledge of your private affairs was that much greater. We waited with bated breath for the judge's reactions. Spiro had his massive head slightly lowered like a bull about to charge.

"I see," said the judge dryly.

He shuffled some papers aimlessly for a moment and then glanced up.

"I understand," he said, "that the prosecution has a witness. I suppose we had better hear her."

It was Lucretia's big moment. She rose to her feet, folded her arms, and stared majestically at the judge, her normally pale face pink with excitement, her soulful eyes glowing.

"You are Lucretia Condos and you are employed by these people as a cook?" inquired the judge.

"Yes," said Lucretia, "and a kinder, more generous family you could not wish to meet. Why, only the other day they gave me a frock for myself and for my daughter and it was only a month or two ago that I asked the *kyrios*..."

"Yes," interrupted the judge, "I see. Well, this has not got much relevance to the case. I understand that you were there when this man called to see about his turkeys. Now tell me in your own words what happened."

Larry groaned.

"If she tells him in her own words, they'll get Leslie for sure," he said.

"Well," said Lucretia, glancing round the court to make sure she had everybody's attention. "The *kyrios* had been very ill, very ill indeed. At times we despaired for his life. I kept suggesting cupping to his mother, but she wouldn't hear of it..."

"Would you mind getting to the point?" said the judge.

"Well," said Lucretia, reluctantly abandoning the subject of illness, which was always a favourite topic with her, "it was the *kyrios'* first day up and he was very weak. Then this man," she said, pointing a scornful finger at Crippenopoulos, "arrived dead drunk and said that their dog had killed five of his turkeys. Now the dog wouldn't do that, *kyrié* judge. A sweeter, kinder, nobler dog was never seen in Corfu."

"The dog is not on trial," said the judge.

"Well," said Lucretia, "when the *kyrios* said, quite rightly, that he would have to see the corpses before he paid the man, the man said he couldn't show them because the dog had eaten them. This is ridiculous, as you can well imagine, *kyrié* judge, as no dog could eat five turkeys."

"You are supposed to be a witness for the prosecution, aren't you?" said the judge. "I ask only because your story doesn't tally with the complainant's."

"Him," said Lucretia, "you don't want to trust him. He's a drunkard and a liar and it is well known in the village that he has got two wives."

"So you are telling me," said the judge, endeavouring to sort out this confusion, "that the *kyrios* didn't swear at him in Greek and refuse payment for the turkeys."

"Of course he didn't," said Lucretia. "A kinder, finer, more upstanding *kyrios…*"

"Yes, yes, all right," said the judge.

He sat pondering for some time while we all waited in suspense, then he glanced up and looked at Crippenopoulos.

"I can see no evidence," he said, "that the Englishman behaved in the way you have suggested. Firstly he does not speak Greek."

"He does speak Greek," shouted Crippenopoulos wrathfully. "He called me a…"

"Will you be quiet," said the judge coldly. "Firstly, as I was saying, he does not speak Greek. Secondly, your own witness denies all knowledge of the incident. It seems to me clear, however, that you endeavoured to extract payment for turkeys which had not, in fact, been killed and eaten by the defendant's dog. However, you are not on trial here for that, so I will merely find the defendant not guilty, and you will have to pay the costs."

Immediately pandemonium reigned. Crippenopoulos was on his feet, purple with rage, shouting at the top of his voice and calling on St Spiridion's aid. Spiro, bellowing like a bull, embraced Leslie, kissed him on both checks, and was followed by the weeping Lucretia who did likewise. It was some time before we managed to extricate ourselves from the court, and jubilantly we went down to the Esplanade and sat at a table under the trees to celebrate.

Presently the judge came past and we rose in a body to thank him and invite him to sit and have a drink with us. He refused the drink shyly and then fixed Leslie with a penetrating eye.

"I wouldn't like you to think," he said, "that justice in Corfu is always dispensed like that, but I had a long conversation with Spiro about the case and after some deliberation I decided that your crime was not as bad as the man's. I hoped it might teach him not to swindle foreigners in future."

"Well, I really am most grateful to you," said Leslie.

The judge gave a little bow. He glanced at his watch. "Well, I must be going," he said. "By the way, thank you so much for those stamps you sent me yesterday. Among them were two quite rare ones which were new to my collection."

Raising his hat he trotted off across the Esplanade.

INTERLUDE FOR SPIRITS

What seest thou else in the dark backward and abysm of time?

— THE TEMPEST

INTERLUDE FOR SPIRITS

Not very long after Leslie's court case, Margo was beset by
another affliction to keep company with her acne. She suddenly
started to put on weight and before long, to her horror, she was
almost circular. Androuchelli, our doctor, was called in to view
this mystery. He uttered a long series of distressed "Po, po, pos"
as he viewed Margo's obesity. He tried her on several pills and
potions and a number of diets, to no effect.

"He says," Margo confided to us tearfully at lunch one day,
"that he thinks it's glandular."

"Glandular?" said Mother, alarmed. "What does he mean,
glandular?"

"I don't know," wailed Margo.

"Must we always discuss your ailments at mealtimes?"
inquired Larry.

"Larry dear, Androuchelli says it's glandular," said Mother.

"Rubbish," said Larry airily. "It's puppy-fat."

"Puppy-fat!" squeaked Margo. "Do you know how much
I weigh?"

"What you want is more exercise," said Leslie. "Why don't
you take up sailing?"

"Don't think the boat's big enough," said Larry.

"Beast," said Margo, bursting into tears. "You wouldn't say things like that if you knew how I felt."

"Larry dear," said Mother placatingly, "that wasn't a very kind thing to say."

"Well, I can't help it if she's wandering around looking like a water-melon covered with spots," said Larry irritably. "One would think it was *my* fault the way you all go on."

"Something will have to be done," said Mother. "I shall see Androuchelli tomorrow."

But Androuchelli repeated that he thought her condition might be glandular and that in his opinion Margo ought to go to London for treatment. So, after a flurry of telegrams and letters, Margo was despatched to London and into the tender care of two of the only worthwhile relatives with whom we were still on speaking terms, my mother's cousin Prudence and her mother, Great-aunt Fan.

Apart from a brief letter saying she had arrived safely and that she, Cousin Prue, and Aunt Fan had taken up residence at a hotel near Notting Hill Gate and that she had been put in touch with a good doctor, we heard nothing further from Margo for a considerable length of time.

"I do wish she would write," Mother said.

"Don't fuss, Mother," said Larry. "What's she got to write about, anyway, except to give you her new dimensions?"

"Well, I like to know what's going on," said Mother. "After all, she's in *London*."

"What's London got to do with it?" asked Larry.

"In a big city like that anything can happen," said Mother darkly. "You hear all sorts of things about girls in big cities."

"Really, Mother, you do worry unnecessarily," said Larry in exasperation. "What do you think's happened to her, for Heaven's sake? Do you think she's being lured into some den of vice? They'd never get her through the door."

"It's no joking matter, Larry," said Mother severely.

"But you get yourself into a panic about nothing," said Larry. "I ask you, what self-respecting white slaver is going to look at Margo twice? I shouldn't think there's one strong enough to carry her off, anyway."

"Well, I'm worried," said Mother, "and I'm going to send a cable."

So she sent a cable to Cousin Prudence, who replied at length saying that Margaret was associating with people she didn't approve of, that she thought it would be a good thing if Mother came to talk some sense into her. Immediately pandemonium reigned. Mother, distraught, despatched Spiro to buy tickets and started packing frantically, until she suddenly remembered me. Feeling it would do more harm than good to leave me in the tender care of my two elder brothers, she decided that I should accompany her. So Spiro was despatched to get more tickets and yet more packing was done. I regarded the whole situation as heaven-sent, for I had just acquired a new tutor, Mr Richard Kralefsky, who was endeavouring – with grim determination in the face of my opposition – to instruct me in irregular French verbs, and this trip to England, I thought, would give me a much-needed respite from this torture.

The journey by train was uneventful, except that Mother was in constant fear of being arrested by the Fascist carabinieri. This fear increased a thousandfold when, at Milan, I drew a caricature of Mussolini on the steamy window of the carriage. Mother scrubbed at it for quite ten minutes with her handkerchief, with all the dedication of a washerwoman in a contest, before she was satisfied that it was obliterated.

Coming from the calm, slow, sunlit days of Corfu, our arrival in London, late in the evening, was a shattering experience. So many people were at the station that we did not *know*, all hurrying to and fro, grey-faced and worried. The almost incomprehensible language that the porters spoke, and London aglitter with lights and churning with people. The taxi nosing its way through Piccadilly like a beetle through a firework display. The cold air that made your breath float like a web of smoke in front of your mouth as you talked, so that you felt like a character in a cartoon strip.

Eventually the taxi drew up outside the fake, soot-encrusted Corinthian columns of Balaklava Mansions. We got our luggage into the hotel with the aid of an elderly, bow-legged, Irish porter, but there was no one to greet us, so apparently the telegram signalling our arrival had gone astray. The young lady, we were informed by the porter, had gone to her meeting, and Miss Hughes and the old lady had gone to feed the dogs.

"What did he say, dear?" asked Mother when he had left the room, for his accent was so thick that it sounded almost as though he were talking a foreign language. I said that Margo had gone to a meeting and that Cousin Prue and Aunt Fan were feeding the dogs.

"What *can* he mean?" said Mother, bewildered. "What meeting has Margo gone to? What dogs is he talking about?"

I said I did not know but, from what I had seen of London, what it needed was a few more dogs around.

"Well," said Mother, inexpertly putting a shilling in the meter and lighting the gas fire, "I suppose we'll just have to make ourselves comfortable and wait until they come back."

We had waited an hour when suddenly the door burst open and Cousin Prue rushed in, arms outstretched, crying "Louise, Louise, Louise," like some strange marsh bird. She embraced us both, her sloe dark eyes glowing with love and excitement. Her beautiful face, delicately scented, was soft as a pansy as I kissed her dutifully.

"I began to think that you were never coming," she said. "Mummy is on her way up. She finds the stairs trying, poor dear. Well, now, *don't* you both look well. You must tell me everything. Do you like this hotel, Louise? It's so cheap and convenient, but full of the most peculiar people."

A gentle wheezing sound made itself heard through the open door.

"Ah, there's Mummy," cried Prue. "Mummy! Mummy! Louise's here."

Through the door appeared my Great-aunt Fan. At first glance she looked, I thought rather uncharitably, like a walking tent. She was enveloped in a rusty-red tweed suit of incredible style and dimensions. It made her look like a russet-red pyramid of tweed. On her head she wore a somewhat battered velveteen hat of the style that pixies are reputedly wont to use. Her spectacles, through which her eyes stared owlishly, glittered.

"Louise!" she cried throwing her arms wide and casting her eyes up as though Mother were some divine apparition. "Louise and Gerald! You have come!"

Mother and I were kissed and embraced heartily. This was not the feathery, petal-soft embrace of Cousin Prue. This was a hearty, rib-cracking embrace and a firm kiss that left your lips feeling bruised.

"I am so sorry we weren't here to greet you, Louise dear," said Prue, "but we weren't sure when you were arriving and we had the dogs to feed."

"What dogs?" asked Mother.

"Why, my Bedlington puppies, of course," said Prue. "Didn't you know? Mummy and I have become dog-breeders." She gave a coy, tinkling laugh.

"But you had something else last time," said Mother. "Goats or something, wasn't it?"

"Oh, we've still got those," said Aunt Fan. "And my bees and the chickens. But Prudence here thought it would be a good thing to start dog-breeding. She's got such a head for business."

"I really think it's a paying concern, Louise dear," said Prue earnestly. "I bought Tinkerbell and then Lucybell…"

"And then Tinybell," interrupted Aunt Fan.

"And Tinybell," said Prue.

"And Lucybell," said Aunt Fan.

"Oh, Mummy, do be quiet. I've already said Lucybell."

"And there's Tinkerbell too," said Aunt Fan.

"Mummy is a little hard of hearing," said Prue unnecessarily, "and they have all had puppies. I brought them up to London to sell and at the same time we have been keeping an eye on Margo."

"Yes, where is Margo?" asked Mother.

Prue tiptoed over to the door and closed it softly.

"She's at a *meeting*, dear," she said.

"I know, but what sort of meeting?" asked Mother.

Prue glanced round nervously.

"A *spiritualist* meeting," she hissed.

"And then there's Lucybell," said Aunt Fan.

"Oh, Mummy, do be quiet."

"Spiritualist meeting?" said Mother. "What on earth's she gone to a spiritualist meeting for?"

"To cure her fatness and her acne," said Prue. "But mark my words, no good will come of it. It's an evil power."

I could see Mother beginning to get alarmed.

"But I don't understand," she said. "I sent Margo home to see that doctor, what's his name?"

"I *know* you did, dear," said Prue. "Then, after she came to this hotel, she fell into the grasp of that evil woman."

"What evil woman?" said Mother, now considerably alarmed.

"The goats are well too," said Aunt Fan, "but their milk yield is down a little this year."

"Oh, Mummy, do shut up," hissed Prue. "I mean that evil woman, Mrs Haddock."

"Haddock, haddock," said Mother, bewildered. Her train of thought was always liable to be interrupted if anything culinary was mentioned.

"She's a medium, my dear," said Prue, "and she's got her hooks on Margo. She's told Margo that she's got a guide."

"A guide?" said Mother feebly. "What sort of guide?"

I could see, in her distraught condition, that she was now beginning to think Margo had taken up mountaineering or some similar occupation

"A spirit guide," said Prue. "It's called Mawake. He's supposed to be a Red Indian."

"I have ten hives now," said Aunt Fan proudly. "We get twice as much honey."

"Mother, be quiet," said Prue.

"I don't understand," said Mother plaintively. "Why isn't she still going to the doctor for her injections?"

"Because Mawake told her not to," said Prue triumphantly. "Three séances ago, he said – according to Margaret, and of course the whole thing comes through Mrs Haddock so you can't trust it for a moment – according to Margaret, Mawake said she was to have no more punctures."

"Punctures?" said Mother.

"Well, I suppose it's Red Indian for injections," said Prue.

"It is nice to see you again, Louise," said Aunt Fan. "I think we ought to have a cup of tea,"

"That's a very good idea," said Mother faintly.

"I'm not going down there to order tea, Mummy," said Prue, glancing at the door as if, behind it, were all the fiends of Hell. "Not when they're having a meeting."

"Why, what happens?" asked Mother.

"And some toast would be nice," said Aunt Fan.

"Oh, Mummy, do be quiet," said Prue. "You have no idea what happens at these meetings, Louise. Mrs Haddock goes into a trance, then becomes covered with ectoplasm."

"Ectoplasm?" said Mother. "What's ectoplasm?"

"I've got a pot of my own honey in my room," said Aunt Fan. "I'm sure you will enjoy it, Louise. So much purer than these synthetic things you buy now."

"It's a sort of stuff that mediums produce," said Prue. "It looks like… Well, it looks like, sort of like – I've never actually seen it, but I'm told that it looks like *brains*. Then they make trumpets fly about and things. I tell you, my dear, I never go into the lower regions of the hotel when they are holding a meeting."

Fascinated though I was by the conversation, I felt the chance of seeing a woman called Mrs Haddock covered with brains, with a couple of trumpets floating about, was too good to miss, so I volunteered to go down and order tea.

However, to my disappointment, I saw nothing in the lower regions of the hotel to resemble remotely Cousin Prudence's description, but I did manage to get a tray of tea brought up by the Irish porter. We were sipping this, and I was endeavouring to explain to Aunt Fan what ectoplasm was, when Margaret arrived, carrying a large cabbage under one arm, accompanied by a dumpy little woman with protruding blue eyes and wispy hair.

"Mother!" said Margo dramatically. "You've come!"

"Yes, dear," said Mother grimly. "And not a moment too soon, apparently."

"This is Mrs Haddock," said Margo. "*She's absolutely marvellous.*"

It became immediately apparent that Mrs Haddock suffered from a strange affliction. For some obscure reason she seemed to be incapable of breathing while talking. The result was that she would gabble, all her words latched together like a daisy-chain and would then, when her breath ran out, pause and suck it in, making a noise that sounded like "Whaaaha".

Now she said to Mother, "IamdelightedtomeetyouMrs-Durrell. Ofcourse,myspiritguideinformedmeofyourcoming. Idohopeyouhadacomfortablejourney… Whaaaha."

Mother, who had been intending to give Mrs Haddock a very frigid and dignified greeting, was somewhat put off by this strange delivery.

"Oh, yes. Did we?" she said nervously, straining her ears to understand what Mrs Haddock was saying.

"Mrs Haddock is a spiritualist, Mother," said Margo proudly, as though she were introducing Leonardo da Vinci or the inventor of the first aeroplane.

"Really, dear?" said Mother, smiling frostily. "How very interesting."

"Itgivesonegreatcomforttoknowthatthosewhohavegone-beforearestillintouchwithone… Whaaaha," said Mrs Haddock earnestly. "Somanypeopleareunaware… Whaa…aha…ofthe-spiritworldthatliessoclose."

"You should have seen the puppies tonight, Margo," observed Aunt Fan. "The little tinkers had torn up all their bedding."

"Mummy, do be quiet," said Prue, eyeing Mrs Haddock as though she expected her to grow horns and a tail at any moment.

"Yourdaughterisveryluckyinasmuchasshehas... Whaa...aha ...managedtoobtainoneofthebetterguides," said Mrs Haddock, rather as though Margaret had riffled through the *Debrett* before settling on her spirit counsellor.

"He's called Mawake," said Margo. "He's *absolutely marvellous!*"

"He doesn't appear to have done you much good so far," said Mother tartly.

"But he has," said Margo indignantly. "I've lost three ounces."

"Ittakestimeandpatienceandimplicitbeliefinthefuturelife... Whaaaha...mydearMrsDurrell," said Mrs Haddock, smiling at Mother with sickly sweetness.

"Yes, I'm sure," said Mother, "but I really would prefer it if Margo were under a medical practitioner one could see."

"I don't think they meant it," said Aunt Fan. "I think they're teething. Their gums get sore, you know."

"Mummy, we are not *talking* about the puppies," said Prue. "We are talking about Margo's guide."

"That will be nice for her," said Aunt Fan, beaming fondly at Margo.

"Thespiritworldissomuchwiserthananyearthlybeing... Whaaaha," said Mrs Haddock. "Youcouldn'thaveyourdaughter-inbetterhands. Mawakewasagreatmedicinemaninhisowntribe. OneofthemostknowledgeableinthewholeofNorthAmerica... Whaaah."

"And he's given me such good advice, Mother," said Margo. "Hasn't he, Mrs Haddock?"

"Nomorepunctures. Thewhitegirlmusthavenomorepunctures ...Whaaaha," intoned Mrs Haddock.

"There you are," hissed Prue triumphantly, "I told you."

"Have some honey," said Aunt Fan companionably. "It's not like that synthetic stuff you buy in the shops nowadays."

"Mummy, be quiet."

"I still feel, Mrs Haddock, that I would prefer my daughter to have sensible medical attention rather than this Mawake."

"Oh, Mother, you're so narrow-minded and Victorian," said Margo in exasperation.

"MydearMrsDurrellyoumustlearntotrustthegreatinfluen-cesofthespiritworldthatareafterallonlytryingtohelpandguideus... Whaaaha," said Mrs Haddock. "Ifeelthatifyoucametooneofour-meetingsyouwouldbeconvincedofthegreatpowersofgoodthatour-spiritguideshave... Whaaaha."

"I prefer to be guided by my own spirit, thank you very much," said Mother, with dignity.

"Honey isn't what it used to be," said Aunt Fan, who had been giving the matter some thought.

"You are just prejudiced, Mother," said Margo. "You're condemning a thing without even *trying*."

"IfeelsurethatifyoucouldpersuadeyourMothertoattendoneof-ourmeetings... Whaaaha," said Mrs Haddock, "shewould-findawholenewworldopeningupbeforeher."

"Yes, Mother," said Margo, "you must come to a meeting. I'm *sure* you'd be convinced. The things you see and hear! After all, there are no bricks without fire."

I could see that Mother was suffering an inward struggle. For many years she had been deeply interested in superstitions, folk magic, witchcraft, and similar subjects, and now the temptation to accept Mrs Haddock's offer was very great. I waited breath-lessly, hoping that she would accept. There was nothing I wanted more at that moment than to see Mrs Haddock covered with brains and with trumpets flying round her head.

"Well," said Mother, undecided, "we'll see. We'll talk about it tomorrow."

"I'msurethatoncewebreakthroughthebarrierforyouwe'll-beabletogiveyoualotofhelpandguidance… Whaaaha," said Mrs Haddock.

"Oh, yes," said Margo. "Mawake's simply *wonderful!*" One would have thought she was talking about her favourite film star.

"Wearehavinganothermeetingtomorroweveningherein-thehotel… Whaaaha," said Mrs Haddock, "andIdohopethat-bothyouandMargowillattend… Whaaaha."

She gave us a pallid smile as though reluctantly forgiving us our sins, patted Margo on the cheek, and left.

"Really, Margo," said Mother as the door closed behind Mrs Haddock, "you do make me cross."

"Oh, Mother, you are so *old-fashioned*," said Margo. "That doctor wasn't doing me any good with his injections, anyway, and Mawake is working miracles."

"Miracles," snorted Mother scornfully. "You still look exactly the same size to me."

"Clover," said Aunt Fan, through a mouthful of toast, "is supposed to be the best, although I prefer heather myself."

"I tell you, dear," said Prue, "this woman's got a grip on you. She's malignant. Be warned before it's too late."

"All I ask is that you just simply come to a meeting and see," said Margo.

"Never," said Prue, shuddering. "My nerves wouldn't stand it."

"It's interesting, too, that they have to have bumble-bees to fertilize the clover," observed Aunt Fan.

"Well," said Mother, "I'm much too tired to discuss it now. We will discuss it in the morning."

"Can you help me with my cabbage?" asked Margo.

"Do what?" inquired Mother.

"Help me with my cabbage," said Margo.

"I have often wondered whether one could not cultivate bumble-bees," said Aunt Fan, thoughtfully.

"What do you do with your cabbage?" inquired Mother.

"She puts it on her face," hissed Prue. "Ridiculous!"

"It isn't ridiculous," said Margo, angrily. "It's done my acne a world of good."

"What? Do you mean you boil it or something?" asked Mother.

"No," said Margo, "I put the leaves on my face and you tie them on for me. Mawake advised it and it works wonders."

"It's ridiculous, Louise dear. You should stop her," said Prue, bristling like a plump kitten. "It's nothing more than witchcraft."

"Well, I'm too tired to argue about it," said Mother. "I don't suppose it can do you any harm."

So Margo sat in a chair and held to her face large crinkly cabbage leaves which Mother solemnly fixed to her head with lengths of red twine. I thought she looked like some curious vegetable mummy.

"It's paganism. That's what it is," said Prue.

"Nonsense, Prue, you do fuss," said Margo, her voice muffled by cabbage leaves.

"I sometimes wonder," said Mother, tying the last knot, "whether my family's *all there.*"

"Is Margo going to a fancy-dress ball?" inquired Aunt Fan, who had watched the procedure with interest.

"No, Mummy," roared Prue, "it's for her spots."

Margo got up and groped her way to the door. "Well, I'm going to bed," she said.

"If you meet anybody on the landing, you'll give them a terrible shock," said Prue.

"Have a good time," said Aunt Fan. "Don't stay out till all hours. I know what you young things are like."

After Margo had gone, Prue turned to Mother.

"You see, Louise dear? I didn't exaggerate," she said. "That woman is an evil influence. Margo's behaving like a mad thing."

"Well," said Mother, whose maxim in life was always defend your young regardless of how much in the wrong they are, "I think she's being a little *unwise.*"

"Unwise!" said Prue. "Cabbage leaves all over her face! Never doing anything that that Mawake doesn't tell her to! It's not healthy!"

"I shouldn't be a bit surprised if she didn't win first prize," said Aunt Fan, chuckling. "I shouldn't think there'd be other people there disguised as a cabbage."

The argument waxed back and forth for a considerable time, interlaced with Aunt Fan's reminiscences of fancy-dress balls she had been to in India. At length Prue and Aunt Fan left us and Mother and I prepared for bed.

"I sometimes think," said Mother, as she pulled the clothes up and switched off the light, "I sometimes think that I'm the only *sane* member of the family."

The following morning we decided to go shopping, since there were a great number of things unobtainable in Corfu that Mother wanted to purchase and take back with us. Prue said this would be an excellent plan, since she could drop her Bedlington puppies off with their new owner en route.

So at nine o'clock we assembled on the pavement outside Balaklava Mansions, and we must have presented a somewhat curious sight to passers-by. Aunt Fan, presumably to celebrate our arrival, had put on a pixie hat with a large feather in it. She stood on the pavement entwined like a maypole by the leashes of the eight Bedlington puppies that romped and fought and urinated round her.

"I think we'd better take a taxi," said Mother, viewing the gambolling puppies with alarm.

"Oh, no, Louise," said Prue. "Think of the expense! We can go by tube."

"With all the puppies?" asked Mother doubtfully.

"Yes, dear," said Prue. "Mummy's quite used to handling them."

Aunt Fan, now bound almost immobile by the puppies' leashes, had to be disentangled before we could walk down the road to the tube station.

"Yeast and maple syrup," said Margo. "You mustn't let me forget yeast and maple syrup, Mother; Mawake says they're excellent for acne."

"If you mention that man once again I shall get seriously angry," said Mother.

Our progress to the tube station was slow, since the puppies circumnavigated any obstacle in their path in different ways, and we had to pause continually to unwind Aunt Fan from the lampposts, pillar-boxes, and occasional passers-by.

"Little tinkers!" she would exclaim breathlessly, after each encounter. "They don't mean any harm."

When we finally arrived at the ticket office, Prue had a prolonged and acrimonious argument over the price charged for the Bedlingtons.

"But they're only eight weeks old," she kept protesting. "You don't charge for *children* under three."

Eventually, however, the tickets were purchased and we made our way to the escalators to face a continuous warm blast of air from the bowels of the earth, which the puppies appeared to find invigorating. Yapping and snarling in a tangle of leads, they forged ahead, dragging Aunt Fan, like a massive galleon, behind them. It was only when they saw the escalators that they began to have misgivings about what, hitherto, had appeared to be an exciting adventure. They did not, it appeared, like to stand on things that move and they were unanimous in their decision. Before long we were all wedged in a tight knot at the top of the escalator, struggling with the screaming, hysterical puppies.

A queue formed behind us.

"It shouldn't be allowed," said a frosty-looking man in a bowler hat. "Dogs shouldn't be allowed on the tube."

"I have paid for them," panted Prue. "They have as much right to travel by tube as you have."

"Bloody 'ell," observed another man. "I'm in an 'urry. Can't you let me get by?"

"Little tinkers!" observed Aunt Fan, laughing. "They're so high-spirited at this age."

"Perhaps if we all picked up a puppy each?" suggested Mother, getting increasingly alarmed by the muttering of the mob.

At that moment Aunt Fan stepped backwards onto the first step of the escalator and slipped and fell in a waterfall of tweeds, dragging the shrieking puppies after her.

"Thank God for that," said the man in the bowler hat. "Perhaps now we can get on."

Prue stood at the top of the escalator and peered down. Aunt Fan had now reached the halfway mark and was finding it impossible to rise, owing to the weight of puppies.

"Mummy, Mummy, are you all right?" screamed Prue.

"I'm sure she is, dear," said Mother soothingly.

"Little tinkers!" said Aunt Fan faintly as she was carried down the escalator.

"Now that your dogs have gone, Madam," said the man in the bowler hat, "would it be possible for us, too, to use the amenities of this station?"

Prue turned, bristling to do battle, but Margo and Mother grabbed her and they slid downwards on the staircase towards the heaving heap of tweed and Bedlingtons that was Great-aunt Fan.

We picked her up and dusted her down and disentangled the puppies. Then we made our way along to the platform. The puppies now would have made a suitable subject for an RSPCA poster. Never, at the best of times, a prepossessing breed, Bedlingtons can, in moments of crisis, look more ill-used than any other dog I know. They stood uttering quavering, high-pitched yelps like miniature seagulls, shivering violently, periodically squatting down bow-legged to decorate the platform with the results of their fear.

"Poor little things," said a fat woman commiseratingly, as she passed. "It's a shame the way some people treat animals."

"Oh! Did you hear her?" said Prue belligerently. "I've a good mind to follow her and give her a piece of my mind."

Mercifully, at that moment the train arrived with a roar and a blast of hot air, and distracted everybody's attention. The effect on the puppies was immediate. One minute they had been standing there shivering and wailing like a group of half-starved grey lambs and the next minute they had taken off down the platform like a team of virile huskies, dragging Aunt Fan in their wake.

"Mummy, Mummy, come back," screamed Prue as we started off in pursuit.

She had forgotten Aunt Fan's method of leading the dogs, which she had explained to me at great length. Never pull on the lead, because it might hurt their necks. Carrying out this novel method of dog-training, Aunt Fan galloped down the platform with the Bedlingtons streaming before her. We finally caught her and restrained the puppies just as the doors closed with a self-satisfied hiss and the train rumbled out of the station. So we had to wait in a pool of Bedlingtons for the next train to arrive. Once we finally got them in the train the puppies' spirits suddenly revived. They fought each other with enjoyment, snarling and screeching. They wound their leads round people's legs, and one of them, in a fit of exuberance, leaped up and tore a copy of *The Times* from the grasp of a man who looked as though he were the manager of the Bank of England.

We all had headaches by the time we arrived at our destination, with the exception of Aunt Fan, who was enchanted by the virility of the puppies. Acting on Mother's advice, we waited until there was a pause in the flow of human traffic before we attempted the escalator. To our surprise, we got the puppies to the top with little or no trouble. They were obviously becoming seasoned travellers.

"Thank goodness that's over," said Mother as we reached the top.

"I'm afraid the puppies were a little bit trying," said Prue, flustered. "But then you see, they are used to the country. In town they think that everything's wrong."

"Eh?" said Aunt Fan.

"Wrong," shouted Prue. "The puppies. They think that everything's wrong."

"What a pity," said Aunt Fan, and before we could stop her she had led the puppies onto the other escalator and they disappeared once again into the bowels of the earth.

Once we had got rid of the puppies, in spite of feeling somewhat jaded by our experiences, we had quite a satisfactory morning's shopping. Mother got all the things she needed, Margo got her yeast and maple syrup, and I, while they were purchasing these quite unnecessary items, managed to procure a beautiful red cardinal, a black-spotted salamander as fat and as shiny as an eiderdown, and a stuffed crocodile.

Each satisfied in our own way with our purchases, we returned to Balaklava Mansions.

At Margaret's insistence, Mother had decided that she would attend the séance that evening.

"Don't do it, Louise dear," Cousin Prue said. "It's dabbling with the unknown."

Mother justified her action with a remarkable piece of logic.

"I feel I ought to meet this Mawake person," she said to Prue. "After all, he's giving Margaret treatment."

"Well, dear," said Prue, seeing that Mother was adamant, "I think it's madness, but I shall have to come with you. I can't let you attend one of those things on your own."

I begged to be allowed to go too, for, as I pointed out to Mother, I had some little time previously borrowed a book from Theodore on the art of exposing fake mediums, so I felt that my knowledge thus acquired might come in exceedingly useful.

"I don't think we ought to take Mummy," said Prue. "I think it might have a bad effect on her."

So at six o'clock that evening, with Prue palpitating in our midst like a newly caught bird, we made our way down to Mrs Haddock's basement room. Here we found quite a collection of people. There was Mrs Glut, the manageress of the hotel; a tall, saturnine Russian with an accent so thick that he sounded as though he were speaking through a mouthful of cheese; a young and very earnest blond girl; and a vapid young man who, rumour had it, was studying to be an actor, but whom we had never seen do anything more strenuous than doze peacefully in the palm-fringed lounge. To my annoyance, Mother would not let me search the room before we started for hidden cords or fake ectoplasm. However, I did manage to tell Mrs Haddock about the book I had been reading, as I thought that if she was genuine it would be of interest to her. The look she bestowed upon me was anything but benevolent.

We sat in a circle holdings hands and got off to a rather inauspicious start, since, as the lights were switched out, Prue uttered a piercing scream and leaped out of the chair she had been sitting in. It was discovered that the handbag she had leaned against the leg of the chair had slipped and touched her leg with a leathery clutch. When we had calmed Prue and assured her that she had not been assaulted by an evil spirit, we all returned to our chairs and held hands again. The illumination was from a night-light that guttered and blinked in a saucer and sent shadows rippling down the room and made our faces look as though they were newly arisen from a very old grave.

"NowIdon'twantanytalkingandImustaskyoualltokeepyourhandsfirmlyclaspedsothatwedon'tloseanyoftheessence… Whaaaha," said Mrs Haddock. "Iknowthereareunbelievers amongstus. NeverthelessIaskyoutomakeyourmindsquietandreceptive."

"What does she mean?" whispered Prue to Mother. "I'm not an unbeliever. My trouble is I believe too much."

Having given us our instructions, Mrs Haddock then took up her position in an armchair, and with deceptive ease, went into a trance. I watched her narrowly. I was determined not to miss the ectoplasm. At first she just sat there with her eyes closed, and there was no sound except for the rustle and quiver of the agitated Prue. Then Mrs Haddock started to breathe deeply; presently she began to snore richly and vibrantly. It sounded like a sack of potatoes being emptied across a loft floor. I was not impressed. Snoring, after all, was one of the easiest things to fake. Prue's hand clutching mine was moist with perspiration and I could feel her shivers of apprehension running down her arm.

"Ahaaaaa," said Mrs Haddock suddenly, and Prue leaped in her chair and uttered a small, despairing squeak as though she had been stabbed.

"Ahaaaaaaaa," said Mrs Haddock, extracting the full dramatic possibilities from this simple utterance.

"I don't like it," whispered Prue shakily. "Louise, dear, I don't like it."

"Be quiet or you'll spoil it all," whispered Margaret. "Relax, and make your mind receptive."

"I see strangers among us," said Mrs Haddock suddenly, with such a strong Indian accent that it made me want to giggle. "Strangers who have come to join our circle. To them I say 'welcome'."

The only extraordinary thing about this, as far as I was concerned, was that Mrs Haddock was no longer stringing her words together and no longer uttering that strange inhalation of breath. She mumbled and muttered for a moment or so, incomprehensibly, and then said clearly, "This is Mawake."

"Ooo!" said Margaret, delighted. "He's come! There you are, Mother! That's Mawake!"

"I think I'm going to faint," said Prue.

I stared at Mrs Haddock in the dim, shaky light and I could not see any signs of ectoplasm or trumpets.

"Mawake says," announced Mrs Haddock, "that the white girl must have no more punctures."

"There!" said Margaret triumphantly.

"White girl must obey Mawake. Must not be influenced by disbelievers."

I heard Mother snort belligerently in the gloom.

"Mawake says that if white girl trusts him, before the coming of two moons she will be cured. Mawake says…"

But what Mawake was about to say was never vouchsafed to us, for, at that moment, a cat that had been drifting round the room, cloudlike and unobserved, jumped onto Prue's lap. Her scream was deafening. She leaped to her feet shouting, "Louise, Louise, Louise!" and blundered like a bedazzled moth round the circle of people, screaming every time she touched anything.

Somebody had the good sense to switch on the lights before Prue, in her chicken-like panic, could do any damage.

"I say, it's a bit much, what?" said the vapid young man.

"You may have done her great harm," said the girl, glaring at Prue and fanning Mrs Haddock with her handkerchief.

"I was touched by something. It touched me. Got into my lap," said Prue tearfully. "Ectoplasm."

"You spoiled everything," said Margaret angrily. "Just as Mawake was coming through."

"I think we have heard quite enough from Mawake," said Mother. "I think it's high time you stopped fooling around with this nonsense."

Mrs Haddock, who had remained snoring with dignity throughout this scene, suddenly woke up.

"Nonsense," she said fixing her protuberant blue eyes on Mother. "Youdaretocallitnonsense?... Whaaaha."

It was one of the very few occasions when I had seen Mother really annoyed. She drew herself up to her full height of 4 feet 3 ½ inches and bristled.

"Charlatan," she said uncharitably to Mrs Haddock. "I said it was nonsense and it is nonsense. I am not having my family mixed up in any jiggery-pokery like this. Come Margo, come Gerry, come Prue. We will leave."

So astonished were we by this display of determination on the part of our normally placid mother, that we followed her meekly out of the room, leaving the raging Mrs Haddock and her several disciples.

As soon as we reached the sanctuary of our room, Margo burst into floods of tears.

"You've spoiled it. You've spoiled it," she said, wringing her hands. "Mrs Haddock will never talk to us again."

"And a good job, too," said Mother grimly, pouring out a brandy for the twitching and still-distraught Prue.

"Did you have a nice time?" asked Aunt Fan, waking suddenly and beaming at us owlishly.

"No," said Mother shortly, "we didn't."

"I can't get the thought of that ectoplasm out of my mind," said Prue, gulping brandy. "It was like a sort of…like…well, you know, squishy."

"Just as Mawake was coming through," howled Margo. "Just as he was going to tell us something *important*."

"I think you are wise to come back early," said Aunt Fan, "because even at this time of year it gets chilly in the evening."

"I felt sure it was coming for my throat," said Prue. "I felt it going for my throat. It was like a sort of…a kind of…well a squishy sort of *hand* thing."

"And Mawake's the only one that's done me any good."

"My father used to say that at this time of the year the weather can be very treacherous," said Aunt Fan.

"Margaret, stop behaving so stupidly," said Mother crossly.

"And Louise dear, I could feel this horrible sort of squishy fingers groping up towards my throat," said Prue, ignoring Margo, busy with the embroidery of her experience.

"My father always used to carry an umbrella, winter and summer," said Aunt Fan. "People used to laugh at him, but many's the time, even on quite hot days, when he found he needed it."

"You always *spoil* everything," said Margo. "You always interfere."

"The trouble is I don't interfere enough," said Mother. "I'm telling you, you're to stop all this nonsense, stop crying, and we are going back to Corfu immediately."

"If I hadn't leaped up when I did," said Prue, "it would have fastened itself in my jugular."

"There's nothing more useful than a pair of galoshes, my father used to say," said Aunt Fan.

"I'm not going back to Corfu. I won't. I won't."

"You will do as you're told."

"It wound itself round my throat in such an evil way."

"He never approved of gumboots, because he said they sent the blood to the head."

I had ceased listening. My whole being was flooded with excitement. We were going back to Corfu. We were leaving the gritty, soulless absurdity of London. We were going back to the enchanted olive groves and blue sea, to the warmth and laughter of our friends, to the long, golden, gentle days.

6

THE OLIVE MERRY-GO-ROUND

By May the olive-picking had been in progress for some time.
The fruit had plumped and ripened throughout the hot summer
days and now it fell and lay shining in the grass like a harvest of
black pearls. The peasant women appeared in droves carrying
tins and baskets on their heads. They would then crouch in
circles round the base of the olive tree, chattering as shrilly as
sparrows as they picked up the fruit and placed it in the
containers. Some of the olive trees had been producing crops
like this for five hundred years, and for five hundred years the
peasants had been gathering the olives in precisely the same way.

It was a great time for gossip and for laughter. I used to move
from tree to tree, joining the different groups, squatting on my
haunches, helping them pick up the glossy olives, hearing gossip
about all the relatives and friends of the olive-pickers and
occasionally joining them as they ate under the trees, wolfing
down the sour black bread and the little flat cakes wrapped in
vine leaves that were made out of last season's dried figs. Songs
would be sung, and it was curious that the peasants' voices, so
sour and raucous in speech, could be plaintively sweet when

raised in harmony together. At that time of year, with the yellow, waxy crocuses just starting to bubble up among the olive roots, and the banks purple with campanulas, the peasants gathered under the trees looked like a moving flower-bed and the songs would echo down the naves between the ancient olives, the sound as melancholy and as sweet as goat bells.

When the containers were piled high with the fruit, they would be hoisted up, and we would carry them down to the olive press in a long, chattering line. The olive press, a gaunt, gloomy building, was down in a valley through which ran a tiny, glittering stream. The press was presided over by Papa Demetrios, a tough old man, as twisted and bent as the olive trees themselves, with a completely bald head and an enormous moustache, snow-white except where it was stained yellow by nicotine, and reputed to be the biggest moustache in the whole of Corfu. Papa Demetrios was a gruff, bad-tempered old man, but for some reason he took a fancy to me and we got along splendidly. He even allowed me into the holy of holies itself, the olive press.

Here was a great circular trough like an ornamental fishpond and mounted in it a gigantic grindstone with a central strut of wood jutting from it. This strut was harnessed to Papa Demetrios' ancient horse, which, with a sack over its head so that it did not get giddy, would circle the trough, thus rolling the great grindstone round and round so that it could crush the olives as they were poured into it in a glinting cascade. As the olives were crushed, a sharp, sour smell rose in the air. The only sounds were the solid ploddings of the horse's hooves and the rumbling of the great grindstone and the steady drip, drip of the oil trickling out of the vents of the trough, golden as distilled sunlight.

In one corner of the press was a huge black crumbling mound that was the residue from the grinding: the crushed seeds, pulp, and skin of the olives forming black crusty cakes, like coarse peat. It had a rich, sweet-sour smell that almost convinced you it was good to eat. It was in fact fed to the cattle and horses with their winter food and it was also used as a remarkably efficient, if somewhat overpungent, fuel.

Papa Demetrios, because of his bad temper, was left severely alone by the peasants, who would deliver their olives and depart from the press with all speed. For you were never certain whether anybody like Papa Demetrios might not have the evil eye. In consequence, the old man was lonely and so he welcomed my intrusion into his domain. From me he would get all the local gossip: who had given birth and whether it was a boy or a girl; who was courting whom; and sometimes a more juicy item such as that Pepe Condos had been arrested for smuggling tobacco. In return for my acting as a sort of newspaper for him, Papa Demetrios would catch specimens for me. Sometimes it would be a pale-pink gulping gecko, or a praying mantis, or the caterpillar of an oleander hawkmoth, striped like a Persian carpet, pink and silver and green. It was Papa Demetrios who got me one of the most charming pets that I had at that time, a spade-footed toad, which I christened Augustus Tickletummy.

I had been down in the olive groves helping the peasants and I started to feel hungry. I knew that Papa Demetrios always kept a good supply of food at the olive press, so I went down to visit him. It was a sparkling day with a rumbustious, laughing wind that thrummed through the olive grove like a harp. There was a nip in the air, so I ran all the way with the dogs leaping and barking about me, and I arrived flushed and panting to find Papa Demetrios crouched over a fire that he had constructed out of slabs of olive "cake".

"Ah!" he said, glaring at me fiercely. "So you've come, have you? Where have you been? I haven't seen you for two days. I suppose now spring is here you've got no time for an old man like me."

I explained that I had been busy with a variety of things, such as making a new cage for my magpies, since they had just raided Larry's room and stood in peril of their lives if they were not incarcerated.

"Hum," said Papa Demetrios. "Ah, well. Do you want some corn?"

I said, as nonchalantly as I could, that there was nothing I would like better than corn.

He got up and strutted bow-legged to the olive press and reappeared carrying a large frying pan, a sheet of tin, a bottle of oil, and five golden-brown cobs of dried maize, like bars of bullion. He put the frying pan on the fire and scattered a small quantity of oil into it, then waited until the heat of the fire made the oil purr and twinkle and smoke gently in the bottom of the pan. Then he seized a cob of maize and twisted it rapidly between his arthritic hands so that the golden beads of corn pattered into the pan with a sound like rain on a roof. He put the flat sheet of tin over the top, gave a little grunt, and sat back, lighting a cigarette.

"Have you heard about Andreas Papoyakis?" he asked, running his fingers through his luxurious moustache.

No, I said I had not heard.

"Ah," he said with relish. "He's in hospital, that foolish one."

I said I was sorry to hear it because I liked Andreas. He was a gay, kind-hearted, exuberant boy who inevitably managed to do the wrong things. They said of him in the village that he would ride a donkey backwards if he could. What, I inquired, was his affliction?

"Dynamite," said Papa Demetrios, waiting to see my reaction.

I gave a slow whistle of horror and nodded my head slowly. Papa Demetrios, now assured of my undivided attention, settled himself more comfortably.

"This was how it happened," he said. "He's a foolish boy, Andreas is, you know. His head is as empty as a winter swallows' nest. But he's a good boy, though. He's never done anybody any harm. Well, he went dynamite fishing. You know that little bay down near Benitses? Ah, well, he took his boat there because he had been told that the country policeman had gone farther down the coast for the day. Of course, foolish boy, he never thought to check and make sure that the policeman was farther down the coast."

I clicked my tongue sorrowfully. The penalty for dynamite fishing was five years in prison and a heavy fine.

"Now," said Papa Demetrios, "he got into his boat and was rowing slowly along when he saw ahead of him, in the shallow water, a big shoal of barbouni. He stopped rowing and lit the fuse on his stick of dynamite."

Papa Demetrios paused dramatically, peered at the corn to see how it was doing, and lit another cigarette.

"That would have been all right," he went on, "but just as he was about to throw the dynamite, the fish swam away, and what do you think that idiot of a boy did? Still holding the dynamite he rowed after them. Bang!"

I said I thought that there could not be very much left of Andreas.

"Oh, yes," said Papa Demetrios scornfully. "He can't even dynamite properly. It was such a tiny stick all it did was blow off his right hand. But even so, he owes his life to the policeman, who *hadn't* gone farther down the coast. Andreas managed to row to the shore and there he fainted from loss of blood and he would undoubtedly have died if the policeman, having heard the bang, had not come down to the shore to see who was dynamiting. Luckily the bus was just passing and the policeman stopped it and they got Andreas into it and into the hospital."

I said I thought it was a great pity that it should happen to anybody as nice as Andreas, but he was lucky to be alive. I presumed that when he was better he would be arrested and sent to Vido for five years.

"No, no," said Papa Demetrios. "The policeman said he thought Andreas had been punished quite enough, so he told the hospital that Andreas had caught his hand in some machinery."

The corn had now started to explode, banging on to the top of the tin like the explosions of miniature cannons. Papa Demetrios lifted the pan off the fire and took the lid off. There was each grain of corn exploded into a little yellow-and-white cumulus cloud, scrunchy and delicious. Papa Demetrios took a twist of paper from his pocket and unwrapped it. It was full of coarse grains of grey sea salt, and into this we dipped the little clouds of corn and scrunched them up with relish.

"I've got something for you," said the old man at last, wiping his moustache carefully with a large red-and-white handkerchief. "Another one of those terrible animals that you are so eager to get."

Stuffing my mouth with the remains of the popcorn and wiping my fingers on the grass, I asked him eagerly what it was.

"I'll fetch it," he said, getting to his feet. "It's a very curious thing. I've never seen one like it before."

I waited impatiently while he went into the olive press and reappeared carrying a battered tin, the neck of which he had stuffed with leaves.

"There you are," he said. "Be careful, because it smells." I pulled out the plug of leaves and peered into the tin and discovered that Papa Demetrios was quite right; it smelt as strongly of garlic as a peasant bus on market-day. In the bottom was crouched a medium-size, rather smooth-skinned, greenish-brown toad with enormous amber eyes and a mouth set in a perpetual, but rather insane, grin. As I put my hand into the tin to pick him up, he ducked his head between his forelegs, retracted his protuberant eyes into his skull in the odd way that toads have, and uttered a sharp bleating cry rather like that of a miniature sheep. I lifted him out of the tin and he struggled violently, exuding a terrible odour of garlic. I noticed that on each hind foot he had a horny black excrescence, blade-shaped, like a ploughshare. I was delighted with him, for I had spent a considerable amount of time and energy trying to track down spade-footed toads without success. Thanking Papa Demetrios profusely, I carried him home triumphantly and installed him in an aquarium in my bedroom.

I had placed earth and sand to a depth of two or three inches at the bottom of the aquarium and Augustus, having been christened and released, immediately set to work to build himself a home. With a curious movement of his hind legs, working backwards, using the blades of his feet as spades, he very rapidly dug himself a hole and disappeared from view with the exception of his protuberant eyes and grinning face.

Augustus, I soon discovered, was a remarkably intelligent beast and had many endearing traits of character which made themselves apparent as he got tamer. When I went into the room, he would scuttle out of his hole and make desperate endeavours to reach me through the glass walls of the aquarium. If I took him out and placed him on the floor, he would hop round the room after me and then, if I sat down, would climb laboriously up my leg until he reached my lap, where he would recline in a variety of undignified attitudes, basking in the heat of my body, blinking his eyes slowly, grinning up at me, and gulping. It was then that I discovered he liked to lie on his back and have his stomach gently massaged by my forefinger, and so from this unusual behaviour he derived the surname of Tickletummy. He would also, I learned, sing for his food. If I held a large, writhing earthworm over the top of the equarium, Augustus would go into paroxysms of delight, his eyes seeming to protrude more and more with excitement, and he would utter a series of little pig-like grunts and the strange bleating cry he had given when I first picked him up. When the worm was finally dropped in front of him, he would nod his head vigorously, as if in thanks, grab one end of it and proceed to stuff it into his mouth with his thumbs. Whenever we had any guests, they were treated to an Augustus Tickletummy recital and they all agreed, gravely, that he had the best voice and repertoire of any toad they had met.

It was round about this time that Larry introduced Donald and Max into our life. Max was an immensely tall Austrian with curly blond hair, a blond moustache perched like an elegant butterfly on his lip, and intensely blue and kindly eyes. Donald, on the other hand, was short and pale-faced; one of those Englishmen who give you a first impression of being not only inarticulate, but completely devoid of personality.

Larry had run into this ill-assorted couple in the town and had lavishly invited them up to have drinks. The fact that they arrived, mellowed by a variety of alcoholic stimuli, at two o'clock in the morning did not strike any of us as being particularly curious, since, by that time, we were inured, or almost inured, to Larry's acquaintances.

Mother had gone to bed early with a severe cold, and the rest of the family had also retired to their rooms. I was the only member of the household awake. The reason for this was that I was waiting for Ulysses to return to the bedroom from his nightly wanderings and devour his supper of meat and minced liver. As I lay there reading, I heard a dim, blurred sound echoing through the olive groves. I thought at first it was a party of peasants returning late from a wedding, and took no notice. Then the cacophony grew closer and closer and from the clop and jingle accompanying it I realized it was some late night revellers passing on the road below in a cab. The song they were singing did not sound particularly Greek and I wondered who they could be. I got out of bed and leaned out the window, staring down through the olive trees. At that moment the cab turned off the road and started up the long drive towards the house. I could see it quite clearly because whoever was sitting in the back had apparently lighted a small bonfire. I watched this, puzzled and intrigued, as it flickered and shook through the trees on its way up to us.

At that moment Ulysses appeared out of the night sky, like a silently drifting dandelion clock, and endeavoured to perch on my naked shoulder. I shook him off and went and fetched his plate of food, which he proceeded to peck and gobble at, uttering tiny throaty noises to himself and blinking his brilliant eyes at me.

By this time the cab had made slow but steady progress and had entered the forecourt of the house. I leaned out the window enraptured by the sight.

It was not, as I had thought, a bonfire in the back of the cab. There were two individuals sitting there, each clasping an enormous silver candelabra in which had been stuck some of the great white candles that one normally bought to put in the church of St Spiridion. They were singing loudly and untunefully, but with great panache, a song from *The Maid of the Mountains*, endeavouring, wherever possible, to harmonize.

The cab rolled to a halt at the steps that led up to the veranda.

"At seventeen…" sighed a very British baritone.

"At seventeen!" intoned the other singer in a rather heavy middle-European accent.

"He falls in love quite madly," said the baritone, waving his candelabra about wildly, "with eyes of tender blue."

"Tender blue," intoned the middle-European accent, giving a lechery to these simple words that had to be heard to be believed.

"At twenty-five," continued the baritone, "he thinks he's got it badly."

"Badly," said the middle-European accent dolefully.

"With eyes of different hue," said the baritone, making such a wild gesture with his candelabra that the candles sped out of their sockets like rockets and fell sizzling onto the grass.

My bedroom door opened and Margo, clad in yards of lace and what appeared to be butter muslin, came in.

"What on earth's that noise?" she asked in a hoarse, accusing whisper. "You know Mother's not well."

I explained that the noise was nothing whatsoever to do with me, but apparently we had company. Margo leaned out the window and peered down at the cab where the singers had just reached the next verse of their song.

"I say," she called, in muted tones, "do you mind not making quite so much noise. My mother's sick."

Immediate silence enveloped the cab and then a tall, gangling figure rose unsteadily to its feet. He held his candelabra aloft and gazed earnestly up at Margo.

"Must not dear lady," he intoned sepulchrally, "must not disturb Muzzer."

"No, by Jove," agreed the English voice from the interior of the cab.

"Who do you think they are?" Margo whispered to me in agitation.

I said that to me the thing was perfectly clear; they must be friends of Larry's.

"Are you friends of my brother's?" Margo fluted out the window.

"A noble being," said the tall figure, waving the candelabra at her. "He invited us for drinks."

"Er… Just a minute, I'll come down," said Margo.

"To look you closer would be to fulfil the ambition of a lifetime," said the tall man, bowing somewhat uncertainly.

"See you closer," corrected a quiet voice from the back of the cab.

"I'll go downstairs," said Margo to me, "and get them inside and keep them quiet. You go and wake Larry."

I pulled on a pair of shorts, picked up Ulysses un-ceremoniously (who, with half-closed eyes, was digesting his food), and went to the window and threw him out.

"Extraordinary!" said the tall man, watching Ulysses fly away over the moon-silvered olive tops. "Dis like the house of Dracula, no, Donald?"

"By Jove, yes," said Donald.

I pattered down the corridor and burst into Larry's room. It took me some time to shake him awake, for, under the firm impression that Mother had been breathing her cold germs over him, he had taken the precaution of consuming half a bottle of whisky before he went to bed. Eventually he sat up blearily and looked at me.

"What the bloody hell do *you* want?" he inquired.

I explained about the two characters in the cab and that they had said they had been invited to drinks.

"Oh, Christ!" said Larry. "Just tell them I've gone to Dubrovnik."

I explained that I could not very well do this as by now Margo would have lured them into the house and that Mother, in her fragile condition, must not be disturbed. Groaning, Larry got out of bed and put on his dressing-gown and slippers and together we went down the creaking stairs to the drawing-room. Here we found Max, lanky, flamboyant, good-natured, sprawled in a chair waving his candelabra at Margo, all the candles of which had gone out. Donald sat hunched and gloomy in another chair, looking like an undertaker's assistant.

"Your eyes, they are tender blue," said Max, waving a long finger at Margo. "Ve vas singing about blue eyes, vere ye not, Donald?"

"We were singing about blue eyes," said Donald.

"Dat's what I said," said Max benevolently.

"You said 'was'," said Donald.

Max thought about this for a brief moment.

"Anyvay," he said, "de eyes vas blue."

"Were blue," said Donald.

"Oh, there you are," said Margo, breathlessly, as Larry and I came in. "I think these are friends of yours, Larry."

"Larry!" bellowed Max, lurching up with the ungainly grace of a giraffe. "Ve have come like you told us."

"How very nice," said Larry, forcing his sleep-crumpled features into something approaching an ingratiating smile. "Do you mind keeping your voice down, because my mother's sick?"

"Muzzers," said Max, with immense conviction, "are de most important thing in de vorld."

He turned to Donald, laid a long finger across his moustache, and said "Shush" with such violence that Roger, who had sunk into a peaceful sleep, immediately leaped to his feet and started barking wildly. Widdle and Puke joined in vociferously.

"Damned bad form that," observed Donald between the barks. "Guest should not make his host's dogs bark."

Max went down on his knees and engulfed the still barking Roger in his long arms, a manoeuvre that I viewed with some alarm, since Roger, I felt, was quite capable of misinterpreting it.

"Hush, Bow Wow," said Max, beaming into Roger's bristling and belligerent face.

To my astonishment, Roger immediately stopped barking and started to lick Max's face extravagantly.

"Would you…em…like a drink?" said Larry. "I can't ask you to stop long, of course, because unfortunately my mother's ill."

"Very civil of you," said Donald. "Very civil indeed. I must apologize for him. Foreigner, you know."

"Well, I think I'll just go back to bed," said Margo, edging tentatively towards the door.

"No, you won't," Larry barked. "Somebody's got to pour out the drinks."

"Do not," said Max, reclining on the floor with Roger in his arms and gazing at her piteously, "do not remove doze eyes from my orbit."

"Well, I'll go and get the drinks, then," said Margo breathlessly.

"And I vill help you," said Max, casting Roger from him and leaping to his feet.

Roger had been under the misguided impression that Max had intended to spend the rest of the night cuddling him in front of the dying fire, and so was not unnaturally put out when he was thrown aside like this. He started barking again.

The door of the drawing-room burst open and Leslie, stark naked except for a shotgun under his arm, made his appearance.

"What the bloody hell's going on?" he asked.

"Leslie, *do* go and put some clothes on," said Margo. "These are friends of Larry's."

"Oh, God," said Leslie dismally, "not *more*."

He turned and made his way back upstairs.

"Drinks!" said Max, rapturously scizing Margo in his arms and waltzing her round to the accompaniment of almost hysterical barks on the part of Roger.

"I do wish you would try to be more quiet," said Larry. "Max, for Christ's sake."

"Damned bad form," said Donald.

"Remember my mother," said Larry, since this reference had obviously struck a chord in Max's soul.

Immediately he ceased waltzing with the breathless Margo and came to a halt.

"Vere is your Muzzer?" he inquired. "De lady is sick…take me to her dat I may secure her."

"Succour," said Donald.

"I'm here," said Mother in a slightly nasal tone of voice from the doorway. "What is going on?"

She was clad in her nightie and wearing, for reasons of her cold, a voluminous shawl over her shoulders. She carried under one arm the drooping, panting, apathetic figure of Dodo, her Dandie Dinmont terrier.

"Why, you're just in time, Mother," said Larry. "I want you to meet Donald and Max."

With the first sign of animation that he had shown, Donald rose to his feet, marched swiftly across the room to Mother, seized her hand, and gave a slight bow over it.

"Enchanted," he said. "Terribly sorry about the disturbance. My friend, you know. Continental."

"How nice to see you," said Mother, summoning up all her resources.

At her entrance, Max had thrown his arms wide and was now gazing upon her with all the devoutness of a Crusader catching his first sight of Jerusalem.

"Muzzer!" he intoned dramatically. "You are de Muzzer!"

"How do you do," said Mother uncertainly.

"You are," Max asked, getting his facts straight, "de sick Muzzer?"

"Oh, it's just a bit of a cold," said Mother deprecatingly. "Ve have voked you," said Max, clasping his breast, his eyes brimming with tears.

"Awoken or woken," said Donald *sotto voce*.

"Come," said Max and put his long arms round Mother and ushered her to a chair near the fire, pressing her into it with the utmost delicacy. He took off his coat and spread it gently about her knees. Then he squatted by her side, took her hand and peered earnestly into her face.

"Vhat," he inquired, "does Muzzer vant?"

"An uninterrupted night's sleep," said Leslie, who had just returned, more conventionally garbed in a pair of pyjama trousers and sandals.

"Max," said Donald sternly, "stop monopolizing the conversation. Remember what we have come for."

"Of course," said Max delightedly. "Ve have vunderful news, Larry. Donald has decided to become an author."

"Had to," murmured Donald modestly. "Seeing all you chaps living in the lap of luxury. Royalties pouring in. Felt I must try my hand at it.

"That's jolly good," said Larry, with a certain lack of enthusiasm.

"I've just completed the first chapter," said Donald, "and so we came out hot-foot, as it were, so that I could read it to you."

"Oh, God," said Larry, horrified. "No, Donald, really. My critical faculties are completely dehydrated at half past two in the morning. Can't you leave it here and I'll read it tomorrow?"

"It's short," said Donald, taking no notice of Larry and producing a small sheet of paper from his pocket, "but I think you will find the style interesting."

Larry gave an exasperated sigh, and we all sat back and listened expectantly while Donald cleared his throat.

"Suddenly," he began in a deep vibrant voice, "suddenly, suddenly, suddenly, there he was and then suddenly, there she was, suddenly, suddenly, suddenly. And suddenly he looked at her, suddenly, suddenly, suddenly, and she suddenly looked at him, suddenly. She suddenly opened her arms, suddenly, suddenly, and he opened his arms, suddenly. Then suddenly they came together and, suddenly, suddenly, suddenly, he could feel the warmth of her body and suddenly, suddenly she could feel the warmth of his mouth on hers as they suddenly, suddenly, suddenly, suddenly fell on the couch together."

There was a long pause while we waited for Donald to go on. He gulped once or twice as though overcome with emotion at his own writing, folded the piece of paper carefully and put it back in his pocket.

"What do you think?" he inquired of Larry.

"Well, it's a bit short," said Larry cautiously.

"Ah, but what do you think of the style?" said Donald. "Well, it's, um, interesting," said Larry. "I think you'll find it's been done before, though."

"Couldn't have been," explained Donald. "You see, I only thought of it tonight."

"I don't think he ought to have any more to drink," said Leslie loudly.

"Hush, dear," said Mother. "What do you intend to call it, Donald?"

"I thought," said Donald owlishly, "I thought I would call it *The Suddenly Book*."

"A very trenchant title," said Larry. "I feel, however, that your main characters could be padded out a little bit, in depth, as it were, before you get them all tangled up on the sofa."

"Yes," said Donald. "You could well be right."

"Well, that *is* interesting," said Mother, sneezing violently. "And now I think we really all ought to have a cup of tea."

"I vill make de tea for you, Muzzer," said Max, leaping to his feet and starting all the dogs barking again.

"I will help you," said Donald.

"Margo, dear, you had better go with them and just make sure they find everything," said Mother.

When the three of them had left the room, Mother looked at Larry.

"And these are the people," she said coldly, "you say are not eccentric."

"Well, Donald's not eccentric," said Larry. "He's just a bit high."

"And suddenly, suddenly, suddenly, suddenly he was drunk," intoned Leslie, putting some more logs on the fire and kicking it into some semblance of a blaze.

"They are both of them very good chaps," said Larry. "Donald's already laid half of Corfu by its ears."

"What do you mean?" said Mother.

"Well, you know how the Corfiotes love to worm every hidden secret out of you," said Larry. "They're all convinced that since he appears to have private means and is so incredibly British that he must have a terribly posh background. So he has been amusing himself by telling them all different stories. He has so far, I have been assured, been the elder son of a duke, the cousin of the Bishop of London, and the illegitimate son of Lord Chesterfield. He has been educated at Eton, Harrow, Oxford, Cambridge, and, to my delight, this morning Mrs Papanopoulos assured me that he had assured her that his formal education had been undertaken at Girton."

Just at that moment Margaret came back into the drawing-room, looking slightly distraught.

"I think you had better come and do something with them, Larry," she said. "Max has just lighted the kitchen fire with a five-pound note and Donald has disappeared and keeps shouting 'Cooee' at us and we can't see where he's gone."

All of us trooped down to the gigantic stone-flagged kitchen where a kettle was starting to sing on one of the charcoal fires and Max was contemplating, woefully, the charred remains of a five-pound note which he held in one hand.

"Really, Max," said Mother, "what a silly thing to do."

Max beamed at her.

"No expense spared for Muzzer," he said, and then, pressing the remains of the flyer into her hand, "Keep it, Muzzer, as a souvenir."

"Cooee," came a doleful, echoing cry.

"That's Donald," said Max proudly.

"Where is he?" said Mother.

"I don't know," said Max. "Ven he vants to hide, he vants to hide."

Leslie strode to the back door and flung it open.

"Donald," he called, "are you there?"

"Cooee," came a quavering cry from Donald with subtle, echoing overtones.

"Christ!" said Leslie. "The silly bastard's fallen down the well."

In the garden at the back of the kitchen there was a large well some fifty feet deep with a thick, round, iron pipe running right down the shaft. From the echoing qualities of Donald's voice, we were quite sure that Leslie's guess was right. Carrying a lamp, we made our way hurriedly up to the edge of the well and peered, in a circle, down into its dark depths. Halfway down the pipe was Donald, his arms and legs entwined firmly round it. He gazed up at us.

"Cooee," he said coyly.

"Donald, don't be a bloody fool," said Larry exasperatedly. "Come up out of there. If you fall into that water you'll drown. Not that I worry about that, but you'll pollute our entire water supply."

"Shan't," said Donald.

"Donald," said Max, "ve vant you. Come. It is cold down dere. Come and have some tea with Muzzer and ve will talk more about your book."

"Do you insist?" asked Donald.

"Yes, yes, we insist," said Larry impatiently.

Slowly and laboriously Donald climbed up the pipe, while we watched him breathlessly. When he was within easy reach, Max and the entire family leaned over the well, grabbed various portions of his anatomy, and hauled him to safety. Then we escorted our guests back into the house and plied them with vast quantities of hot tea until they seemed as sober as they were likely to be without having slept.

"I think you had better go home now," said Larry firmly, "and we'll meet you in town tomorrow."

We escorted them out onto the veranda. The cab stood, with the horse drooping forlornly between the shafts. The cab driver was nowhere to be seen.

"Did they have a cab driver?" Larry asked of me.

I said that, quite honestly, I had been so captivated by the sight of their candelabras that I had not noticed.

"I vill drive," said Max, "and Donald shall sing to me."

Donald arranged himself carefully in the back of the cab with the candelabras and Max took to the driving seat. He cracked the whip in a most professional manner and the horse aroused itself from its comatose condition, gave a sigh, and then shambled off down the drive.

"Good night," shouted Max, waving his whip.

We waited until they had disappeared from sight behind the olive trees and then trooped back inside the house and with sighs of heartfelt relief, closed the front door.

"Really, Larry, you shouldn't invite people at this hour of night," said Mother.

"I didn't *invite* them at this hour of the night," said Larry, annoyed. "They just *came*. I invited them for drinks."

Just at that moment there was a thunderous knocking on the front door.

"Well, I'm off," said Mother and scuttled upstairs with considerable alacrity.

Larry opened the front door and there stood the distraught figure of the cab driver.

"Where's my carrochino?" he shouted.

"Where were you?" retorted Larry. "The kyrios have taken it."

"They have stolen my carrochino?" shouted the man.

"Of course they haven't stolen it, foolish one," said Larry, now tried beyond endurance. "Because you weren't waiting here they took it to get back into town. If you run quickly you can catch them up."

Imploring St Spiridion to help him, the man ran off through the olive trees and down towards the road.

Determined not to miss the last act in this drama, I ran to a vantage point where I got a clear view of the entrance to our drive and a stretch of moonlit roadway which led into town. The cab had just left the drive and arrived on the road at a brisk walk, Donald and Max singing happily together. At that moment the cab driver appeared through the olives, and screaming imprecations, he started to run after them.

Max, startled, looked over his shoulder.

"Volves, Donald," he shouted. "Hold tight!" He proceeded to belabour the behind of the unfortunate horse who, startled, broke into a gallop. But it was the sort of gallop that only a Corfu cab horse could achieve. It was just sufficiently fast to keep the cab owner running at full stretch some ten paces behind the cab. He was shouting and imploring and almost weeping with rage. Max, determined to save Donald, at all costs, was belabouring the horse unmercifully while Donald leant over the back of the cab and shouted "Bang!" at intervals, and thus they disappeared out of my sight along the Corfu road.

The following morning, at breakfast, all of us felt slightly jaded, and Mother was lecturing Larry severely for allowing people to turn up at two o'clock in the morning for drinks. Just at that moment, Spiro's car drove up to the front of the house and he waddled onto the veranda where we were sitting, clasping in his arms an enormous, flat brown-paper parcel.

"This is for yous, Mrs Durrells," he said.

"For me?" said Mother, adjusting her spectacles. "What on earth can it be?"

She unwrapped the brown paper cautiously and there inside, as bright as a rainbow, was the biggest box of chocolates I had ever seen in my life. Pinned to it was a little white card on which had been written in a rather shaky hand, "With apologies for last night. Donald and Max."

7

OWLS AND ARISTOCRACY

Now winter was upon us. Everything was redolent with the smoke of olive-wood fires. The shutters creaked and slapped the sides of the house as the wind caught them, and the birds and leaves were tumbled across a dark lowering sky. The brown mountains of the mainland wore tattered caps of snow and the rain filled the eroded, rocky valleys, turning them into foaming torrents that fled eagerly to the sea carrying mud and debris with them. Once they reached the sea they spread like yellow veins through the blue water, and the surface was dotted with squill bulbs, logs and twisted branches, dead beetles and butterflies, clumps of brown grass and splintered canes. Storms would be brewed in among the whitened spikes of the Albanian mountains and then tumble across to us, great black piles of cumulus, spitting a stinging rain, with sheet lightning blooming and dying like yellow ferns across the sky.

It was at the beginning of the winter that I received a letter.

Dear Gerald Durrell,
I understand from our mutual friend, Dr Stephanides, that you are a keen naturalist and possess a number of pets.

I was wondering, therefore, if you would care to have a white owl which my workmen found in an old shed they were demolishing? He has, unfortunately, a broken wing, but is otherwise in good health and feeding well.

If you would like him, I suggest you come to lunch on Friday and take him with you when you return home. Perhaps you would be kind enough to let me know. A quarter to one or one o'clock would be suitable.

Yours sincerely,

Countess Mavrodaki

This letter excited me for two reasons. Firstly, because I had always wanted a barn owl, for that was what it obviously was, and secondly, because the whole of Corfu society had been trying unavailingly for years to get to know the Countess. She was the recluse par excellence. Immensely wealthy, she lived in a gigantic, rambling, Venetian villa deep in the country and never entertained or saw anybody except the workmen on her vast estate. Her acquaintance with Theodore was due only to the fact that he was her medical adviser. The Countess was reputed to possess a large and valuable library and for this reason Larry had been most anxious to try to get himself invited to her villa, but without success.

"Dear God," he said bitterly when I showed him my invitation. "Here I've been trying for months to get that old harpy to let me see her books and she invites you to lunch – there's no justice in the world."

I said that after I had lunched with the Countess, maybe I could ask her if he could see her books.

"After she's had lunch with *you* I shouldn't think she would be willing to show me a copy of *The Times*, let alone her library," said Larry witheringly.

However, in spite of my brother's low opinion of my social graces, I was determined to put in a good word for him if I saw a suitable opportunity. It was, I felt, an important, even solemn occasion, and so I dressed with care. My shirt and shorts were carefully laundered and I had prevailed upon Mother to buy me a new pair of sandals and a new straw hat. I rode on Sally – who had a new blanket as a saddle to honour the occasion – for the Countess' estate was some distance away.

The day was dark and the ground mushy underfoot. It looked as though we would have a storm, but I hoped this would not be until after I had arrived, for the rain would spoil the crisp whiteness of my shirt. As we jogged along through the olives, the occasional woodcock zooming up from the myrtles in front of us, I became increasingly nervous. I discovered that I was ill-prepared for this occasion. To begin with, I had forgotten to bring my four-legged chicken in spirits. I had felt sure that the Countess would want to see this and in any case I felt it would provide a subject of conversation that would help us in the initial awkward stages of our meeting. Secondly, I had forgotten to consult anybody on the correct way to address a countess. "Your Majesty" would surely be too formal, I thought, especially as she was giving me an owl? Perhaps "Highness" would be better – or maybe just a simple "Mam"?

Puzzling over the intricacies of protocol, I had left Sally to her own devices and so she had promptly fallen into a donkey-doze. Of all the beasts of burden, only the donkey seems capable of falling asleep while still moving. The result was that she ambled close to the ditch at the side of the road, suddenly stumbled and lurched and I, deep in thought, fell off her back into six inches of mud and water. Sally stared down at me with an expression of accusing astonishment that she always wore when she knew she was in the wrong. I was so furious, I could have strangled her. My new sandals oozed, my shorts and shirt – so crisp, so clean, so *well-behaved-looking* a moment before – were now bespattered with mud and bits of decaying water-weed. I could have wept with rage and frustration. We were too far from home to retrace our footsteps so that I could change; there was nothing for it but to go on, damp and miserable, convinced now that it did not matter how I addressed the Countess. She would, I felt sure, take one look at my gypsy-like condition and order me home. Not only would I lose my owl, but any chance I had of getting Larry in to see her library. I was a fool, I thought bitterly. I should have walked instead of trusting myself to this hopeless creature, who was now trotting along at a brisk pace, her ears pricked like furry arum lilies.

Presently we came to the Countess' villa, lying deep in the olive groves, approached by a drive lined with tall green-and-pink-trunked eucalyptus trees. The entrance to the drive was guarded by two columns on which were perched a pair of white-winged lions who stared scornfully at Sally and me as we trotted down the drive. The house was immense, built in a hollow square. It had at one time been a lovely, rich, Venetian red, but this had now faded to a rose-pink, the plaster bulged and cracked in places by the damp, and I noticed that a number of brown tiles were missing from the roof. The eaves had slung under them more swallows' nests – now empty, like small, forgotten, brown ovens – than I had ever seen congregated in one spot before.

I tied Sally up under a convenient tree and made my way to the archway that led into the central patio. Here a rusty chain hung down and when I pulled it I heard a bell jangle faintly somewhere in the depths of the house. I waited patiently for some time and was just about to ring the bell again when the massive wooden doors were opened. There stood a man who looked to me exactly like a bandit. He was tall and powerful, with a great jutting hawk-nose, sweeping flamboyant white moustaches, and a mane of curling white hair. He was wearing a scarlet tarbush, a loose white blouse beautifully embroidered with scarlet-and-gold thread, baggy pleated black pants, and on his feet upturned *charukias* decorated with enormous red-and-white pom-poms. His brown face cracked into a grin and I saw that all his teeth were gold. It was like looking into a mint.

"*Kyrié* Durrell?" he inquired. "Welcome."

I followed him through the patio, full of magnolia trees and forlorn winter flower-beds, and into the house. He led me down a long corridor tiled in scarlet and blue, threw open a door, and ushered me into a great, gloomy room lined from ceiling to floor with bookshelves. At one end was a large fireplace in which a blaze flapped and hissed and crackled. Over the fireplace was an enormous gold-framed mirror, nearly black with age. Sitting by the fire on a long couch, almost obliterated by coloured shawls and cushions, was the Countess.

She was not a bit what I had expected. I had visualized her as being tall, gaunt, and rather forbidding, but as she rose to her feet and danced across the room to me I saw she was tiny, very fat, and as pink and dimpled as a rosebud. Her honey coloured hair was piled high on her head in a pompadour style and her eyes, under permanently arched and surprised eyebrows, were as green and shiny as unripe olives. She took my hand in both her warm little pudgy ones and clasped it to her ample breast.

"How kind, how *kind* of you to come," she exclaimed in a musical, little girl's voice, exuding an overpowering odour of Parma violets and brandy in equal quantities. "How very, very kind. May I call you Gerry? Of course I may. My friends call me Matilda…it isn't my *real* name, of course. That's Stephani Zinia…so uncouth – like a patent medicine. I *much* prefer Matilda, don't you?"

I said, cautiously, that I thought Matilda a very nice name.

"Yes, a comforting *old-fashioned* name. Names are so important, don't you think? Now he there," she said, gesturing at the man who had shown me in, "*he* calls himself Demetrios. I call him Mustapha."

She glanced at the man and then leaned forward, nearly asphyxiating me with brandy and Parma violets, and hissed suddenly, in Greek, "He's a misbegotten Turk."

The man's face grew red and his moustache bristled, making him look more like a bandit than ever. "I am not a Turk," he snarled. "You lie."

"You are a Turk and your name's Mustapha," she retorted.

"It isn't… I'm not… It isn't… I'm not," said the man, almost incoherent with rage. "You are lying."

"I'm not."

"You are."

"I'm not."

"You are."

"I'm *not*."

"You're a damned elderly liar."

"Elderly," she squeaked, her face growing red. "You dare to call me elderly…you…you *Turk* you."

"You are elderly and you're fat," said Demetrios-Mustapha coldly.

"That's too much," she screamed. "Elderly…fat…that's too much. You're sacked. Take a month's notice. No, leave this instant, you son of a misbegotten Turk."

Demetrios-Mustapha drew himself up regally.

"Very well," he said. "Do you wish me to serve the drinks and lunch before I go?"

"Of course," she said.

In silence he crossed the room and extracted a bottle of champagne from an ice bucket behind the sofa. He opened it and poured equal quantities of brandy and champagne into three large glasses. He handed us one each and lifted the third himself.

"I give you a toast," he said to me solemnly. "We will drink to the health of a fat, elderly liar."

I was in a quandary. If I drank the toast it would seem that I was concurring in his opinion of the Countess, and that would scarcely seem polite; and yet, if I did not drink the toast, he looked quite capable of doing me an injury. As I hesitated, the Countess, to my astonishment, burst into delighted giggles, her smooth fat cheeks dimpling charmingly.

"You mustn't tease our guest, Mustapha. But I must admit the toast was a good touch," she said, gulping at her drink.

Demetrios-Mustapha grinned at me, his teeth glittering and winking in the firelight.

"Drink, *kyrié*," he said. "Take no notice of us. She lives for food, drink, and fighting, and it is my job to provide all three."

"Nonsense," said the Countess, seizing my hand and leading me to the sofa, so that I felt as though I were hitched to a small, fat, pink cloud. "Nonsense, I live for a lot of things, a lot of things. Now, don't stand there drinking my drink, you drunkard. Go and see to the food."

Demetrios-Mustapha drained his glass and left the room, while the Countess seated herself on the sofa, clasping my hand in hers, and beamed at me.

"This *is* cosy," she said delightedly. "Just you and I. Tell me, do you always wear mud all over your clothes?"

I hastily and embarrassedly explained about Sally.

"So you came by *donkey*," she said, making it sound a very exotic form of transport. "How *wise* of you. I distrust motor cars myself, noisy, uncontrollable things. Unreliable.

"I remember we had one when my husband was alive, a big yellow one. But my dear, it was a brute. It would obey my husband, but it would not do a thing I told it to do. One day it deliberately backed into a large stall containing fruit and vegetables – in spite of all I was trying to do to stop it – and then went over the edge of the harbour into the sea. When I came out of hospital, I said to my husband, 'Henri,' I said – that was his name – such a nice, *bourgeois* name, don't you think? Where was I? Oh, yes. Well, 'Henri,' I said, 'that car's malevolent,'

I said. 'It's possessed of an evil spirit. You must sell it.' And so he did."

Brandy and champagne on an empty stomach combined with the fire to make me feel extremely mellow. My head whirled pleasantly and I nodded and smiled as the Countess chattered on eagerly.

"My husband was a very cultured man, very cultured indeed. He collected books, you know. Books, paintings, stamps, beer-bottle tops, anything cultural appealed to him. Just before he died, he started collecting busts of Napoleon. You would be surprised how many busts they had made of that horrible little Corsican. My husband had five hundred and eighty-two. 'Henri,' I said to him. 'Henri, this must stop. Either you give up collecting busts of Napoleon or I will leave you and go to St Helena.' I said it as a joke, though, only as a joke, and you know what he said? He said he had been thinking about going to St Helena for a holiday – with all his busts. My God, what dedication! It was not to be borne! I believe in a little bit of culture in its place, but not to become *obsessed* with it."

Demetrios-Mustapha came into the room, refilled our glasses and said, "Lunch in five minutes," and departed again.

"He was what you might call a *compulsive* collector, my dear. The times that I trembled when I saw that fanatical gleam in his eye. At a state fair once he saw a combine harvester, simply immense it was, and I could *see* the gleam in his eyes, but I put my foot down. 'Henri,' I said to him. 'Henri, we are not going to have combine harvesters all over the place. If you must collect, why not something sensible? Jewels or furs or something?' It may seem harsh, my dear, but what could I do?

If I had relaxed for an *instant* he would have had the whole house full of farm machinery."

Demetrios-Mustapha came into the room again. "Lunch is ready," he said.

Still chattering, the Countess led me by the hand out of the room, down the tiled corridor, then down some creaking wooden stairs into a huge kitchen in the cellars. The kitchen at our villa was enormous enough, but this kitchen simply dwarfed it. It was stone-flagged and at one end a positive battery of charcoal fires glowed and winked under the bubbling pots. The walls were covered with a great variety of copper pots, kettles, platters, coffee pots, huge serving dishes, and soup tureens. They all glowed with a pinky-red gleam in the firelight, glinting and winking like tiger beetles. In the centre of the floor was a twelve-foot-long dining-table of beautiful polished walnut. This was carefully set for two with snowy-white serviettes and gleaming cutlery. In the centre of the table two giant silver candelabras each held a white forest of lighted candles. The whole effect of a kitchen and a state dining-room combined was very odd. It was very hot and so redolent with delicious smells they almost suffocated the Countess' scent.

"I hope you don't mind eating in the kitchen," said the Countess, making it sound as though it were really the most degrading thing to eat food in such humble surroundings.

I said I thought eating in the kitchen was a most sensible idea, especially in winter, as it was warmer.

"Quite right," said the Countess, seating herself as Demetrios-Mustapha held her chair for her. "And, you see, if we eat upstairs I get complaints from this elderly Turk about how far he has to walk."

"It isn't the distance I complain of, it's the weight of the food," said Demetrios-Mustapha, pouring a pale green-gold wine into our glasses. "If you didn't eat so much, it wouldn't be so bad."

"Oh, stop complaining and get on with serving," said the Countess plaintively, tucking her serviette carefully under her dimpled chin.

I, filled with champagne and brandy, was now more than a little drunk and ravenously hungry. I viewed with alarm the number of eating utensils that were flanking my plate, for I was not quite sure which to use first. I remembered Mother's maxim that you started on the outside and worked in, but there were so many utensils that I was uneasy. I decided to wait and see what the Countess used and then follow suit. It was an unwise decision for I soon discovered that she used any and every knife, fork, or spoon with a fine lack of discrimination and so, before long, I became so muddled I was doing the same.

The first course that Demetrios-Mustapha set before us was a fine, clear soup, sequinned with tiny golden bubbles of fat, with fingernail-sized croutons floating like crisp little rafts on an amber sea. It was delicious, and the Countess had two helpings, scrunching up the croutons, the noise like someone walking over crisp leaves. Demetrios-Mustapha filled our glasses with more of the pale, musky wine and placed before us a platter of minute baby fish, each one fried a golden brown. Slices of yellow-green lemons in a large dish and a brimming sauce-boat of some exotic sauce unknown to me accompanied it. The

Countess piled her plate high with fish, added a lava flow of sauce, and then squeezed lemon juice lavishly over the fish, the table, and herself. She beamed at me, her face now a bright rose-pink, her forehead slightly beaded with sweat. Her prodigious appetite did not appear to impair her conversational powers one jot, for she talked incessantly.

"Don't you love these little fish? Heavenly! Of course, it's such a pity that they should die so *young*, but there we are. *So* nice to be able to eat *all* of them without worrying about the bones. *Such* a relief! Henri, my husband, you know, started to collect skeletons once. My dear, the house looked and smelt like a mortuary. 'Henri,' I said to him. 'Henri, this must stop. This is an unhealthy death-wish you have developed. You must go and see a psychiatrist.' "

Demetrios-Mustapha removed our empty plates, poured for us a red wine, dark as the heart of a dragon, and then placed before us a dish in which lay snipe, the heads twisted round so that their long beaks could skewer themselves and their empty eye sockets look at us accusingly. They were plump and brown with cooking, each having its own little square of toast. They were surrounded by thin wafers of fried potatoes like drifts of autumn leaves, pale greeny-white candles of asparagus and small peas.

"I simply cannot understand people who are vegetarians," said the Countess, banging vigorously at a snipe's skull with her fork so that she might crack it and get to the brain. "Henri once tried to be a vegetarian. Would you believe it? But I couldn't endure it. 'Henri,' I said to him, 'this must stop. We have enough food in the larder to feed an army, and I can't eat it single-handed.' Imagine, my dear, I had just ordered two dozen hares. 'Henri,' I said, 'you will have to give up this foolish fad.' "

It struck me that Henri, although obviously a bit of a trial as a husband, had nevertheless led a very frustrated existence.

Demetrios-Mustapha cleared away the debris of the snipe and poured out more wine. I was beginning to feel bloated with food and I hoped that there was not too much more to come. But there was still an army of knives and forks and spoons, unused, beside my plate, so it was with alarm I saw Demetrios-Mustapha approaching through the gloomy kitchen bearing a huge dish.

"Ah!" said the Countess, holding up her plump hands in excitement. "The main dish! What is it, Mustapha, what is it?"

"The wild boar that Makroyannis sent," said Demetrios-Mustapha.

"Oh, the boar! The *boar!*" squeaked the Countess, clasping her fat cheeks in her hands. "Oh, lovely! I had forgotten all about it. You do like wild boar, I hope?"

I said that it was one of my favourite meats, which was true, but could I have a very small helping, please?

"But of course you shall," she said, leaning over the great, brown, gravy-glistening haunch and starting to cut thick pink slabs of it. She placed three of these on a plate – obviously under the impression that this was, by anyone's standards, a small portion – and then proceeded to surround them with the accoutrements. There were piles of the lovely little golden wild mushrooms, chanterelles, with their delicate, almost winy flavour; tiny marrows stuffed with sour cream and capers; potatoes baked in their skins, neatly split and annointed with butter; carrots red as a frosty winter sun and great tree trunks of white leeks, poached in cream. I surveyed this dish of food and surreptitiously undid the top three buttons of my shorts.

"We used to get wild boar *such* a lot when Henri was alive. He used to go to Albania and shoot them, you know. But now we seldom have it. What a *treat*! Will you have some more mushrooms? No? So good for one. After this, I think we will have a pause. A pause is essential, I always think, for a good digestion," said the Countess, adding naïvely, "and it enables you to eat so much *more*."

The wild bore was fragrant and succulent, having been marinaded well with herb-scented wine and stuffed with garlic cloves, but even so I only just managed to finish it. The Countess had two helpings, both identical in size, and then leaned back, her face congested to a pale puce colour, and mopped the sweat from her brow with an inadequate lace handkerchief.

"A pause, eh?" she said thickly, smiling at me. "A pause to marshal our resources."

I felt that I had not any resources to marshal, but I did not like to say so. I nodded and smiled and undid all the rest of the buttons on my shorts,

During the pause, the Countess smoked a long thin cheroot and ate salted peanuts, chatting on interminably about her husband. The pause did me good. I felt a little less solid and somnolent with food. When the Countess eventually decided that we had rested our internal organs sufficiently, she called for the next course, and Demetrios-Mustapha produced two mercifully small omelets, crispy brown on the outside and liquid and succulent on the inside, stuffed with tiny pink shrimps.

"What have you got for a sweet?" inquired the Countess, her mouth full of omelet.

"I didn't make one," said Demetrios-Mustapha.

The Countess' eyes grew round and fixed.

"You didn't make a sweet?" she said, in tones of horror, as though he were confessing to some heinous crime.

"I didn't have time," said Demetrios-Mustapha. "You can't expect me to do all this cooking and all the housework."

"But no *sweet*," said the Countess despairingly. "You can't have a lunch without a sweet."

"Well, I bought you some meringues," said Mustapha. "You'll have to make do with those."

"Oh, lovely!" said the Countess glowing and happy again. "Just what's needed."

It was the last thing I needed. The meringues were large and white and brittle as coral and stuffed to overflowing with cream. I wished fervently that I had brought Roger with me, as he could have sat under the table and accepted half my food, since the Countess was far too occupied with her own plate and her reminiscences really to concentrate on me.

"Now," she said at last, swallowing the last mouthful of meringue and brushing the white crumbs from her chin. "Now, do you feel replete? Or would you care for a little something more? Some fruit perhaps? Not that there's very much at this time of the year."

I said no thank you very much, I had had quite sufficient. The Countess sighed and looked at me soulfully. I think nothing would have pleased her more than to ply me with another two or three courses.

"You don't eat enough," she said. "A growing boy like you should eat more. You're far too thin for your age. Does your Mother feed you properly?"

I could imagine Mother's wrath if she had heard this innuendo. I said yes, Mother was an excellent cook and we all fed like lords.

"I'm glad to hear it," said the Countess. "But you still look a little peaky to me."

I could not say so, but the reason I was beginning to look peaky was that the assault of food upon my stomach was beginning to make itself felt. I said, as politely as I could, that I thought I ought to be getting back.

"But of course, dear," said the Countess. "Dear me, a quarter past four already. How time flies!"

She sighed at the thought, then brightened perceptibly.

"However, it's nearly time for tea. Are you sure you wouldn't like to stay and have something?"

I said no, that Mother would be worried about me.

"Now, let me see," said the Countess. "What did you come for? Oh, yes, the owl. Mustapha, bring the boy his owl and bring me some coffee and some of those nice Turkish delights up in the lounge."

Mustapha appeared with a cardboard box done up with string and handed it to me.

"I wouldn't open it until you get home," he said. "That's a wild one, that."

I was overcome with the terrifying thought that if I did not hurry my departure, the Countess would ask me to partake of Turkish delight with her. So I thanked them both sincerely for my owl, and made my way to the front door.

"Well," said the Countess, "it has been enchanting having you, *absolutely enchanting.* You must come again. You must come in the spring or the summer when we have more choice of fruit and vegetables. Mustapha's got a way of cooking octopus which makes it simply melt in your mouth."

I said I would love to come again, making a mental vow that if I did, I would starve for three days in advance.

"Here," said the Countess, pressing an orange into my pocket, "take this. You might feel peckish on the way home."

As I mounted Sally and trotted off down the drive, she called, "Drive carefully."

Grim-faced, I sat there with the owl clasped to my bosom till we were outside the gates of the Countess' estate. Then the jogging I was subjected to on Sally's back was too much. I dismounted, went behind an olive tree, and was deliciously and flamboyantly sick.

When I got home I carried the owl up to my bedroom, untied the box and lifted him, struggling and beak-clicking, out onto the floor. The dogs, who had gathered round in a circle to view the new addition, backed away hurriedly. They knew what Ulysses could do when he was in a bad temper, and this owl was three times his size. He was, I thought, one of the most beautiful birds I had ever seen. The feathers on his back and wings were honeycomb golden, smudged with pale ash-grey; his breast was a spotless cream-white; and the mask of white feathers round his dark, strangely Oriental-looking eyes was as crisp and as starched-looking as any Elizabethan's ruff.

His wing was not as bad as I had feared. It was a clean break, and after half an hour's struggle, during which he managed to draw blood on several occasions, I had it splinted up to my satisfaction. The owl, which I had decided to call Lampadusa, simply because the name appealed to me, seemed to be belligerently scared of the dogs, totally unwilling to make friends with Ulysses, and viewed Augustus Tickletummy with undisguised loathing. I felt he might be happier, till he settled down, in a dark, secluded place, so I carried him up to the attic. One of the attic rooms was very tiny and lit by one small window which was so covered with cobwebs and dust that it allowed little light to penetrate the room. It was quiet and as dim as a cave, and I thought that here Lampadusa would enjoy his convalescence. I put him on the floor with a large saucer of chopped meat and locked the door carefully so that he would not be disturbed. That evening, when I went to visit him, taking him a dead mouse by way of a present, he seemed very much improved. He had eaten most of his meat and now hissed and beak-clicked at me with outspread wings and blazing eyes as he pitter-pattered about the floor. Encouraged by his obvious progress, I left him with his mouse and went to bed.

Some hours later I was awakened by the sound of voices emanating from Mother's room. Wondering, sleepily, what on earth the family could be doing at that hour, I got out of bed and stuck my head out of the bedroom door to listen.

"I tell you," Larry was saying, "it's a damned great poltergeist."

"It can't be a poltergeist, dear," said Mother. "Poltergeists throw things."

"Well, whatever it is, it's up there clanking its chains," said Larry, "and I want it exorcised. You and Margo are supposed to be the experts on the afterlife. You go up and do it."

"I'm not going up there," said Margo tremulously. "It might be anything. It might be a malignant spirit."

"It's bloody malignant all right," said Larry. "It's been keeping me awake for the last hour."

"Are you sure it isn't the wind or something, dear?" asked Mother.

"I know the difference between wind and a damned ghost playing around with balls and chains," said Larry.

"Perhaps it's burglars," said Margo, more to give herself confidence than anything else. "Perhaps it's burglars and we ought to wake Leslie."

Half-asleep and still bee-drowsy from the liquor I had consumed that day, I could not think what the family were talking about. It seemed as intriguing as any of the other crises that they seemed capable of evoking at the most unexpected hours of the day or night, so I went to Mother's door and peered into the room. Larry was marching up and down, his dressing-gown swishing imperially.

"Something's got to be done," he said. "I can't sleep with rattling chains over my head, and if I can't sleep I can't write."

"I don't see what you expect *us* to do about it, dear," said Mother. "I'm sure it must be the wind."

"Yes, you can't expect us to go up there," said Margo. "You're a man, *you* go."

"Look," said Larry, "you are the one who came back from London covered with ectoplasm and talking about the infinite. It's probably some hellish thing you've conjured up from one of your séances that's followed you here. That makes it *your* pet. You go and deal with it."

The word "pet" penetrated. Surely it could not be Lampadusa? Like all owls, barn owls have wings as soft and as silent as dandelion clocks. Surely he could not be responsible for making a noise like a ball and chain?

I went into the room and inquired what they were all talking about.

"It's only a ghost, dear," said Mother. "Larry's found a ghost."

"It's in the attic," said Margo, excitedly. "Larry thinks it followed me from England. I wonder if it's Mawake?"

"We're not going to start *that* all over again," said Mother firmly.

"I don't care *who* it is," said Larry, "which one of your disembodied friends. I want it removed."

I said I thought there was just the faintest possibility that it might be Lampadusa.

"What's that?" inquired Mother.

I explained that it was the owl the Countess had given me.

"I might have known it," said Larry. "I might have known it. Why it didn't occur to me instantly, I don't know."

"Now, now, dear," said Mother. "It's only an owl."

"Only an owl!" said Larry. "It sounds like a battalion of tanks crashing about up there. Tell him to get it out of the loft."

I said I could not understand why Lampadusa was making a noise since owls were the quietest of things... I said they drifted through the night on silent wings like flakes of ash...

"This one hasn't got silent wings," said Larry. "It sounds like a one-owl jazz band. Go and get it *out*."

Hurriedly I took a lamp and made my way up to the attic. When I opened the door I saw at once what the trouble was. Lampadusa had devoured his mouse and then discovered that there was a long shred of meat still lying in his saucer. This, during the course of the long, hot day, had solidified and become welded to the surface of the saucer. Lampadusa, feeling that this shred of meat would do well as a light snack to keep body and soul together until dawn, had endeavoured to pick it off the plate. The curve of his sharp amber beak had gone through the meat, but the meat had refused to part company with the saucer, so that there he was, effectively trapped, flapping ineffectually round the floor, banging and clattering the saucer against the wooden boards in an effort to disentangle it from his beak. So I extricated him from this predicament and carried him down to my bedroom where I shut him in his cardboard box for safe-keeping.

PART THREE

Criseda

This place is wonderfully lovely. I wish you could see it; if you came I could put you up beautifully, and feed you on Ginger-beer and claret and prawns and figs.

— EDWARD LEAR

8

HEDGEHOGS AND SEA-DOGS

When spring came, we moved to a new villa, an elegant, snow-white one shaded by a huge magnolia tree, that lay in the olive groves not far from where our very first villa had been. It was on a hillside overlooking a great flat area marked out like a gigantic chessboard by irrigation ditches, which I knew as the fields. They were in fact the old Venetian salt-pans used long ago for collecting the brine that floated into the channels from the big salt-water lake on whose shores they lay. The lake had long since silted up and the channels, now flooded by fresh water from the hills, provided a grid-work of lush fields. This was an area overflowing with wildlife, and so it was one of my happiest hunting grounds.

Spring in Corfu never seemed to be half-hearted. Almost overnight, it seemed, the winter winds had blown the skies clean of clouds, so that they shone a clear delphinium blue, and overnight the winter rains had flooded the valleys with wildflowers; the pink of pyramid orchids, yellow of crocus, tall pale spikes of the asphodels, the blue eyes of the grape hyacinths peering at you from the grass, and the wine-dipped anemones that bowed in the slightest breeze. The olive groves were alive and rustling with the newly arrived birds: the hoopoes, salmon-pink and black with surprised crests, probed their long, curved beaks at the soft earth between the clumps of emerald grass; goldfinches, chiming and wheezing, danced merrily from twig to twig, their plumage glowing gold and scarlet and black. In the irrigation ditches in the fields, the waters became green with weed, interlaced with the strings of toad spawn, like black-pearl necklaces; emerald-green frogs croaked at each other, and the water tortoises, their shells as black as ebony, crawled up the banks to dig their holes and lay their eggs. Steel-blue dragonflies, slender as threads, hatched and drifted like smoke through the undergrowth, moving in a curious stiff flight. Now was the time when the banks at night were lit by the throbbing, green-white light of a thousand glow-worms and in the daytime by the glint of wild strawberries hanging like scarlet lanterns in the shade. It was an exciting time, a time for explorations and new discoveries, a time when an overturned log might reveal almost anything from a field-vole's nest to a wriggling glitter of baby slow-worms, looking as though they were cast in burnished bronze.

I was down in the fields one day, endeavouring to catch some of the brown water snakes that inhabited the irrigation ditches, when an old woman, whom I knew slightly, called me from some six fields away. She had been digging up the ground with her short-handled, broad-bladed hoe, standing up to her ankles in the rich loam, wearing the thick, ungainly sheep's-wool stockings the peasants put on for this operation.

"I've found you something," she called. "Come quickly."

It was impossible for me to get there quickly, for each field was surrounded by an irrigation ditch on all four sides and finding the bridges across these was like finding your way through a maze.

"Quickly! Quickly!" screamed the old woman. "They are running away. Quickly!"

I ran and leaped and scuttled, almost falling into the ditches, racing across the rickety plank bridges, until, panting, I reached her side.

"There," she said, pointing. "There. Mind they don't bite you."

I saw that she had dug up a bundle of leaves from under the earth in which something white was moving. Gingerly I parted the leaves with the handle of my butterfly net and saw to my delight four fat, newly born, baby hedgehogs, pink as cyclamen, with soft, snow-white spines. They were still blind and they wriggled and nosed at each other like a litter of tiny pigs. I picked them up and put them carefully inside my shirt, thanked the old woman, and made my way homewards. I was excited about my new pets, principally because they were so young. I already had two adult hedgehogs, called Itch and Scratch because of the vast quantities of fleas they harboured, but they were not really tame. These babies I thought would grow up differently. I would be, as far as they were concerned, their mother. I visualized myself walking proudly through the olive groves, preceded by the dogs, Ulysses, and my two magpies, and trotting at my heels, four tame hedgehogs, all of which I would have taught to do tricks.

The family were arranged on the veranda under the grapevine, each occupied with his or her own affairs. Mother was knitting, counting the stitches audibly at intervals to herself and saying "damn" periodically when she went wrong. Leslie was squatting on the flagstones, carefully weighing gunpowder and little piles of silver shot as he filled shiny red cartridge cases. Larry was reading a massive tome and occasionally glancing irritably at Margaret, who was clattering away at her machine, making some diaphanous garment, and singing, off-key, the only line she knew of her favourite song of the moment.

"She wore her little jacket of blue," she warbled. "She wore her little jacket of blue, She wore her little jacket of blue, She wore her little jacket of blue."

"The only remarkable thing about your singing is your tenacity," said Larry. "Anybody else, faced with the fact that they could not carry a tune and couldn't remember the simplest lyric, would have given up, defeated, a long time ago."

He threw his cigarette butt down on the flagstones and this produced a roar of rage from Leslie.

"Watch the gunpowder," he shouted.

"Leslie dear," said Mother, "I do wish you wouldn't shout like that, you've made me lose count."

I produced my hedgehogs proudly and showed them to Mother.

"Aren't they sweet," she said, peering at them benignly through her spectacles.

"Oh, God! He hasn't got something new has he?" asked Larry. He peered at my pink progeny in their white fur coats with distaste.

"What are they?" he inquired.

I explained that they were baby hedgehogs.

"They can't be," he said. "Hedgehogs are all brown."

My family's ignorance of the world they lived in was always a source of worry to me, and I never lost an opportunity of imparting information. I explained that female hedgehogs could not, without suffering the most refined torture, give birth to babies covered with hard spines, and so they were born with these little rubbery white spikes which could be bent between the fingers as easily as a feather. Later, as they grew, the spines would darken and harden.

"How are you going to feed them, dear? They've got such tiny mouths," said Mother, "and they must still be drinking milk, surely?"

I said that I had seen, in a shop in the town, a complete do-it-yourself baby outfit for children, which consisted of several worthless items such as a celluloid doll, nappies, a potty, and so forth, but one article had caught my attention; a miniature feeding bottle with a supply of tiny red teats. This, I said, would be ideal for feeding the baby hedgehogs with, but the potty, doll, and other accoutrements could be given to some deserving peasant child. There was only one slight snag, and that was that I had had some rather heavy expenses to meet recently (such as the wire for the magpie cage) and so I had overspent on my pocket-money.

"Well, dear," said Mother doubtfully, "if it isn't too expensive I suppose I could buy it for you."

I said it was not expensive at all, when you considered that it was more like an investment, for not only would you be getting an invaluable feeding bottle which would come in useful for other animals, but you would be rearing four tame hedgehogs and getting a grateful peasant child into the bargain. What finer way, I asked, of spending money? So the outfit was purchased. A young peasant girl, whom I rather fancied, received with the most satisfactory joy the doll, potty, and other rubbish, and I went about the stern task of rearing my babies.

They lived in a large cardboard box, full of cotton wool, under my bed, and at night, in order to keep them warm, I placed their box on top of a hot-water bottle. I had wanted to have them sleeping in the bed with me, but Mother pointed out that this was not only unhygienic, but that I risked rolling on them in the night and killing them. I found they thrived best on watered cow's milk and I fed them assiduously three times a day and once in the middle of the night. The night feed proved to be a little difficult, for in order to make sure that I woke up I had borrowed a large tin alarm clock from Spiro. This used to go off like a rattle of musketry, and unfortunately woke not only me but the entire family as well. Eventually, so vociferous were the family in their complaints, Mother suggested I give them an extra feed late at night when I went to bed, in lieu of the feed at two o'clock in the morning that woke everybody up. This I did and the hedgehogs thrived and grew. Their eyes opened and their spines turned from snow-white to grey and became firmer. They had now, as I anticipated, convinced themselves that I was their mother, and would come scrambling onto the edge of the box when I opened it, jostling and pushing for first suck at the bottle, uttering tiny wheezy squeaks and grunts. I was immensely proud of them and looked forward happily to the day when they would trot at my heels through the olive groves.

Then Mother and I were invited to spend a weekend with some friends in the extreme south of the island, and I found myself in a quandary. I longed to go, for the sandy, shallow coasts of the south were a fine place for finding heart-urchins which, in fact, looked not unlike baby hedgehogs. Heart-shaped, they were covered with soft spines which formed a tufted tail at one end and a spiky Red-Indian-like head-dress along the back. I had found only one of these, and that had been crushed by the sea and was scarcely recognizable, but I knew from Theodore that they were found in abundance two or three inches under the sand in the south of the island. However, I had my brood of hedgehogs to consider, for I could not very well take them with me, and as Mother was coming too, there was nobody I really trusted to look after them.

"I'll look after them," offered Margo. "Dear little things." I was doubtful. Did she realize, I asked, the intricacies of looking after the hedgehogs? The fact that, for example, the cotton wool in their box had to be changed three times a day? That they must have only diluted cow's milk? That the milk had to be warmed to blood heat and no more? And most important of all, that they were allowed only half a bottle of milk each at every feed? For I had very soon found out that, if you let them, they would drink themselves comatose at every meal, with the most dire results that entailed the changing of the cotton wool even more frequently.

"Don't be silly," said Margo. "Of course I can look after them. I know about babies and things. You just write down on a piece of paper what I am supposed to do, and they'll be quite all right."

I was torn. I desperately wanted to search for heart-urchins in the golden sands covered by the warm, shallow sea, and yet I doubted Margo's proclivities as a nursemaid. However, Margo grew so indignant at my doubting her that eventually, reluctantly, I gave in. I had prevailed upon Larry, who happened to be in a good mood, to type out a detailed list of do's and don't's for hedgehog-rearers and I gave Margo a practical course in bottle warming and cotton wool changing.

"They seem awfully hungry," she said as she lifted each writhing, squeaking baby out of the box and pushed the end of the teat into its groping, eager mouth.

I said that they were always like that. One should take no notice of it. They were just naturally greedy.

"Poor little things," said Margo.

I should have been warned.

I spent an exhilarating weekend. I got myself badly sunburnt, for the fragile spring sun was deceptive, but I came back, triumphant, with eight heart-urchins, four shells new to my collection, and a baby sparrow that had fallen out of its nest. At the villa, after I had suffered the barks and licks and nibbles of greeting that the dogs always bestowed upon you if you had been away for more than two hours, I asked Margo eagerly how my baby hedgehogs were.

"They're doing all right now," she said. "But really, Gerry, I do think you ill-treat your pets. You were starving those poor little things to death. They were so hungry. You've no idea."

With a sinking feeling in the pit of my stomach, I listened to my sister.

"Ravenous, poor little dears. Do you know, they've been taking two bottles each at every feed?"

Horrified, I rushed up to my bedroom and pulled the cardboard box out from under my bed. In it lay my four hedgehogs, bloated beyond belief. Their stomachs were so large that they could only paw feebly with their legs without making any progress. They had degenerated into pink sacks full of milk, frosted with spines. They all died that night and Margo wept copiously over their balloon-like corpses. But her grief did not give me any pleasure, for never would my hedgehogs trot obediently at my heels through the olive groves. As a punishment to my overindulgent sister, I dug four little graves and erected four little crosses in the garden as a permanent reminder, and for four days I did not speak to her.

My grief over the death of my hedgehogs was, however, short-lived, for at that time Donald and Max reappeared on the island, triumphantly, with a thirty-foot yacht, and Larry introduced into our midst Captain Creech.

Mother and I had spent a very pleasant afternoon in the olive groves, she collecting wild flowers and herbs and I collecting newly emerged butterflies. Tired but happy, we made our way back to the villa for tea. When we came in sight of the villa, she came to a sudden halt.

"Who's that man sitting on the veranda?" she asked.

I had been busy throwing sticks for the dogs, so I was not really concentrating. Now I saw, stretched out on the veranda, a strange figure in crumpled white ducks.

"Who is he? Can you see?" asked Mother, agitated.

At that time she was suffering under the delusion that the manager of our bank in England was liable, at any moment, to pay a flying visit to Corfu for the express purpose of discussing our overdraft, so this unknown figure on the veranda fermented her fears.

I examined the stranger carefully. He was old, almost completely bald, and what little hair he had adhering to the back of his skull was long and as white and wispy as late summer thistledown. He had an equally unkempt white beard and moustache. I assured Mother that, as far as I could see, he bore no resemblance to the bank manager.

"Oh, dear," said Mother, annoyed. "He would arrive now. I've got absolutely nothing for tea. I wonder who he is?"

As we got nearer, the stranger, who had been dozing peacefully, suddenly woke up and spotted us.

"Ahoy!" he shouted, so loudly and suddenly that Mother tripped and almost fell down. "Ahoy! You must be Mother Durrell, and the boy, of course. Larry told me all about you. Welcome aboard."

"Oh, dear," whispered Mother to me, "it's another one of Larry's."

As we got closer, I could see that our guest had a most extraordinary face, pink and as carunculated as a walnut. The cartilage of his nose had obviously received, at one time or another, so many severe blows that it twisted down his face like a snake. His jaw too had suffered the same fate and was now twisted to one side, as though hitched up to his right earlobe by an invisible thread.

"Delighted to meet you," he said, as though he owned the villa, his rheumy eyes beaming. "My, you're a better-looking wench than your son described."

Mother stiffened and dropped an anemone from the bunch of flowers she carried.

"I," she said with frigid dignity, "am Mrs Durrell, and this is my son Gerald."

"My name's Creech," said the old man. "Captain Patrick Creech." He paused and spat accurately and copiously over the veranda rail into Mother's favourite bed of zinnias. "Welcome aboard," he said again, exuding bonhomie. "Glad to know you."

Mother cleared her throat nervously. "Is my son Lawrence here?" she inquired, adopting her fruity, aristocratic voice, which she did only in moments of extreme stress.

"No, no," said Captain Creech. "I left him in town. He told me to come out here for tea. He said he would be aboard shortly."

"Well," said Mother, making the best of a bad job, "do sit down. If you will excuse me a moment I'll just go and make some scones."

"Scones, eh?" said Captain Creech, eyeing Mother with such lasciviousness that she dropped two more wild flowers. "I like scones, and I like a woman that's handy in the galley."

"Gerry," said Mother frostily, "you entertain Captain Creech while I get the tea."

She made a hurried and slightly undignified exit and I was left to cope with Captain Creech.

He had reslumped himself in his chair and was staring at me with watery eyes from under his tattered white eyebrows. His stare was so fixed that I became slightly unnerved. Conscious of my duties as host, however, I offered him a box full of cigarettes. He peered into it, as though it were a well, his jaw moving to and fro like a ventriloquist's dummy.

"Death!" he shouted so suddenly and so vigorously that I almost dropped the cigarettes. He lay back in his chair and fixed me with his blue eyes.

"Cigarettes are death, boyo," he said. He felt in the pocket of his white ducks and produced a stubby pipe as blackened and as gnarled as a piece of charcoal. He stuck it between his teeth, which made his jaw look even more lopsided than ever.

"Never forget," he said, "a man's best friend is his pipe."

He laughed uproariously at his own joke and dutifully I laughed too. He got up and spat copiously over the veranda rail and then flopped back into his chair. I searched my mind for a topic of conversation. Nothing seemed to present itself. He would surely not be interested in the fact that today I had heard the first cicada, nor that Agathi's chicken laid six eggs the size of hazelnuts. Since he was nautically inclined, I wondered whether the exciting news that Taki, who could not afford a boat, had been night-fishing (holding a light above his head with one hand and a trident in the other) and had successfully driven the trident through his own foot, imagining it was an exotic form of fish? But Captain Creech, peering at me from behind the oily fumes of his pipe, started the conversation himself.

"You're wondering about my face, aren't you boyo?" he said accusingly, and I noticed that the skin on his cheeks became pinker and more shiny, like satin, as he said it. Before I could voice a denial, he went on.

"Wind-jammers. That's what did it. Wind-jammers. Going round the Horn. Tearing wind, straight out of the arsehole of the earth. I fell, see? The canvas flapping and roaring like God's thunder. The rope slipped through my fingers like an oiled snake. Straight onto the deck. They did what they could with it…of course, we hadn't a doctor on board." He paused and felt his jaw meditatively. I sat riveted in my chair, fascinated. "By the time we got round to Chile the whole thing had set as hard as Portland," he said, still fondling his jaw. "I was sixteen years old."

I wondered whether to commiserate with him or not, but he had fallen into a reverie, his blue eyes blank. Mother came onto the veranda and paused, struck by our immobility.

"Chile," said the Captain with relish. "Chile. That was the first time I got gonorrhoea."

Mother started and then cleared her throat loudly.

"Gerry, come and help me bring out the tea," she said.

Together we brought out the teapot, milk jug and cups, and the plates with golden-yellow scones and toast Mother had prepared.

"Tucker," said Captain Creech, filling his mouth with scone. "Stops your belly rumbling."

"Are you, um, staying here long?" asked Mother, obviously hoping that he was not.

"Might retire here," said Captain Creech indistinctly, wiping scone crumbs off his moustache. "Looks a pretty little place. Might go to anchor here."

He was forced, because of his jaw, to slurp his tea noisily. I could see Mother getting increasingly alarmed.

"Don't you, um, have a ship?" she asked.

"No bloody fear," said Captain Creech, seizing another scone. "Retired, that's me. Got time now to look a little more closely at the wenches."

He eyed Mother meditatively as he spoke, masticating his scone with great vigour.

"A bed without a woman is like a ship without a hold," he observed.

Mercifully Mother was saved from having to reply to this remark by the arrival of the car containing the rest of the family and Donald and Max,

"Muzzer, we have come," announced Max, beaming at her and embracing her tenderly. "And I see we are in time for tea. Strumpets! How lovely! Donald, we have strumpets for tea!"

"Crumpets," corrected Donald.

"They're scones," said Mother.

"I remember a strumpet in Montevideo," said Captain Creech. "Marvellous bitch. Kept the whole ship entertained for two days. They don't breed them with stamina like that nowadays."

"Who is this disgusting old man?" asked Mother as soon as she had an opportunity of backing Larry into a corner away from the tea party, which was now in full swing.

"He's called Creech," said Larry.

"I know *that*," said Mother, "but what did you bring him here for?"

"He's an interesting old boy," said Larry, "and I don't think he's got a lot of money. He's come here to retire on a minute pension, I think."

"Well, he's not going to retire on us," said Mother firmly. "Don't invite him again."

"I thought you'd like him," said Larry. "He's travelled all over the world. He's even been to India. He's full of the most fascinating stories."

"As far as I am concerned he can go on travelling," said Mother. "The stories he's been telling up to now aren't what I call fascinating."

Captain Creech, once having discovered our "anchorage," as he put it, became a frequent visitor. He would arrive generally, we noticed, just in time for a meal, shouting, "Ahoy there! Can I come aboard and have a chin-wag?" As he had obviously walked two and a half miles through the olive groves to reach us, it was difficult to deny him this privilege, and so Mother, muttering evilly, would rush into the kitchen and water the soup and bisect the sausages so that Captain Creech could join us. He would regale us with tales of his life at sea and the names of the places that he had visited. Names that I knew only from maps would slide enticingly out of his disjointed mouth. Trincomalee, Darwin and Durban, Buenos Aires, Wellington and Calcutta, the Galapagos, the Seychelles and the Friendly Islands. It seemed that there was no corner of the globe that he had not penetrated. He would intersperse these stories with prolonged and exceptionally vulgar sea-shanties and limericks of such biological complexity that, fortunately, Mother could not understand them.

Then came the never-to-be-forgotten day when Captain Creech arrived, uninvited, for tea as we were entertaining the local English minister and his wife, more out of a sense of duty than of religion. To our amazement, Captain Creech behaved remarkably well. He exchanged views on sea-serpents and the height of tidal waves with the padre and explained the difference between longitude and latitude to the padre's wife. His manners were exemplary and we were quite proud of him, but towards the end of tea the padre's wife had, with extreme cunning, managed to steer the conversation on to her children. This subject was all-absorbing to her. You would have thought that not only was she the only woman in the world to have given birth, but that they had been immaculately conceived as well. Having treated us to a ten-minute monologue on the incredible perspicacity of her offspring, she paused momentarily to drink her tea.

"I'm a bit too old to have babies," said Captain Creech.

The padre's wife choked.

"But," he went on with satisfaction, "I have a lot of fun trying."

The tea party was not a success.

Shortly after this, Donald and Max turned up one day at the villa.

"Muzzer," said Max, "we are going to carry you away."

"Yacht party," said Donald. "Fabulous idea. Max's idea, of course."

"Yacht party where?" inquired Mother.

"Round ze island," said Max, throwing out his long arms in an all-embracing gesture.

"But I thought you didn't know how to sail her," said Leslie.

"No, no. We don't sail her. Larry sails her," said Max.

"Larry?" said Leslie incredulously. "But Larry doesn't know the first thing about boats."

"Oh, no," said Donald earnestly. "Oh, no. He's quite an expert. He's been taking lessons from Captain Creech. The Captain's coming along too, as crew."

"Well, that settles it then," said Mother. "I'm not coming on a yacht with that disgusting old man, apart from the danger involved if Larry's going to sail it."

They tried their best to persuade her, but Mother was adamant. The most she would concede was that the rest of the family, with Theodore, would drive across the island and rendezvous with them at a certain bay where we could picnic and, if it was warm enough, bathe.

It was a bright, clean morning when we set off and it looked as though it were going to be ideal for both sailing and picnicking; but by the time we reached the other side of the island and had unpacked the picnic things, it began to look as though we were in for a sirocco. Theodore and I made our way down through the trees to the edge of the bay. The sea had turned a cold steel-grey and the wind had stretched and starched a number of white clouds across the blue sky. Suddenly, along the rim of the sea, three waterspouts appeared, loping along the horizon like the huge undulating necks of some prehistoric monsters. Bowing and swaying, graceful as swans they danced along the horizon and disappeared.

"Aha," said Theodore, who had been watching this phenomenon interestedly, "I have never seen *three* of them together. Very curious. Did you notice how they moved together, almost as if they were…er…you know, animals in a herd?"

I said that I wished they had been closer.

"Um," said Theodore rasping his beard with his thumb. "I don't think waterspouts are things one wants to get on…er…um…intimate terms with. I remember once I visited a place in Macedonia where one had…er…you know, come ashore. It had left a trail of damage about two hundred yards wide and a quarter of a mile long, that is to say *inland*. Even quite big olive trees had been, er, you know, damaged and the smaller ones were broken up like matchwood. And of course, at the point where the waterspout finally broke up, the ground was saturated by tons of salt water and so it was…you know…completely unsuitable for agriculture."

"I say, did you see those bloody great waterspouts?" asked Leslie, joining us.

"Yes, very curious," said Theodore.

"Mother's in a panic," said Leslie. "She's convinced they're heading straight for Larry."

"I don't think there's any danger of that," said Theodore, "they look too far out to me."

By the time we had installed ourselves in the olive groves at the edge of the bay, it was obvious that we were in for one of those sudden and exceedingly sharp siroccos which blew up at that time of the year. The wind lashed the olive trees and churned up the bay to white-capped rollers.

"We might as well go home," said Leslie. "It isn't going to be much fun picnicking in this."

"We can't, dear," said Mother. "We promised to meet Larry here."

"If they've got any sense, they'll have put in somewhere else," said Leslie.

"I can't say I envy them being out in this," said Theodore, gazing at the waves pounding the rocks.

"Oh, dear, I do hope they will be all right," said Mother. "Larry really is foolish."

We waited an hour, with Mother getting increasingly panicky with each passing moment. Then Leslie, who had climbed to a neighbouring headland, came back with the news that he could see them.

"I must say I think it's surprising they got this far," said Leslie. "The boom's swinging about all over the place and they're tacking practically in circles."

Presently the yacht headed into the narrow mouth of the bay and we could see Donald and Max dodging about, pulling at ropes and canvas while Larry and Captain Creech clung to the tiller and were obviously shouting instructions. We watched their progress interestedly.

"I hope they remember that reef," said Leslie.

"What reef?" said Mother in alarm.

"There's a damn great reef just there where that white water is," said Leslie.

Spiro had been standing gazing out to sea like a brown gargoyle, his face scowling.

"I don't likes it, Master Leslies," he said in a hoarse whisper. "They don't looks as though they knows how to sails."

"Oh, dear," said Mother. "Why ever did I agree to this?" At that moment (owing to the fact, we discovered later, that Donald and Max misinterpreted their instructions and had hauled up a length of canvas instead of taking it down) several things happened simultaneously. The yacht's sails were suddenly caught by an errant gust of wind. They puffed out. The boom came over with a splintering crash that one could hear quite clearly on shore and knocked Max overboard. The yacht turned almost on her side and, propelled by the gust of wind, ran with a remarkably loud scrunching noise straight onto the reef, where she remained upright for a brief moment and then, as if despairing of the yachtsmen on board, she lay down languidly on her side. Immediately all was confusion.

Mother shouting "Oh, my God! Oh, my God!" had to sit down hurriedly on an olive root. Margaret burst into tears, waving her hands and screaming, "They'll drown! They'll drown!" Spiro, Leslie, and I made our way to the edge of the bay. There was not much we could do as there was no boat available to launch as a rescue vessel. But presently we saw the four expert sailors swimming away from the wreck of the yacht, Larry and Donald apparently propelling Captain Creech through the water. Leslie and I and Spiro stripped off our clothes hurriedly and plunged into the sea. The water was icy cold and the waves had considerably more force in them than I gave them credit for.

"Are you all right?" shouted Leslie as the flotilla of shipwrecked mariners came towards us.

"Yes," said Max. "Right as rain."

He had a four-inch gash on his forehead and the blood was running down his face and into his moustache. Larry had one eye bruised and scraped and rapidly swelling. Captain Creech's face, bobbing between Larry's and Donald's, had achieved an extraordinary mauve colour, rather like the bloom of a plum.

"Give us a hand with the Captain," said Larry. "Silly old bastard only told me as we went over that he couldn't swim."

Spiro, Leslie, and I laid hands upon Captain Creech and relieved the panting Donald and Larry of their rescue work. We must have made an arresting tableau as we staggered, gasping, through the shallows and out onto the shore. Leslie and Spiro were supporting Captain Creech, one on each side of him, as his legs seemed in imminent danger of buckling.

"Ahoy there!" he called to Mother. "Ahoy there, my wench."

"Look at Max's head!" screamed Margo. "He'll bleed to death!"

We staggered up into the shelter of the olive groves, and while Mother, Margo, and Theodore did hasty first-aid on Max's head and Larry's eye, we laid Captain Creech under an olive tree, since he seemed incapable of standing up.

"Port at last," he said with satisfaction. "Port at last. I'll make sailors of you lads yet."

It became obvious, now that we had time to concentrate, that Captain Creech was extremely drunk.

"Really, Larry, you do make me cross," said Mother. "You might all have been drowned."

"It wasn't my fault," said Larry aggrievedly. "We were doing what the Captain told us to do. Donald and Max went and pulled the wrong ropes."

"How can you take instructions from him?" said Mother. "He's drunk."

"He wasn't drunk when he started," said Larry. "He must have had a secret supply somewhere on board. He did seem to pop down to the cabin rather a lot, now I come to think about it."

"Do not trust him, gentle maiden," sang Captain Creech in a wavering baritone. "Though his heart be pure as gold, He'll leave you one fine morning, With a cargo in your hold."

"Disgusting old brute," said Mother. "Really, Larry, I'm extremely cross with you."

"A drink, me boyos," called Captain Creech hoarsely, gesturing at the dishevelled Max and Donald. "You can't sail without a drink."

At length we had dried ourselves as best we could and wrung the water out of everybody's clothes; then we made our way, shivering, up the hill to the car.

"What are we going to do about the yacht?" said Leslie, since Donald and Max, as the owners, appeared to be unperturbed by her fate.

"We'll stops at the next village," said Spiro. "I knows a fishermans there. He'll fix it."

"I think, you know," said Theodore, "if we've got any stimulant with us, it would be an idea to give some to Max. He may possibly suffer from concussion after a blow like that."

"Yes, we've got some brandy," said Mother, delving into the car.

She produced a bottle and a cup.

"Darling girl," said Captain Creech, fixing his wavering eye upon the bottle. "Just what the doctor ordered."

"You're not having any of this," said Mother firmly. "This is for Max."

We had to dispose ourselves in the car as best we could, sitting on each other's laps, trying to give as much space as possible to Max, who had now gone a very nasty leaden colour and was shivering violently in spite of the brandy. To Mother's annoyance, she found herself, willy-nilly, having to be wedged in alongside Captain Creech.

"Sit on my lap," said the Captain hospitably. "Sit on my lap and we can have a little cuddle to keep warm."

"Certainly not," said Mother primly. "I'd rather sit on Donald's lap."

As we drove back across the island to town, the Captain regaled us with his version of some sea shanties. The family argued acrimoniously.

"I do wish you'd stop him singing these songs, Larry," said Mother.

"How can I stop him? *You're* in the back. *You* stop him."

"He's *your* friend," said Mother.

"Ain't it a pity, she's only one titty to feed the baby on. The poor little bugger will never play rugger and grow up big and strong."

"Might have killed you all, filthy old brute," said Mother.

"Actually, most of it was Larry's fault," said Leslie.

"It was not," said Larry indignantly. "You weren't there, so you don't know. It's extremely difficult when someone shouts at you to luff your helm, or whatever it is, when there's a howling gale blowing."

"There was a young lady from Chichester," observed Captain Creech with relish, "who made all the saints in their niches stir."

"The one I'm sorry for is poor Max," said Margo, looking at him commiseratingly.

"I don't know why he should get the sympathy," said Larry, whose eye had now almost completely disappeared and was a rich shiny black. "He's the fool who caused it all. I had the boat under perfect control till he hauled up that sail."

"Well, I don't call you a sailor," said Margo. "If you'd been a sailor you wouldn't have told him to haul it up."

"That's just the point," snarled Larry. "I didn't tell him to haul it up. He hauled it up on his own."

"It was the good ship Venus," began the Captain, whose repertoire appeared to be inexhaustible.

"Don't argue about it, dear," said Mother. "I've got a severe headache. The sooner we get into town, the better."

We got to town eventually and dropped Donald and Max at their hotel and the still caroling Captain Creech at his and drove home, wet and cold and acrimonious.

The following morning we were sitting, all feeling slightly wilted, finishing our breakfast on the veranda. Larry's eye had now achieved sunset hues which could only have been captured by the brush of Turner. Spiro drove up honking his horn, the dogs racing in front of the car, snarling and trying to bite the wheels.

"I do wish Spiro wouldn't make quite so much noise when he arrives," said Larry.

Spiro stumped up onto the veranda and went through his normal morning routine.

"Morning, Mrs Durrells, morning Missy Margo, morning Master Larrys, morning Master Leslies, morning Master Gerrys.

How's your eyes, Master Larrys?" he said, screwing up his face into a commiserating scowl.

"At the moment I feel as if I shall probably be going round with a white stick for the rest of my days," said Larry.

"I've got a letters for yous," said Spiro to Mother. Mother put on her glasses and opened it. We waited expectantly. Her face went red.

"The impertinence! The insolence! Disgusting old *brute*! Really, I have never heard anything like it."

"What on earth's the matter?" asked Larry.

"That revolting old Creech creature," said Mother, waving the letter at him.

"It's *your* fault, *you* introduced him to the house."

"What have I done now?" asked Larry, bewildered.

"That filthy old brute has written and proposed to me," said Mother.

There was a moment's stunned silence while we took in this remarkable information.

"Proposal?" said Larry cautiously. "An indecent proposal, I presume?"

"No, no," said Mother. "He says he wants to marry me. What a fine little woman I am and a lot of sentimental twaddle like that."

The family, united for once, sat back and laughed until tears came.

"It's no laughing matter," said Mother, stamping about the veranda. "You've got to *do* something about it."

"Oh," said Larry, mopping his eyes. "Oh, this is the best thing that's happened for ages. I suppose he thinks since he took his trousers off in front of you yesterday to wring them out, he must make an honest woman of you."

"Do stop laughing," said Mother angrily. "It isn't *funny*."

"I can see it all," said Larry unctuously. "You in white muslin, Leslie and me in toppers to give you away, Margo as your bridesmaid, and Gerry as your page. It will be very affecting scene. I expect the church will be full of jaded ladies of pleasure, all waiting to forbid the bans."

Mother glared at him. "When there's a *real* crisis," she said angrily, "you children are of absolutely no use whatsoever."

"But I think you would look lovely in white," said Margo, giggling.

"Where have you decided on for your honeymoon?" asked Larry. "They say Capri is awfully nice at this time of year."

But Mother was not listening. She turned to Spiro, registering determination from top to toe.

"Spiro, you are to tell the Captain the answer is *no*, and that I never want him to set foot in this house again."

"Oh, come now, Mother," protested Larry. "What we children *want* is a father."

"And you all," said Mother, rounding on us in a fury, "are not to tell anybody about this. I will not have my name linked with that disgusting...disgusting *reprobate*."

And so that was the last we saw of Captain Creech. But what we all referred to as Mother's great romance made an auspicious start to the year.

9

THE TALKING HEAD

Summer gaped upon the island like the mouth of a great oven. Even in the shade of the olive groves it was not cool and the incessant, penetrating cries of the cicadas seemed to swell and become more insistent with each hot, blue noon. The water in the ponds and ditches shrank and the mud at the edges became jigsawed, cracked and curled by the sun. The sea lay as breathless and still as a bale of silk, the shallow waters too warm to be refreshing. You had to row the boat out into deep water, you and your reflection the only moving things, and dive over the side to get cool. It was like diving into the sky.

Now was the time for butterflies and moths. In the day, on the hillsides, which seemed sucked free of every drop of moisture by the beating sun, you would get the great languid swallowtails, flapping elegantly and erratically from bush to bush; fritillaries, glowing almost as hot and angry an orange as a live coal, skittered quickly and efficiently from flower to flower; cabbage whites; clouded yellows; and the lemon-yellow-and-orange brimstones bumbled to and fro on untidy wings. Among the grasses the skippers, like little brown furry

247

aeroplanes, would skim and purr, and on glittering slabs of gypsum the red admirals, as flamboyant as a cluster of Woolworth jewellery, would sit opening and closing their wings as though expiring from the heat. At night the lamps would become a teeming metropolis of moths, and the pink geckos on the ceiling, big-eyed and splay-footed, would gorge until they could hardly move. Oleander hawkmoths, green and silver, would zoom into the room suddenly, from nowhere, and in a frenzy of love, dive at the lamp, hitting it with such force that the glass shattered. Death's-head hawkmoths, mottled ginger and black, with the macabre skull and crossbones embroidered on the plush fur of their thoraxes, would come tumbling down the chimney to lie fluttering and twitching in the grate, squeaking like mice.

Up on the hillsides where the great beds of heather were burnt crisp and warm by the sun, the tortoises, lizards, and snakes would prowl, and praying mantises would hang among the green leaves of the myrtle, swaying slowly and evilly from side to side. The afternoon was the best time to investigate life on the hills, but it was also the hottest. The sun played a tattoo on your skull, and the baked ground was as hot as a griddle under your sandalled feet. Widdle and Puke were cowards about the sun and would never accompany me in the afternoons, but Roger, that indefatigable student of natural history, would always be with me, panting vigorously, swallowing his drooling saliva in great gulps.

Together we shared many adventures. There was the time when we watched, entranced, two hedgehogs, drunk as lords on the fallen and semi-fermented grapes they had eaten from under the vines, staggering in circles, snapping at each other belligerently, uttering high-pitched screams and hiccups. There was a time we watched a fox cub, red as an autumn leaf, discover his first tortoise among the heather. The tortoise, in the phlegmatic way they have, folded himself up in his shell, tightly closed as a portmanteau. But the fox had seen a movement and, prick-eared, it moved round him cautiously. Then, for it was still only a puppy, it dabbed quickly at the tortoise's shell with its paw and then jumped away, expecting retaliation. Then it lay down and examined the tortoise for several minutes, its head between its paws. Finally it went forward rather gingerly and after several unsuccessful attempts managed to pick the tortoise up with its jaws, and with head held high, trotted off proudly through the heather. It was on these hills that we watched the baby tortoises hatching out of their papery-shelled eggs, each one looking as wizened and as crinkled as though it were a thousand years old at the moment of birth, and it was here that I witnessed for the first time the mating dance of the snakes.

Roger and I were sitting under a large clump of myrtles that offered a small patch of shade and some concealment. We had disturbed a hawk in a cypress tree near by and were waiting patiently for him to return so that we could identify him. Suddenly, some ten feet from where we had crouched, I saw two snakes weaving their way out of a brown web of heather stalks. Roger, who for some obscure reason was frightened of snakes, uttered an uneasy little whine and put his ears back. I shushed him violently and watched to see what the snakes would do. One appeared to be following close on the heels of the other. Was he, I wondered, perhaps in pursuit of it in order to eat it? They slid out of the heather and into some clumps of sun-whitened grass and I lost sight of them. Cursing my luck, I was just about to shift my position in the hopes of seeing them again when they reappeared on a comparatively open piece of ground.

Here the one that was leading paused and the one that had been following it slid up alongside. They lay like this for a moment or so and then the pursuer started to nose tentatively at the other one's head. I decided that the first snake was a female and that her follower was her mate. He continued butting his head at her throat until eventually he had raised her head and neck slightly off the ground. She froze in that position and the male, backing away a few inches, raised his head also and they stayed like that, immobile, staring at each other for some considerable time. Then slowly the male slid forward and twined himself round the female's body and they both rose as high as they could without overbalancing, as entwined together as two convolvulus. Again they remained motionless for a time and then started to sway like two wrestlers pushing against each other in the ring, their tails curling and grasping at the grass roots around them to give themselves better purchase. Suddenly they flopped sideways, the hinder ends of their bodies met and they mated lying there in the sun, as entangled as streamers at a carnival.

At this moment Roger, who had viewed with increasing distress my interest in the snakes, got to his feet and shook himself before I could stop him, indicating that, as far as he was concerned, it would be far better if we moved on. The snakes unfortunately saw his movement. They convulsed in a tangled heap for a moment, their skins gleaming in the sun, and then the female disentangled herself and sped rapidly towards the sanctuary of the heather, dragging the male, still fastened to her, helplessly behind her. Roger looked at me, gave a small sneeze of pleasure, and wagged his stumpy tail. But I was annoyed with him and told him so in no uncertain terms. After all, as I pointed out to him, on the numerous occasions when he was latched to a bitch how would he like to be overtaken by some danger and dragged so ignominiously from the field of love?

With the summer came the bands of gypsies to the island to help harvest the crops and to steal what they could while they were there. Sloe-eyed, their dusky skins burnt almost black by the sun, their hair unkempt and their clothing in rags, you would see them moving in family groups along the white, dusty roads, riding on donkeys or on lithe little ponies, shiny as chestnuts. Their encampments were always a squalid enchantment, with a dozen pots bubbling with different ingredients over the fires, the old women squatting in the shadow of their grubby lean-tos with the heads of the younger children in their laps, carefully searching them for lice, while the older children, tattered as dandelion leaves, rolled and screamed and played in the dust. Those of the men who had a sideline would be busy with it, one twisting and tying multi-coloured balloons together, so that they screeched in protest, making strange animal shapes. Another, perhaps, who was the proud possessor of a Karaghiozi shadow show, would be refurbishing the highly coloured cut-out figures and practising some of Karaghiozi's vulgarities and innuendoes to the giggling delight of the handsome young women who stirred the cooking pots or knitted in the shade.

I had always wanted to get on intimate terms with the gypsies, but they were a shy and hostile people, barely tolerating the Greeks. So that my mop of hair, bleached almost white by the sun, and my blue eyes made me automatically suspect, and although they would allow me to visit their camps, they were never forthcoming, in the way that the peasants were in telling me about their private lives and their aspirations. But it was, nevertheless, the gypsies who were indirectly responsible for an uproar in the family. For once I was entirely innocent.

It was the tail-end of an exceptionally hot summer's afternoon. Roger and I had been having an exhausting time pursuing a large and indignant king snake along a length of dry stone wall. No sooner had we dismantled one section of it than the snake would ease himself fluidly along into the next section, and by the time we had rebuilt the section we had pulled down, it would take half an hour or so to locate him again in the jigsaw of rocks. Finally we had to concede defeat and we were now making our way home to tea, thirsty, sweating, and covered with dust. As we rounded an elbow of the road, I glanced into the olive grove that sloped down the hillside into a small valley, and saw what, at first glance, I took to be a man with an exceptionally large dog. A closer look, however, and I realized, incredulously, that it was a man with a bear. I was so astonished that I cried out involuntarily. The bear stood up on its hind legs and turned to look up at me, as did the man. They stared at me for a moment and then the man waved his hand in casual greeting and turned back to the task of spreading his belongings under the olive tree while the bear got down again on its haunches and squatted, watching him with interest. I made my way hurriedly down the hillside, filled with excitement. I had heard that there were dancing bears in Greece, but I had never actually seen one. This was an opportunity too good to be missed. As I drew near, I called a greeting to the man and he turned from his jumble of possessions and replied courteously enough. I saw that he was indeed a gypsy, with the dark, wild eyes and the blue-black hair, but he was infinitely more prosperous-looking than most of them, for his suit was in good repair and he wore shoes, a mark of distinction in those days, even among the landed peasantry of the island.

I asked whether it was safe to approach, for the bear, although wearing a leather muzzle, was untethered.

"Yes, come," called the man. "Pavlo won't hurt you, but leave your dog."

I turned to Roger and I could see that, brave though he was, he did not like the look of the bear and was staying by me only out of a sense of duty. When I told him to go home, he gave me a grateful look and trotted off up the hillside, trying to pretend that he was ignorant of the whole scene. In spite of the man's assurances that Pavlo was harmless, I approached with caution, for although it was only a youngster, the bear, when it reared on its hind legs, was a good foot or so taller than I was and possessed on each broad, furry paw a formidable and very serviceable array of glittering claws. It squatted on its haunches and peered at me out of tiny, twinkling brown eyes, panting gently. It looked like a large pile of animated, unkempt seaweed. To me it was the most desirable animal I had ever set eyes on and I walked round it, viewing its excellence from every possible vantage point.

I plied the man with eager questions. How old was it? Where did he get it? What was he doing with it?

"He dances for his living and for my living," said the man, obviously amused by my enthusiasm over the bear. "Here, I'll show you."

He picked up a stick with a small hook at the end and slid it into a ring set into the leather muzzle the bear wore.

"Come, dance with your papa."

In one swift movement the bear rose on its hind legs. The man clicked his fingers and whistled a plaintive tune, starting to shuffle his feet in time to the music and the bear followed suit. Together they shuffled in a slow, stately minuet among the electric blue thistles and the dried asphodel stalks. I could have watched them forever. When the man reached the end of his tune, the bear, as of habit, got down on all fours again and sneezed.

"Bravo!" said the man softly. "Bravo!"

I clapped enthusiastically. Never, I said earnestly, had I seen such a fine dance, nor such an accomplished performer as Pavlo. Could I, perhaps, pat him?

"You can do what you like with him," said the man, chuckling, as he unhooked his stick from the bear's muzzle. "He's a fool, this one. He wouldn't even hurt a bandit who was robbing him of his food."

To prove it he started scratching the bear's back and the bear, pointing its head up into the sky, uttered throaty, wheezy murmurings of pleasure and sank gradually down onto the ground in ecstasy, until he was spread out looking almost, I thought, like a bearskin rug.

"He likes to be tickled," said the man. "Come and tickle him."

The next half-hour was pure delight for me. I tickled the bear while he crooned with delight. I examined his great claws and his ears and his tiny bright eyes and he lay there and suffered me as though he were asleep. Then I leaned against his warm bulk and talked to his owner. A plan was forming in my mind. The bear, I decided, had got to become mine. The dogs and my other animals would soon get used to it and together we could go waltzing over the hillsides. I convinced myself that the family would be overjoyed at my acquisition of such an intelligent pet. But first I had to get the man into a suitable frame of mind for bargaining. With the peasants, bargaining was a loud, protracted, and difficult business. But this man was a gypsy and what they did not know about bargaining would fit conveniently into an acorn cup. The man seemed much less taciturn and reticent than the other gypsies I had come into contact with, and I took this as a good sign. I asked him where he had come from.

"Way beyond, way beyond," he said, covering his possessions with a shabby tarpaulin and shaking out some threadbare blankets which were obviously going to serve as his bed. "Landed at Lefkimi last night and we've been walking ever since, Pavlo, the Head, and I. You see, they wouldn't take Pavlo on the buses; they were frightened of him. So we got no sleep last night, but tonight we'll sleep here and then tomorrow we'll reach the town."

Intrigued, I asked him what he meant by "he, Pavlo, and the Head" walking up from Lefkimi?

"My Head, of course," he said. "My little talking Head." And he picked up the bear stick and slapped it on a pile of goods under the tarpaulin, grinning at me.

I had unearthed the battered remains of a bar of chocolate from the pocket of my shorts and I was busy feeding this to the bear, who received each fragment with great moans and slobberings of satisfaction. I said to the man that I did not understand what he was talking about. He squatted on his haunches in front of me and lit a cigarette, peering at me out of dark eyes, as enigmatic as a lizard's.

"I have a Head," he said, jerking his thumb towards his pile of belongings, "a living Head. It talks and answers questions. It is without doubt the most remarkable thing in the world."

I was puzzled. Did he mean, I asked, a head without a body?

"Of course without a body. Just a head," and he cupped his hands in front of him, as though holding a coconut.

"It sits on a little stick and talks to you. Nothing like it has ever been seen in the world."

But how, I inquired, if the head were a disembodied head, could it live?

"Magic," said the man solemnly. "Magic that my great-great-grandfather passed down to me."

I felt sure that he was pulling my leg, but intriguing though the discussion on talking heads was, I felt we were wandering away from my main objective, which was to acquire the immediate freehold of Pavlo, now sucking in through his muzzle, with wheezy sighs of satisfaction, my very last bit of chocolate. I studied the man carefully as he squatted, dreamy-eyed, his head enveloped in a cloud of smoke. I decided that with him the bold approach was the best. I asked him bluntly whether he would consider selling the bear and for how much.

"Sell Pavlo?" he said. "Never! He's like my own son."

Surely, I said, if he went to a good home? Somewhere where he was loved and allowed to dance, surely then he might be tempted to sell? The man looked at me, meditatively puffing on his cigarette.

"Twenty million drachmas?" he inquired, and then laughed at my look of consternation. "Men who have fields must have donkeys to work them," he said. "They don't part with them easily. Pavlo is my donkey. He dances for his living and he dances for mine, and until he is too old to dance, I will not part with him."

I was bitterly disappointed, but I could see that he was adamant. I rose from my recumbent position on the broad, warm, faintly snoring back of Pavlo and dusted myself down. Well, I said, there was nothing more I could do. I understood his wanting to keep the bear, but if he changed his mind, would he get in touch with me? He nodded gravely. And if he was performing in town, could he possibly let me know where, so that I could attend?

"Of course," he said, "but I think people will tell you where I am, for my Head is extraordinary."

I nodded and shook his hand. Pavlo got to his feet and I patted his head.

When I reached the top of the valley I looked back. They were both standing side by side. The man waved briefly and

Pavlo, swaying on his hind legs, had his muzzle in the air, questing after me with his nose. I liked to feel it was a gesture of farewell.

I walked slowly home thinking about the man and his talking head and the wonderful Pavlo. Would it be possible, I wondered, for me to get a bear cub from somewhere and rear it? Perhaps if I advertised in a newspaper in Athens it might bring results.

The family were in the drawing-room having tea and I decided to put my problem to them. As I entered the room, however, a startling change came over what had been a placid scene. Margo uttered a piercing scream, Larry dropped a cup full of tea into his lap and then leaped up and took refuge behind the table, while Leslie picked up a chair and Mother gaped at me with a look of horror on her face. I had never known my presence to provoke quite such a positive reaction on the part of the family.

"Get it out of here," roared Larry.

"Yes, get the bloody thing out," said Leslie.

"It'll kill us all!" screamed Margo.

"Get a gun," said Mother faintly. "Get a gun and save Gerry."

I couldn't, for the life of me, think what was the matter with them. They were all staring at something behind me. I turned and looked and there, standing in the doorway, sniffing hopefully towards the tea–table, was Pavlo. I went up to him and caught hold of his muzzle. He nuzzled at me affectionately. I explained to the family that it was only Pavlo.

"I am not *having* it," said Larry throatily. "I am not *having* it. Birds and dogs and hedgehogs all over the house and now a bear. What does he think this is, for Christ's sake? A bloody Roman arena?"

"Gerry, dear, do be careful," said Mother quaveringly. "It looks rather fierce."

"It will kill us all," quavered Margo with conviction.

"I can't get past it to get to my guns," said Leslie.

"You are *not* going to have it. I forbid it," said Larry. "I will not have the place turned into a bear-pit."

"Where did you get it, dear?" asked Mother.

"I don't care *where* he got it," said Larry. "He's to take it back this instant, quickly, before it rips us to pieces. The boy's got no sense of responsibility. I am not going to be turned into an early Christian martyr at my time of life."

Pavlo got up on his hind legs and uttered a long wheezing moan which I took to mean that he desired to join us in partaking of whatever delicacies there were on the tea-table. The family interpreted it differently.

"Ow!" screeched Margo, as though she had been bitten. "It's attacking."

"Gerry, *do* be careful," said Mother.

"I'll not be responsible for what I do to that boy," said Larry.

"If you survive," said Leslie. "Do shut up, Margo, you're only making matters worse. You'll provoke the bloody thing."

"I can scream if I want to," said Margaret indignantly. So raucous in their fear were the family that they had not given me a chance to explain. Now I attempted to. I said that, first of all, Pavlo was not mine, and secondly, he was as tame as a dog and would not hurt a fly.

"Two statements I refuse to believe," said Larry. "You pinched it from some flaming circus. Not only are we to be disembowelled, but arrested for harbouring stolen goods as well."

"Now, now, dear," said Mother, "let Gerry explain."

"Explain?" said Larry. "Explain? How do you explain a bloody great bear in the drawing-room?"

I said that the bear belonged to a gypsy who had a talking head.

"What do you mean, a talking head?" asked Margo.

I said that it was a disembodied head that talked.

"The boy's mad," said Larry with conviction. "The sooner we have him certified the better."

The family had now all backed away to the farthest corner of the room in a trembling group. I said, indignantly, that my story was perfectly true and that, to prove it, I'd make Pavlo dance. I seized a piece of cake from the table, hooked my finger into the ring on his muzzle, and uttered the same commands as his master had done. His eyes fixed greedily on the cake, Pavlo roared up and danced with me.

"Oo, look!" said Margo. "Look! It's dancing!"

"I don't care if it's behaving like a whole *corps de ballet*," said Larry. "I want the damn thing out of here."

I shovelled the cake in through Pavlo's muzzle and he sucked it down greedily.

"He really is rather sweet," said Mother, adjusting her spectacles and staring at him with interest. "I remember my brother had a bear in India once. She was a very nice pet."

"No!" said Larry and Leslie simultaneously. "He's not having it."

I said I could not have it anyway, because the man did not want to sell it.

"A jolly good thing, too," said Larry.

"Why don't you now return it to him, if you have quite finished doing a cabaret act all over the tea-table?"

Getting another slice of cake as a bribe, I hooked my finger once more in the ring on Pavlo's muzzle and led him out of the house. Halfway back to the olive grove, I met the distraught owner.

"There he is! There he is! The wicked one. I couldn't think where he had got to. He never leaves my side normally, that's why I don't keep him tied up. He must have taken a great fancy to you."

Honesty made me admit that I thought the only reason Pavlo had followed me was because he viewed me in the light of a purveyor of chocolates.

"Phew!" said the man. "It is a relief to me. I thought he might have gone down to the village and that would have got me into trouble with the police."

Reluctantly, I handed Pavlo over to his owner and watched them make their way back to their camp under the trees. And then, in some trepidation, I went back to face the family. Although it had not been my fault that Pavlo had followed me, I'm afraid that my activities in the past stood against me, and the family took a lot of convincing that, on this occasion, the guilt was not mine.

The following morning, my head still filled with thoughts of Pavlo, I dutifully went into town – as I did every morning – to the house of my tutor, Richard Kralefsky. Kralefsky was a little gnome of a man with a slightly humped back and great, earnest, amber eyes, who suffered from real tortures in his unsuccessful attempts to educate me. He had two most endearing qualities: one was a deep love for natural history (the whole attic of his house was devoted to an enormous variety of canaries and other birds); the other was the fact that, for at least a part of the time, he lived in a dreamworld where he was always the hero. These adventures he would relate to me. He was inevitably accompanied in them by a heroine who was never named, but known simply as "a lady".

The first half of the morning was devoted to mathematics, and with my head full of thoughts of Pavlo, I proved to be even duller than usual, to the consternation of Kralefsky, who had hitherto been under the impression that he had plumbed the depths of my ignorance.

"My dear boy, you simply aren't concentrating this morning," he said earnestly. "You don't seem able to grasp the simplest fact. Perhaps you are a trifle overtired? We'll have a short rest from it, shall we?"

Kralefsky enjoyed these short rests as much as I did. He would potter about in the kitchen and bring back two cups of coffee and some biscuits, and we would sit companionably while he told me highly coloured stories of his imaginary adventures. But this particular morning he did not get a chance. As soon as we were sitting comfortably, sipping our coffee, I told him all about Pavlo and the man with the talking head and the bear.

"Quite extraordinary!" he said. "Not the sort of thing one expects to find in an olive grove. It must have surprised you, I'll be bound."

Then his eyes glazed and he fell into a reverie, staring at the ceiling, tipping his cup of coffee so that it slopped into the saucer. It was obvious that my interest in the bear had set off a train of thought in his mind. It had been several days since I had had an instalment of his memoirs, and so I waited eagerly to see what the result would be.

"When I was a *young* man," began Kralefsky, glancing at me earnestly to see whether I was listening, "when I was a young man, I'm afraid I was a bit of a harum-scarum. Always getting into trouble, you know."

He chuckled reminiscently and brushed a few biscuit crumbs from his waistcoat. With his delicately manicured hands and his large, gentle eyes it was difficult to imagine him as a harum-scarum, but I tried dutifully.

"I thought at one time I would even join a *circus*," he said, with the air of one confessing to infanticide. "I remember a large circus came to the village where we were living and I attended every performance. Every single performance. I got to know the circus folk quite well, and they even taught me some of their tricks. They said I was *excellent* on the trapeze." He glanced at me, shyly, to see how I would take this. I nodded seriously, as though there were nothing ludicrous in the thought of Kralefsky, in a pair of spangled tights, on a trapeze.

"Have another biscuit?" he inquired. "Yes? That's the ticket! I think I'll have one, too."

Munching my biscuit I waited patiently for him to resume.

"Well," he continued, "the week simply flew past and the evening came for the final performance. I wouldn't have missed it for the world. I was accompanied by a lady, a young friend of mine, who was desirous of seeing the performance. How she laughed at the clowns! *And* admired the horses. She little knew of the horror that was soon to strike."

He took out his delicately scented handkerchief and patted his moist brow with it. He always tended to get a trifle over-excited as he reached the climax of a story.

"The final act," he said, "was the lion-tamer." He paused so that the full portent of this statement could sink in. "Five beasts he had. Huge Nubian lions with black manes, fresh from the jungle, so he told me. The lady and I were sitting in the front row where we could obtain the best possible view of the ring. You know the sort of cage affair that they put up in the ring for the lion act? Well, in the middle of the act, one of the sections, which had not been securely bolted, fell inwards. To our horror, we saw it fall on the lion-tamer, knocking him unconscious instantly." He paused, took a nervous sip of coffee and then wiped his brow once more.

"What was to be done?" he inquired rhetorically. "There were five huge, snarling lions and I had a lady by my side. My thoughts worked fast. If the lady was to be saved, there was only one thing I could think of. Seizing my walking-stick, I leaped into the ring and marched into the cage."

I made just audible sounds, indicative of admiration.

"During the week when I had been visiting the circus, I had studied the lion-tamer's method with great care, and now I thanked my lucky stars for it. The snarling beasts on their pedestals towered over me, but I looked them straight in the eye. The human eye, you know, has great power over the animal world. Slowly, fixing them with a piercing gaze and pointing my walking-stick at them, I got them under control and drove them inch by inch out of the ring and back into their cage. A dreadful tragedy had been averted."

I said that the lady must have been grateful to him.

"She was indeed. She was indeed," said Kralefsky, pleased. "She even went so far as to say that I gave a better performance than the lion-tamer himself."

Had he, I wondered, during his circus days, ever had anything to do with dancing bears?

"All sorts of animals," said Kralefsky lavishly. "Elephants, seals, performing dogs, bears. They were all there."

In that case, I said tentatively, would he not like to come and see the dancing bear. It was only just down the road, and although it was not exactly a circus, I felt it might interest him.

"By Jove, that's an idea," said Kralefsky. He pulled his watch out of his waistcoat pocket and consulted it. "Ten minutes, eh? It'll help blow the cobwebs away."

He got his hat and stick and together we made our way eagerly through the narrow, crowded streets of the town, redolent with the smell of fruits and vegetables, drains, and freshly baked bread. By dint of questioning several small boys, we discovered where Pavlo's owner was holding his show. It was a large, dim barn at the back of a shop in the centre of town.

On the way there I had borrowed some money of Kralefsky and purchased a bar of sticky nougat, for I felt I could not go to see Pavlo without taking him a present.

"Ah, Pavlo's friend! Welcome," said the gypsy as we appeared in the doorway of the barn.

To my delight, Pavlo recognized me and came shuffling forward, uttering little grunts, and then reared up on his hind legs in front of me. Kralefskv backed away, rather hurriedly, I thought, for one of his circus training, and took a firmer grip on his stick.

"Do be careful, my boy," he said.

I fed the nougat to Pavlo and when finally he had squelched the last sticky lump off his back teeth and swallowed it, he gave a contented sigh and lay down with his head between his paws.

"Do you want to see the Head?" asked the gypsy. He gestured towards the back of the barn where there was a plain deal table on which was a square box, apparently made out of cloth.

"Wait," he said, "and I'll light the candles."

He had a dozen or so large candles soldered to the top of a box in their own wax, and these he now lit so they flickered and quivered and made the shadows dance. Then he went forward to the table and rapped on it with his bear stick.

"Head, are you ready?" he asked.

I waited with a delicate prickle of apprehension in my spine. Then from the interior of the cloth box a clear treble voice said, "Yes, I'm ready."

The man lifted the cloth at one side of the box and I saw that the box was formed of slender lathes on which thin cloth had been loosely tacked. The box was about three feet square. In the centre of it was a small pedestal with a flattened top and on it, looking macabre in the flickering light of the candles, was the head of a seven-year-old boy.

"By Jove!" said Kralefsky in admiration. "That is clever!" What astonished me was that the head was *alive*. It was obviously the head of a young gypsy lad, made up rather crudely with black greasepaint to look like a Negro. It stared at us and blinked its eyes.

"Are you ready to answer questions now?" asked the gypsy, looking, with obvious satisfaction, at the entranced Kralefsky.

The Head licked its lips and then said, "Yes, I am ready."

"How old are you?" asked the gypsy.

"Over a thousand years old," said the Head.

"Where do you come from?"

"I come from Africa and my name is Ngo."

The gypsy droned on with his questions and the Head answered them, but I was not interested in that. What I wanted to know was how the trick was done. When he first told me about the Head, I had expected something carved out of wood or plaster which, by ventriloquism, could be made to speak, but this was a living head perched on a little wooden pedestal, the circumference of a candle. I had no doubt that the Head was alive for its eyes wandered to and fro as it answered the questions automatically, and once, when Pavlo got up and shook himself, a look of apprehension came over its face.

"There," said the gypsy proudly when he had finished his questioning. "I told you, didn't I? It's the most remarkable thing in the world."

I asked him whether I could examine the whole thing more closely. I had suddenly remembered that Theodore had told me of a similar illusion which was created with the aid of mirrors. I did not see where it was possible to conceal the body that obviously belonged to the Head, but I felt that the table and the box needed investigation.

"Certainly," said the gypsy, somewhat to my surprise. "Here, take my stick. But all I ask is that you don't touch the Head itself."

Carefully, with the aid of the stick, I poked all round the pedestal to see if there were any concealed mirrors or wires, and the Head watched me with a slightly amused expression in its black eyes. The sides of the box were definitely only of cloth and the floor of the box was, in fact, the top of the table on which it stood. I walked round the back of it and I could see nothing. I even crawled under the table, but there was nothing there and certainly no room to conceal a body. I was completely mystified.

"Ah," said the gypsy in triumph. "You didn't expect that, did you? You thought I had a boy concealed in there, didn't you?"

I admitted the charge humbly and begged him to tell me how it was done.

"Oh, no. I can't tell you," he said. "It's magic. If I told you, the head would disappear in a puff of smoke."

I examined both the box and the table for a second time, but, even bringing a candle closer to aid my investigations, I still could not see how it was possible.

"Come," said the gypsy. "Enough of the Head. Come and dance with Pavlo."

He hooked the stick into the bear's muzzle and Pavlo rose on his hind legs. The gypsy handed the stick to me and then picked up a small wooden flute and started to play, and Pavlo and I did a solemn dance together.

"Excellent, by Jove! Excellent!" said Kralefsky, clapping his hands with enthusiasm. I suggested that he might like to dance with Pavlo too, since he had such vast circus experience.

"Well, now," said Kralefsky. "I wonder whether it would be altogether wise? The animal, you see, is not familiar with me."

"Oh, he'll be all right," said the gypsy. "He's tame with anyone."

"Well," said Kralefsky reluctantly, "if you're sure. If you insist."

He took the bear stick gingerly from me and stood facing Pavlo, looking extremely apprehensive.

"And now," said the gypsy, "you will dance."

And he started to play a lilting little tune on his pipe.

I stood enchanted by the sight. The yellow, flickering light of tile candles showed the shadows of Kralefsky's little humpbacked figure and the shaggy form of the bear on the wall as they pirouetted round and round, and squatting on its pedestal in the box, the Head watched them, grinning and chuckling to itself.

10

THE ANGRY BARRELS

At the tail-end of the summer came the grape harvest. Throughout the year you had been aware of the vineyards as part of the scenery, but it was only when the grape harvest came that you remembered the sequence of events that led up to it: the vineyards in winter, when the vines looked dead, like so many pieces of driftwood stuck in lines in the soil; and then the day in spring when you first noticed a green sheen on each vine as the delicate, frilly little leaves uncurled. And then the leaves grew larger and hung on the vines, like green hands warming themselves in the heat of the sun. After that the grapes started to appear, tiny nodules on a branched stem, which gradually grew and plumped themselves in the sunlight until they looked like the jade eggs of some strange sea-monster. Then was the time for the washing of the vines. The lime and copper sulphate in big barrels would be dragged to the vineyards in little wooden carts pulled by the ever-patient donkeys. The sprayers would appear in their uniforms that made them look like visitors from another planet: goggles and masks, a great canister strapped on their backs from which led a rubber pipe, as mobile as an elephant's trunk, through which the liquid would run. This mixture was of a blue that put the sky and the sea to shame. It was the distilled blueness of everything blue in the world. Tanks would be filled and the sprayers would move through the frilly groves of vine, covering each leaf, wrapping each bunch of green grapes in a delicate web of Madonna blue. Under this protective blue mantle, the grapes swelled and ripened until at last, in the hot dog-days of summer, they were ready to be plucked and eased of their juice.

The grape harvest was so important that it naturally became a time of visiting, a time of picnics and of celebrations, a time when you brought out last year's wine and mused over it.

We had been invited to attend a wine harvest by a Mr Stavrodakis, a tiny, kindly, wizened little man with a face like that of a half-starved tortoise, who owned a villa and some big vineyards towards the north of the island. He was a man who lived for his wine, who thought that was the most important thing in the world; and so his invitation was delivered with all the solemnity befitting such an occasion and was received with equal solemnity by the family. In his note of invitation, written in bold copperplate, embellished with little frills and flourishes so that it looked like a wrought-iron tracery, he had said, "Do please feel free to bring those of your friends that you think might enjoy this."

"Wonderful," said Larry. "He's supposed to have the best cellar in Corfu."

"Well, I suppose we can go if you want to," said Mother doubtfully.

"Of course I want to," said Larry. "Think of all that wine. I tell you what, we'll hire a benzina and make up a party."

"Oh, yes," said Margo eagerly. "He's got that marvellous beach on his estate. We must get in some more swimming before the summer ends."

"We can invite Sven," said Larry. "He should be back by then. And we'll ask Donald and Max to come along."

"And Theodore," said Leslie.

"Larry dear," said Mother, "the man's only invited us to watch his grapes being pressed or whatever it is they do; you can't take a whole assortment of people along with you."

"He says in his letter to bring any of our friends we want to," said Larry.

"Yes, but you can't take a whole circus," said Mother. "How's the poor man going to feed us all?"

"Well, that's easily solved," said Larry. "Write and tell him that we'll bring our own food."

"I suppose that means I'll have to cook it," said Mother.

"Nonsense," said Larry vaguely. "We'll just take a few chops or something and grill them over an open fire."

"I know what that means," said Mother.

"Well, surely you can organize it somehow," said Larry. "After all, it seems to me a perfectly simple thing to do."

"Well," said Mother reluctantly, "I'll have a word with Spiro in the morning and see what can be done."

The result was that Mother penned a careful note to Mr Stavrodakis saying that we would be delighted to accept his invitation and bring a few friends. We would bring our own food and picnic on the beach, if we might. Mr Stavrodakis sent back another piece of copperplate topiary expressing himself overwhelmed at our kindness in accepting his invitation and saying that he looked forward to seeing us. He added, "Do please come undressed as we are in the family way." The phrase puzzled us all considerably – since he was a bachelor of long standing – until we realized he had translated it literally from the French.

The party finally consisted of Donald and Max, Theodore, Kralefsky, Sven, who had turned up in the nick of time from Athens, Spiro, and the family. We assembled at six-thirty in the morning at the sunken steps behind the king's palace in the town, where a dumpy, freshly painted benzina waited, bobbing a greeting to us on the tiny ripples. Getting on board took us quite some time. There were the numerous hampers of food and wine, the cooking utensils, and Mother's enormous umbrella which she refused to travel without during the summer months. Then Kralefsky, bowing and beaming, had to go through the performance of handing Mother and Margo on board.

"Gently now. Don't stumble. That's the ticket!" he said as he escorted them both onto the boat with all the courtesy of a doge handing his latest mistress into a gondola.

"Fortunately," said Theodore, peering up at the blue sky penetratingly from under the brim of his Homburg, "fortunately it looks as though it's going to be er…um…you know, a fine day. I'm glad of that, for, as you know, the slightest motion upsets me."

Sven missed his footing as he was getting on board and almost dropped his precious accordion into the sea, but it was retrieved from a watery death by Max's long arm. Eventually we were all on board. The benzina was pushed out, the engine was started, and we were off. In the pale, pearly, early morning haze, the town looked like a child's town, built of toppling bricks. The façades of tall, elderly Venetian houses of the town, crumbling gently, coloured in pale shades of cream and brown and white and cyclamen pink, were blurred by the haze so they looked like a smudged pastel drawing.

"A life on the ocean wave!" said Kralefsky, inhaling the warm, still air dramatically. "That's the ticket!"

"Although the sea *looks* so calm," observed Theodore, "there is, I think, a slight – almost imperceptible – motion."

"What rubbish, Theodore," said Larry. "You could lay a spirit-level on this sea and you wouldn't get a wink out of the bubble."

"Is Muzzer comfortable?" inquired Max lovingly of Mother.

"Oh, yes, dear, thank you, quite comfortable," she said, "but I'm a little bit worried. I'm not sure whether Spiro remembered the garlic."

"Don't you worries Mrs Durrells," said Spiro, who had overheard the remark. "I gots all the things that you tells me to get."

Sven, having examined his accordion with the utmost care to make sure that it had come to no harm, now lashed it round himself and ran an experimental series of fingers up its keyboard.

"A rousing sea shanty," said Donald. "That's what we need. Yo, ho, ho, and a bottle of rum."

I left them and made my way up into the bow of the benzina where I lay, staring down over the prow as it sheared its way through the glassy blue sea. Occasionally little flocks of flying fish would break the surface ahead of us, glittering blue and moon silver in the sun, as they burst from the water and skimmed along the surface, like insect-gleaning summer swallows across a blue meadow.

At eight o'clock we reached our destination, a half-mile long beach that lay under the flanks of Pandokrator. Here the olive grove came almost to the sea, separated from it only by a wide strip of shingle. As we approached the shore, the engine was switched off and we drifted in gently under our own momentum. Now that there was no engine noise we could hear the cries of the cicadas welcoming us to land. The benzina, with an enormous sigh, pressed its bow into the pebbles of the shallows. The lithe, brown boy, whose boat it was, came forward from the engine and leaped from the bow with the anchor, which he lodged firmly in the shingle. Then he piled a collection of boxes alongside the bow of the benzina in a sort of tottering staircase down which Mother and Margo were escorted by Kralefsky, who bowed elegantly as each reached the shingle, but somewhat marred the effect by inadvertently stepping backwards into six inches of seawater and irretrievably ruining the crease of his elegant trousering. Eventually we and all our goods and chattels were ashore, and leaving our possessions under the olive trees, strewn haphazardly like something from a wrecked ship that had been disgorged by the sea, we made our way up the hill to Stavrodakis' villa.

The villa was large and square, faded red with green shutters and built up high so that the lower floor formed a spacious cellar. Streams of peasant girls were walking up the drive carrying baskets of grapes on their heads, moving with the lithe gracefulness of cats. Stavrodakis came scuttling among them to greet us.

"So kind, so kind! Really so kind!" he kept repeating as each introduction was made.

He seated us all on his veranda under a great carnival-red wig of bougainvillea and opened several bottles of his best wine. It was heavy and sharp and glowed a sullen red as though he were pouring garnets into our glasses. When we were fortified and slightly light-headed with this brew, he led us, skittering ahead like an amiable black beetle, down to his cellars.

The cellars were so big that their dimmest recesses had to be lit by oil lamps, little flickering wicks floating in pots of amber oil. The cellar was divided into two parts, and he led us first to where the treading was taking place. Looming over everything else in the dim light were three gigantic barrels. One of them was being filled with grapes by a constant procession of peasant women. The other two were occupied by the treaders. In the corner, seated on an upturned keg, was a grey, fragile-looking old man who, with great solemnity, was playing on a fiddle.

"That's Taki and that's Yani," said Stavrodakis, pointing to the two wine-treaders.

Taki's head could only just be seen above the rim of the barrel, whereas Yani's head and shoulders were still visible.

277

"Taki's been treading since last night," said Stavrodakis, glancing nervously at Mother and Margo, "so I'm afraid he's a little bit inebriated."

Indeed, from where we stood we could smell the heady fumes of the grape pulp and they were intoxicating enough, so their force must have been trebled when concentrated in the warm depths of the barrel. From the base of the barrel the crude young wine dribbled out into a trough, where it lay smouldering with patches of froth on top as pink as almond blossom. From here it was syphoned off into barrels.

"This is, of course, the end of the harvest," Stavrodakis was explaining. "These are the last of the red grapes. They come from a little vineyard high up and produce, I venture to think, one of the better wines of Corfu."

Taki momentarily stopped his jig on the grapes, hooked arms over the side of the barrel and hung there like a drunken swallow on its nest, his arms and hands stained with wine and covered with a crust of grape skins and seeds.

"It's time I came out," he said thickly, "or I shall be as drunk as a lord."

"Yes, yes, in a minute, my Taki," said Stavrodakis, looking round him nervously. "In a minute Costos will be here to relieve you."

"One must pee," Taki explained aggrievedly. "A man can't work unless he pees."

The old man put down his fiddle, and presumably by way of compensation, handed Taki a lump of coarse bread, which he ate wolfishly.

Theodore was giving Sven an erudite lecture on wines, pointing at both treaders and the barrels with his walking-stick as though they had been objects in a museum.

"Who was it?" said Max to Larry, "that drownded in a butt of malmsey?"

"One of Shakespeare's more sensible heroes," said Larry. "I remember once," Kralefsky said to Donald, "taking a lady round one of the biggest cellars in France. Halfway round the cellar I began to feel uneasy. I had a premonition of danger and so I escorted the lady out and at that moment fourteen of the barrels burst with a roar like cannons..."

"Here, as you have seen, we do the treading," said Stayrodakis. "Now if you will just follow me this way, I'll show you where the wine is stored."

He led us through an archway into the other gloomy section of the cellar. Here rank after rank of barrels lay on their sides and the noise was incredible. At first I thought it must have some outside source. until I realized that it emanated from the barrels. As the wine fermented in their brown bellies, the barrels gurgled and squeaked and growled at each other like an angry mob. The sound was fascinating, but slightly horrific. It was as though in each barrel there were incarcerated some frightful demon mouthing incomprehensible abuse.

"The peasants say," said Theodore with macabre relish, tapping one of the barrels lightly with his stick, "the peasants say that it sounds like a drowning man."

"Malmsey!" said Max excitedly. "Barrels and barrels of malmsey! Larry, we'll get drownded together!"

"Drowned," said Donald.

"Most interesting," Mother was saying insincerely to Stavrodakis, "but if you will excuse us, I think Margo and I had better go back to the beach and see about lunch."

"I wonder what force it generates in there," said Leslie, glancing round moodily. "I mean, if it generated sufficient force to push one of those bungs out, I wonder what power it would have?"

"Quite considerable," said Theodore. "I remember once seeing a man who was quite badly injured by the bung from a barrel." As if to demonstrate this, he tapped a barrel sharply with his stick and we all jumped.

"Yes, well, if you will excuse us," said Mother nervously, "I think Margo and I had better be going."

"But the rest of you, the rest of you will come up to the house and have some wine?" pleaded Stavrodakis.

"Of course we will," said Larry, as though he were doing him a favour.

"Malmsey!" said Max, rolling his eyes in ecstasy. "We will have malmsey!"

So while Margo and Mother went back to the beach to help Spiro in the preparations for lunch, Stavrodakis fussily hurried us back onto the veranda and plied us with wine, so that when it was time for us to go back to the beach, we were mellow, warm, and flushed.

" 'I dreamt,' " carolled Max as we walked through the olives, taking a delighted Stavrodakis with us to share our lunch, " 'I dreamt that I dwelt in marble halls with vessels and turfs by my side.' "

"He just does it to annoy me," Donald confided to Theodore. "He knows that song perfectly well."

Under the trees at the edge of the sea, three charcoal fires had been lighted and they glowed, shuddered, and smoked gently, and over them popped and sizzled a variety of foods. Margo had laid a great cloth in the shade and was putting cutlery and glasses on it, singing untunefully to herself while Mother and Spiro crouched like witches over the fires, larding the brown sizzling carcass of a kid with oil and squeezed garlic and anointing the great body of a fish – its skin bubbled and crisped enticingly by the heat – with lemon juice.

Lunch we ate in a leisurely fashion, sprawled round the bright cloth, the glasses glowing with wine. The mouthfuls of kid were rich and succulent, woven with herbs, and the sections of fish melted like snowflakes in your mouth. The conversation drifted and sprang up and then coiled languidly again, like the smoke from the fires.

"You have to be in love with a piece of stone," said Sven solemnly. "You see a dozen pieces of stone. You say, 'Pah! That's not for me,' and then you see a piece, delicate and elegant, and you fall in love with it. It's like women. But then comes the marriage and that can be terrible. You fight with it and you find that the stone is hard. You are in despair, then suddenly, like wax, it melts under your hands and you create a shape."

"I remember," said Theodore, "being asked by Berlincourt – you know, that French painter who lives over at Paleocastritsa – being asked by him to go and look at his work. He said, er, you know, quite distinctly, 'come and see my *paintings*.' So I went one afternoon and he was most hospitable. He gave me, um, you know, little cakes and tea and then I said I would like to see his paintings, and he pointed to one large canvas which was on the, um, what is it, that thing that painters use? Ah, yes, *easel*. It was quite a pretty painting, really. It showed the bay at Paleocastritsa with the monastery quite clearly and when I had admired it, I looked round to see where the rest of his work was, but there didn't appear to be any. So I, um, asked him where the *rest* of his paintings were and he pointed to the easel and said, um, 'under there.' It appeared that he couldn't afford canvases and so he painted one picture on top of another."

"Great artists have to suffer," said Sven lugubriously.

"When winter comes, I'll take you over to the Butrinto marshes," said Leslie with enthusiasm. "Masses of duck there and damned great wild boars up in the hills."

"Ducks I like, but vild boars I think are a bit big for me," said Max, with the conviction of one who knows his limitations.

"I don't think Max is up to it," said Donald. "He'd probably cut and run at a crucial moment. A foreigner, you know."

"And then," said Mother to Kralefsky, "you put your bay leaf and sorrel in just *before* it starts to simmer."

"So I says to him, Misses Margos, I says, I don't care if he is the French Ambassador, he's a bastard."

"Then, at the edge of the marsh – it's a bit difficult walking, of course, because the ground's so mushy – you can get woodcock and snipe."

"I remember once I visited a village in Macedonia where they did very curious, um, you know, wood sculptures."

"I knew a lady once who used to make it without the bay leaf, but with a pinch of mint."

It was the hottest hour of the day when even the cicadas seem to slow down and falter occasionally in their song. The black ants moved busily across the cloth, gathering the crumbs of our food. A horsefly, its eyes gleaming like malevolent emeralds, settled for a brief moment on Theodore's beard and then zoomed away.

Slowly, full of food and wine, I got up and made my way down to the sea. "And sometimes," I could hear Stavrodakis say to Margo, "sometimes the barrels really shout. They make a noise as if they were fighting. It keeps me awake."

"Oh, don't," said Margo, shuddering. "It makes me creepy just to think of it."

The sea was still and warm, looking as though it had been varnished, with just a tiny ripple patting languidly at the shore. The shingle scrunched and shifted, hot under my bare feet. The rocks and pebbles that made up this beach were incredible in shape and colour, moulded by the waves and the gentle rubbing and polishing one against the other. They had been sculptured into a million shapes. Arrowheads, sickles, cockerels, horses, dragons, and starfish. Their colouring was as bizarre as their shapes, for they had been patterned by the earth's juices millions of years before and now their decorations had been buffed and polished by the sea. White with gold or red filigree, blood-red with white spots, green, blue, and pale fawn, hen's-egg, brown with a deep rusty-red pattern like a fern sprawled across them, pink as a peony with white Egyptian hieroglyphics forming a mysterious, undecipherable message across them. It was like a vast treasure trove of jewels spread along the rim of the sea.

I waded into the warm shallows and then dived and swam out to cooler water. Here, if you held your breath and let yourself sink to the bottom, the soft velvety blanket of the sea momentarily stunned and crippled your ears. Then, after a moment, they became attuned to the underwater symphony. The distant throb of a boat engine, soft as a heartbeat, the gentle whisper of the sand as the sea's movement shuffled and rearranged it and, above all, the musical clink of the pebbles on the shore's edge. To hear the sea at work on its great store of pebbles, rubbing and polishing them lovingly, I swam from the deep waters into the shallows. I anchored myself with a handful of multi-coloured stones, then, ducking my head below the surface, listened to the beach singing under the gentle touch of the small waves. If walnuts could sing, I reflected, they would sound like this. Scrunch, tinkle, squeak, mumble, cough (silence while the wave retreats) and then the whole thing in different keys repeated with the next wave. The sea played on the beach as though it were an instrument. I lay and dozed for a time in the warm shallows and then, feeling heavy with sleep, I made my way back into the olive groves.

Everyone lay about disjointedly, sleeping round the ruins of our meal. It looked like the aftermath of some terrible battle. I curled up like a dormouse in the protective roots of a great olive and drifted off to sleep myself.

I woke to the gentle clinking of teacups as Margo and Mother laid the cloth for tea. Spiro brooded with immense concentration over a fire on which he had set a kettle. As I watched drowsily, the kettle lifted its lid and waved pertly at him, hissing steam. He seized it in one massive hand and poured the contents into a teapot, then, turning, he scowled at our recumbent bodies.

"Teas," he roared thunderously. "Teas is readys."

Everybody started and woke.

"Dear God! Must you yell like that, Spiro?" asked Larry plaintively, his voice thickened by sleep.

"Tea," said Kralefsky, waking up and glancing round him, looking like a dishevelled moth. "Tea, by Jove. Excellent."

"God, my head aches," said Leslie. "It must be that wine. It's got a kick like a mule."

"Yes, I'm feeling a bit fragile myself," said Larry, yawning and stretching.

"I feel as though I've been drowned," said Max with conviction. "Drowned in malmsey and then brought back by artificial inspiration."

"Must you always massacre the English tongue?" said Donald irritably. "God knows it's bad enough having thousands of Englishmen doing it, without you foreigners starting."

"I remember reading somewhere" – began Theodore, who had awakened instantly, like a cat, and who, having slept like one, looked as immaculate as though he had not been to sleep at all – "I remember reading once that there's a tribe up in the mountains of Ceylon that speaks a language that nobody can understand. I mean to say, not even expert linguists have been able to understand it."

"It sounds just like Max's English," said Donald.

Under the influence of tea, buttered toast, salt biscuits, watercress sandwiches, and an enormous fruit cake as damp and as fragile and as rich-smelling as loam, we started to wake up.

Presently we went down to the sea and swam in the warm waters until the sun sank and pushed the mountain's shadow over the beach suddenly, making it look cold and drained of colour. Then we went up to Stavrodakis' villa and sat under the bougainvillea watching the sunset colours blur and mingle over the sea. We left Stavrodakis, who insisted on giving us a dozen great jars of his best wine to commemorate our visit, and made our way back to the benzina.

As we headed out to sea we left the shadow of the mountain and came into the warm glow of the sun again, which was sinking, smudged blood-red behind the bulk of Pandokrator, casting a shimmering reflection across the water like a flaming cypress tree. A few tiny clouds turned pink and vine-yellow, then the sun dipped behind the mountain and the sky turned from blue to pale green and the smooth surface of the sea became for a brief moment all the magical colours of a fire-opal. The engine throbbed as we edged our way back towards the town, unrolling a white bale of lace wake behind us. Sven played the opening of "The Almond Tree" very softly and everyone started to sing.

> "She shook the flowering almond tree one sunny day
>   With her soft little hands,
>   The snowy blossoms on her breast and shoulders lay
>   And in her hair's dark strands
>   The snowy blossoms on her breast and shoulders lay
>   And in her hair's dark strands…"

Spiro's voice, deep, rich, and smooth as black velvet, harmonizing with Theodore's pleasant baritone and Larry's tenor. Two flying fish skimmed up from the blue depths beneath our bow, skittered along the water, and were lost in the twilight sea.

Now it was getting dark enough to see the tiny green coruscations of phosphorus as our bow slid through the water. The dark wine glugged pleasantly from the earthenware pitchers into the glasses, the red wine that, last year, had lain snarling to itself in the brown barrels. A tiny wind, warm and soft as a kitten's paw, stroked the boat. Kralefsky, his head thrown back, his large eyes full of tears, sang at the velvet blue sky, shuddering with stars. The sea crisped itself along the sides of the boat with the sound of winter leaves, wind-lifted, rubbing themselves affectionately against the trunks of the trees that gave them birth.

"But when I saw my darling thus in snow arrayed,
   To her sweet side I sped
   I brushed the gleaming petals from each lock and braid,
   I kissed her and I said:
   I brushed the gleaming petals from each lock and braid,
   I kissed her and I said…"

Far out in the channel between Corfu and the mainland, the darkness was freckled and picked out with the lights of the fishing boats. It was as though a small section of the Milky Way had fallen into the sea. Slowly the moon edged up over the carapace of the Albanian mountains, at first red like the sun, then fading to copper, to yellow, and at last to white. The tiny wind-shimmers on the sea glittered like a thousand fish scales.

The warm air, the wine, and the melancholy beauty of the night filled me with a delicious sadness. It would always be like this, I thought. The brilliant, friendly island, full of secrets, my family and my animals round me and, for good measure, our friends. Theodore's bearded head outlined against the moon wanting only horns to make him Pan; Kralefsky crying unashamedly now like a black gnome weeping over his banishment from fairyland; Spiro with his scowling brown face, his voice becoming as richly vibrant as a million summer bees; Donald and Max, frowning as they endeavoured to remember the words of the song and harmonize at the same time. Sven, like a great ugly white baby, gently squeezing the soulful music from his ungainly instrument.

> "Oh, foolish one, to deck your hair so soon with snow,
>   Long may you have to wait;
>   The dreary winter days when chilling north winds blow
>   Do not anticipate!
>   The dreary winter days when chilling north winds blow
>   Do not anticipate!"

Now, I thought, we were edging into winter, but soon it would be spring again, burnished, glittering, bright as a goldfinch; and then it would be summer, the long, hot, daffodil-yellow days.

> "Oh, foolish one, to deck your hair so soon with snow,
>   Long may you have to wait;
>   The dreary winter days when chilling north winds blow

Do not anticipate!
The dreary winter days when chilling north winds blow
Do not anticipate!"

Lulled by the wine and the throbbing heart of the boat's engine, lulled by the warm night and the singing, I fell asleep while the boat carried us back across the warm, smooth waters to our island and the brilliant days that were not to be.

EPILOGUE

Corfu is of such importance to me that its loss would deal a fatal blow to my projects. Remember this: in the present state of Europe, the greatest misfortune which could befall me is the loss of Corfu.

— NAPOLEON

MAIL

Letter

Dear Mrs Durrell,

It seems at last war can no longer be avoided and I think perhaps you were wise to leave Corfu. One can only hope that we can all meet in happier times when mankind has regained its senses. I will look forward to that.

Should you wish to reach me, my address is c/o The Ionian Bank, Athens.

I wish you and your family the very best of luck in the future.

Love to you all,

Yours,

Theodore

Postcard

Mother,

Have moved to Athens, so keep in touch. Place marvellous. Acropolis like pink flesh in the sun. Have sent my things to you. In a trunk marked "3" you will find book called *An Evaluation of Marlowe*. Can you send it to me? Everyone here wearing tin hats and looking like war. Am buying myself large spear.

Love,
Larry

Letter

Dear Mother,

I have had all my travellers' cheques pinched by some bloody Italian. They nearly arrested me because I punched him in the snoot. Give me the Greeks any day.

Can you send some more money to me at the Magnifica Hotel, Plaza de Contina, Milan? Will be home soon. Don't worry.

Love,
Les

PS. It looks like war, doesn't it?

Letter

Darling Mother,

Just a hurried note to tell you I'm leaving on the boat on Monday so I should be in England in about three weeks.

Things here are rather hectic, but what can you expect? It never rains but it snows. I think it's simply disgusting the way the Germans are carrying on. If I had my way I'd tell them.

Will see you soon.
Love to you,
Margo

PS. I enclose a letter from Spiro. Most odd.

Letter

Dear Missy Margo,

This is to tell you that war has been declared. Don't tell a soul.

Spiro

A MESSAGE FROM THE
DURRELL WILDLIFE CONSERVATION TRUST

The living creatures Gerald Durrell collected in jam-jars and biscuit tins greatly influenced the work he did subsequently to save endangered species all over the world. His childhood experiences on Corfu inspired his lifetime crusade to preserve the rich diversity of animal life on our planet.

This crusade to preserve endangered species did not end with Gerald Durrell's death in 1995. His work goes on through the untiring efforts of the Durrell Wildlife Conservation Trust.

Over the years many readers of Gerald Durrell's books have been so motivated by his experiences and vision that they have wanted to continue the story for themselves by supporting the work of his Trust. We hope that you will feel the same way today because through his books and life, Gerald Durrell set us all a challenge. 'Animals are the great voteless and voiceless majority,' he wrote, 'who can only survive with our help.'

Please don't let your interest in conservation end when you turn this page. Write to us now and we'll tell you how you can be part of our crusade to save animals from extinction.

**FOR FURTHER INFORMATION,
OR TO SEND A DONATION, WRITE TO**

Durrell Wildlife Conservation Trust
Les Augrès Manor
Jersey, English Channel Islands, JE3 5BP
UK
www.durrellwildlife.org

GERALD DURRELL

MY FAMILY AND OTHER ANIMALS
Corfu Trilogy – One

The azure skies, the olive groves and the mountains of Corfu provide the stunning setting for *My Family and Other Animals*. Here, the Durrell family live in chaotic harmony, welcoming a constant stream of eccentric visitors to their villa. This island paradise is exquisitely described by the keen young naturalist, Gerald. With a sense of wonder he evokes the magical world of the creatures he observes and collects: spiders, cicadas, tortoises, toads, fireflies and scorpions. Written with wit and insight, Gerald Durrell masterfully captures the excitement and awe he feels at the natural world around him.

GERALD DURRELL

THE GARDEN OF THE GODS

Corfu Trilogy — Three

The enchanted island of Corfu was home to Gerald Durrell and his family for five years before the Second World War. For the passionate young zoologist, Corfu was a natural paradise, teeming with strange birds and beasts that he could collect, watch and care for. But life was not without its problems — Gerald's family often objected to his animal-collecting activities, especially when the beasts wound up in the family's villa or even worse — the fridge.

Gerald Durrell evokes his island paradise with the passion and wonder of a small boy in the concluding book of the warm and humorous trilogy begun with *My Family and Other Animals* and *Birds, Beasts and Relatives*.

GERALD DURRELL

THE AYE-AYE AND I
A RESCUE MISSION IN MADAGASCAR

Victim of 'slash and burn' agriculture, the Aye-aye is threatened with extinction in its native Madagascar. Gerald Durrell and his wife, Lee, lead an expedition to the island to bring pairs of the endangered species into captivity and to start a breeding programme in their Jersey Zoo.

The Aye-aye and I is the tale of their hunt for the creature with the magical finger, but it is also the search for Giant Jumping rats, Flat-tailed tortoises and Gentle lemurs. From one of the most fascinating islands in the world, this is a compelling story of ecological destruction and the hope that conservation engenders.

GERALD DURRELL

GOLDEN BATS AND PINK PIGEONS

Over millions of years, the island of Mauritius, in its isolated position in the Indian Ocean, developed a unique flora and fauna. But when man arrived with his attendant scourges of dog, rat, pig and monkey he wreaked havoc upon the island's delicate ecosystem, an action which led, amongst other things, to the extinction of the dodo.

In co-operation with the Mauritian Government, Gerald Durrell and his team visited the island to help rescue some of the rapidly dwindling creatures from almost certain extinction. Durrell succeeded in taking some of these threatened animals to his Jersey sanctuary where they could live and breed in safety and from where their progeny could be reintroduced into their natural home. In this revealing and absorbing account of the preservation of endangered species, we also learn of the dangers and challenges this work can entail.

GERALD DURRELL

MENAGERIE MANOR

Menagerie Manor is Gerald Durrell's account of how he set up his zoo in Jersey. Surrounded by a team of devoted helpers, this is a tale of teamwork and devotion to the cause. Besides the human dramas, Durrell reveals a host of fascinating practical details about animal health and behaviour, as well as stories of the individual animals themselves. This is an extremely entertaining and informative book chronicling the fulfilment of Gerald Durrell's lifelong ambition.

OTHER TITLES BY GERALD DURRELL AVAILABLE DIRECT
FROM HOUSE OF STRATUS

Quantity		£	$(US)	$(CAN)	€
NON-FICTION					
☐	THE AYE-AYE AND I: A RESCUE				
	MISSION IN MADAGASCAR	6.99	14.95	21.00	14.00
☐	GOLDEN BATS AND PINK PIGEONS	6.99	14.95	21.00	14.00
☐	MENAGERIE MANOR	6.99	14.95	21.00	14.00
	CORFU TRILOGY				
☐	MY FAMILY AND				
	OTHER ANIMALS (HARDBACK)	7.99	14.95	21.00	14.00
☐	THE GARDEN OF THE GODS	6.99	14.95	21.00	14.00
	CHILDREN'S FICTION				
☐	THE FANTASTIC DINOSAUR				
	ADVENTURE	9.99	14.95	22.95	16.50
☐	THE FANTASTIC FLYING				
	JOURNEY	9.99	14.95	22.95	16.50

THE FANTASTIC FLYING JOURNEY also available in hardback version, £12.99

ALL HOUSE OF STRATUS BOOKS ARE AVAILABLE FROM GOOD BOOKSHOPS
OR DIRECT FROM THE PUBLISHER:

Internet:	www.houseofstratus.com including synopses and features.
Email:	sales@houseofstratus.com
	info@houseofstratus.com
	(please quote author, title and credit card details.)
Tel:	Order Line
	0800 169 1780 (UK)
	International
	+44 (0) 1845 527700 (UK)
Fax:	+44 (0) 1845 527711 (UK)
	(please quote author, title and credit card details.)
Send to:	House of Stratus Sales Department
	Thirsk Industrial Park
	York Road, Thirsk
	North Yorkshire, YO7 3BX
	UK

PAYMENT

Please tick currency you wish to use:

☐ £ (Sterling)   ☐ $ (US)   ☐ $ (CAN)   ☐ € (Euros)

Allow for shipping costs charged per order plus an amount per book as set out in the tables below:

CURRENCY/DESTINATION

	£(Sterling)	$(US)	$(CAN)	€(Euros)
Cost per order				
UK	1.50	2.25	3.50	2.50
Europe	3.00	4.50	6.75	5.00
North America	3.00	3.50	5.25	5.00
Rest of World	3.00	4.50	6.75	5.00
Additional cost per book				
UK	0.50	0.75	1.15	0.85
Europe	1.00	1.50	2.25	1.70
North America	1.00	1.00	1.50	1.70
Rest of World	1.50	2.25	3.50	3.00

PLEASE SEND CHEQUE OR INTERNATIONAL MONEY ORDER
payable to: HOUSE OF STRATUS LTD or card payment as indicated

STERLING EXAMPLE

Cost of book(s):..................... Example: 3 x books at £6.99 each: £20.97

Cost of order:..................... Example: £1.50 (Delivery to UK address)

Additional cost per book:.............. Example: 3 x £0.50: £1.50

Order total including shipping:.......... Example: £23.97

VISA, MASTERCARD, SWITCH, AMEX:

☐☐☐☐☐☐☐☐☐☐☐☐☐☐☐☐☐☐☐☐☐☐

Issue number (Switch only):

☐☐☐

Start Date: **Expiry Date:**

☐☐/☐☐   ☐☐/☐☐

Signature: _____

NAME: _____

ADDRESS: _____

COUNTRY: _____

ZIP/POSTCODE: _____

Please allow 28 days for delivery. Despatch normally within 48 hours.

Prices subject to change without notice.
Please tick box if you do not wish to receive any additional information. ☐

House of Stratus publishes many other titles in this genre; please check our website (**www.houseofstratus.com**) for more details.